LABOUR
LAWS

Everybody
Should Know

LABOUR LAWS
Everybody Should Know

Fifth Edition

H.L. KUMAR
Advocate, Supreme Court of India
Editor, Labour Law Reporter

GAURAV KUMAR
MBA, LL.M., Advocate

Universal
Law Publishing Co. Pvt. Ltd.

First Edition   1995
Second Edition 2003
Third Edition   2005
Fourth Edition 2007
Fifth Edition   2008

ISBN : 978-81-7534-680-2

Published by
UNIVERSAL LAW PUBLISHING CO. PVT. LTD.
C-FF-1A, Dilkhush Industrial Estate,
(Opp. Hans Cinema, Azadpur) G.T. Karnal Road,
Delhi-110 033
Tel : 011-27438103, 27215334, 42381334
Fax : 011-27458529
E-mail *(For sales inquiries)* : sales@unilawbooks.com
E-mail *(For editorial inquiries)* : edit@unilawbooks.com
Website : www.unilawbooks.com

Recommended citation: *Labour Laws—Everybody Should Know*, H.L. Kumar, 5th Edn. (New Delhi: Universal Law Publishing Co. Pvt. Ltd., 2008)

Although every care has been taken to avoid errors or omissions in this publication, inspite of this, inadvertently, errors may creep in. The publication is being sold on the condition and understanding that information given herein is merely for guidance and reference. It must not be taken as having authority of, or binding in any way on, the authors, editors, publishers and sellers who do not owe any responsibility for any damage or loss to any person, who may or may not be a purchaser of this publication on account of any action taken on the basis of this publication. For authoritative text information, please contact the department concerned or refer to the Government publication or the gazette notification. The publishers shall be obliged if any mistake, error or discrepancy is brought to their notice for carrying out correction in the next edition. In case of binding mistake, misprint or for missing pages etc., the publishers liability is limited to replacement within one month of the purchase by similar edition/ reprint. All disputes are subject to Delhi Jurisdiction only.

Computer Typeset at Aesthetic & *Printed at* Taj Press, (Noida)

Preface to Fifth Edition

This book seeks to serve as a reliable guide and companion to both employers and employees as well. Although efforts are required for a drastic change in the labour laws, yet it will still take quite some time to get those proposals translated into reality. With more emphasis on workers acquiring skill and education, the old concept of 'master-servant' relationship is fast shaping into the 'employer and employee relationship. That is why the need to know the rudimentary rules and rubrics of law for both, as all these are necessary. Much has been changing in labour laws, both in nature of litigation before the courts and Industrial Tribunals, in its practice besides amendments and procedure hence the contents of this edition have undergone significant changes, both by way of additions and deletions.

The earlier editions of the book were more focused and centric towards employer but in this time it has been ensured that employees also get benefited. The basic tenet and underpinning philosophy of labour laws is to protect the interests of the employees by saving them from exploitation and harassment on the one hand and providing enough leverage and stick of good governance to employers so as to have conductive work culture on the other hand. The cordial and congenial relationship can be had only when both the limbs of organization have better understanding in the light of the limits of their rights, responsibilities and duties.

The archaic labour laws and slow peace of legislation have proved woefully ineffective, prolix and repetitive, bogged in lengthy procedures and delayed justice. It should be made simple and easily accessible, quick in decision and immediate relief. It is also unsuited to the tempo of modern life where speed and efficiency are of utmost importance.

The provisions of labour laws are generally very complex but in this book, it has been tried to interpret and project those laws with the help of case laws as simple as possible. I am sure that the book will cater to the needs managers, trade union leaders, employers, employees, the practitioners, consultants of the laws and HRM executives.

I must record here my sincere appreciation and thanks to Mr. M.R. Gera, former Director (Projects), All India Management Association who has to the credit of organizing many seminars all over India and has immensely helped me with his vast, varied and rich experiences. I must admit that I have learnt a lot during the seminars and by interacting with the thousands of participants at different places all over the country. My assignment at the seminars, generally pertained to interactive sessions for clarifications to the queries as raised by the participants. Such 'questions-answers sessions' have been provided an opportunity for self learning and were helpful to incorporate the practical aspects in this small but useful book wherein all the important Acts for day-to-day working are explained in this book to make it informative.

H.L. KUMAR

CONTENTS

4. The Child Labour (Prohibition and Regulation) Act, 1986

5. The Employees' Provident Funds and Miscellaneous Provisions Act, 1952

Contents

5A. The Employees' Pension Scheme, 1995

6. The Employees' State Insurance Act, 1948

7. The Employment Exchanges (Compulsory Notification of Vacancies) Act, 1959

8. The Employers' Liability Act, 1938

9. The Equal Remuneration Act, 1976

10. The Factories Act, 1948

11. The Industrial Disputes Act, 1947

11A. Industrial Employment (Standing Order) Act, 1946

12. The Maternity Benefit Act, 1961

13. The Mines Act, 1952

14. The Minimum Wages Act, 1948

15. The Motor Transport Workers Act, 1961

16. The Payment of Bonus Act, 1965

17. The Payment of Gratuity Act, 1972

18. The Payment of Wages Act, 1936

19. The Sales Promotion Employees (Conditions of Service) Act, 1976

20. The Trade Unions Act, 1926

21. The Workmen's Compensation Act, 1923

22. Other Related Matters

TABLE OF CASES

APPRENTICES ACT, 1961

CHECKLIST

Object of the Act
Promotion of new manpower at skills. Improvement/refinement of old skills through theoretical and practical training in number of trades and occupations.

Applicability of the Act
Areas and industries as notified by the Central Government.
Sec. 1

Apprenticeship Advisor
Central Apprenticeship Advisor - when appointed by Central Government.
Sec. 2(b)

Industry

Industry means any industry, or business or in which any trade, occupation or subject/field in engineering or technology or any vocational course may be specified as a designated trade.
Sec. 2(k)

Qualification for being trained as an Apprentice
A person cannot be an apprentice in any designated trade unless
* He is not less than 14 years of age;
* He satisfies such standard of education and physical fitness as may be prescribed.
Sec. 3

Contract of Apprenticeship
To contain such terms and conditions as may be agreed to by the apprentice, or his guardian (in case he is a minor) and employers.
Sec. 4

Conditions for Novation of contract of Apprenticeship
* There exists an apprenticeship contract.
* The employer is unable to fulfil his obligation.
* The approval of the Apprenticeship Advisor is obtained.

  * Agreement must be registered with the Apprenticeship Advisor.
Sec. 5

Period of Apprenticeship
Training to be determined by the National Council

Termination of Apprenticeship
On the expiry of the period of apprenticeship training. On the application by either of the parties to the contract to the Apprenticeship Advisor.
Sec.6

Payment to Apprentices
The employer to pay such stipend at a rate of not less than the prescribed minimum rate as may be specified.

Number of Apprentices in Designated Trade
To be determined by the Central Government after consulting the Central Apprenticeship Council
Sec. 8

Obligations of employers
* To provide the apprentice with the training in his trade.
* To ensure that a person duly qualified is placed in charge of the training of the apprentice.
* To carry out contractual obligations.
Sec. 11

Obligations of Apprentice
* To learn his trade conscientiously, diligently.
* To attend practical and instructional classes regularly.
* To carry out all lawful orders.
* To carry out his contractual obligations.

Health safety & Welfare measures for Apprentices.
As per Factories Act or Mines Act as the case may be when undergoing training.

Hours of Work
* 42 to 48 in a week while on theoretical training.
* 42 in a week while on basic training.
* 42 to 45 in a week in second year of training.
* As per other workers (in the third year).
* Not allowed to work between 10 PM to 4 AM unless approved by Apprenticeship Advisor.

Leave and Holidays
* Casual leave for the maximum period of 12 days in a year.
* Medical leave for the maximum period of 15 days and the accumulated leave upto 40 days in a year.
* Extraordinary leave upto a maximum period of 10 days in a year.
Sec. 15

Employer's liability to pay compensation for injury
As per provisions of Workmen's Compensation Act.
Sec. 16

Offences & Punishment
Imprisonment of a term upto 6 months or with fine when employer (i) engages as an apprentice a person who is not qualified for being so engaged or (ii) fails to carry out the terms and conditions of a contract of apprenticeship, or (iii) contravenes the provisions of the Act relating to the number of apprentices which he is required to engage under those provisions.
Secs. 30 & 31

1. The Apprentices Act, 1961

THE OBJECT

The primary object with which the Apprentices Act, 1961 was passed was to meet the increasing demand for skilled craftsmen in the development of the country. It was intended by the Government to utilise facilities available for training apprentices and to ensure their training in accordance with planned programme.

The Apprentices Act amongst others has two important objectives, *e.g.*, promotion of new manpower skills and improvement and refinement of old skills through theoretical and practical training in number of trades and occupations. It is now a statutory obligation on the part of every employer covered under the Act to train a prescribed number of persons. The Act envisages to regulate and control the training of apprentices in trade and to supplement the availability of the technical persons for the industry.

The Act as amended in 1973 and 1986 defines the technician (vocational) as apprentice who holds or is undergoing training in order that he may hold a certificate in vocational course involving two years of study after completion of the secondary stage of school education recognised by the All India Council and undergoes apprenticeship training in any such subject field in any vocation course as may be prescribed. The Act provides an important instrument for sharpening the capability, ingenuity, resourcefulness and skill of the workers and through this eventually helps to enrich their life style.

In exercise of powers conferred by section 37 of the Act, the Apprenticeship Rules have been amended and published in Gazette of India (Dated 1-8-1992, Part II, Section 3(i) at page 1405).

STANDARD OF EDUCATION FOR APPRENTICES

A person shall be eligible for being engaged as a trade apprentice if he satisfies the minimum educational qualifications as specified in Schedule I.

A person shall be eligible for being engaged as a graduate or technician or technician vocational apprentice if he satisfies one of the minimum educational qualifications specified in Schedule IA:

Provided that:—

no Engineering Graduate or Diploma holder or Vocational Certificate holder who had training or job experience for a period of one year or more, after the attainment of these qualifications shall be eligible for being engaged as an apprentice under the Act;

no Sandwich Course Student shall be eligible for being engaged as an apprentice under the Act after passing the final examination of the technical institution wherein such student is undergoing the course, unless so approved by the Regional Central Apprenticeship Advisers;

A person who has been a Graduate or Technician or Technician (Vocational) apprentice under the Act and in whose case the contract of apprenticeship was terminated for any reason whatsoever shall not be eligible for being engaged as an apprentice again under the Act without the prior approval of the Apprenticeship Adviser.

PERIOD OF APPRENTICESHIP TRAINING

The period of apprenticeship training, which shall be specified in the contract of apprenticeship, shall be as follows:—

(i) In the case of trade apprentices who, having undergone institutional training in a school or other institution recognized by the National Council, have passed the trade tests conducted by the Council, the period of apprenticeship training shall be such as may be determined by the Council or by an institution recognized by that Council;

(ii) In the case of trade apprentices who, having undergone institutional training in a school or other institution affiliated to or recognized by a Board or State Council of Technical Education or any other authority which the Central Government may, by notification in the Official Gazette, specify in this behalf, have passed the trade tests conducted by that Board or State Council or Authority, the period of apprenticeship training shall be such as may be prescribed;

(iii) In the case of other trade apprentices, the period of apprenticeship training shall be such as may be prescribed;

(iv) In the case of graduate or technician apprentices, the period of apprenticeship training shall be such as may be prescribed.

ESSENTIAL INGREDIENTS OF CONTRACT OF APPRENTICESHIP

(i) No person shall be engaged as an apprentice to undergo apprenticeship training in a designated trade unless such person or, if he is a minor, his guardian has entered into a contract of apprenticeship with the employer;

(ii) The apprenticeship training shall be deemed to have commenced on the date on which the contract of apprenticeship has been entered into as per clause (i);

(iii) Every contract of apprenticeship may contain such terms and conditions as may be agreed to by the parties to the contract. Provided that no such term or condition shall be inconsistent with any provision of Apprentices Act or any rule made thereunder;

(iv) Every contract of apprenticeship as entered into shall be sent by the employer within such period as may be prescribed to Apprenticeship Adviser for registration;

(v) The Apprenticeship Adviser shall not register a contract of apprenticeship unless he is satisfied that the person described as an apprentice in the contract is qualified under this Act for being engaged as apprentice to undergo apprenticeship training in the designated trade specified in the contract;

(vi) Where the Central Government after contacting the Central Apprenticeship Council, makes any rule varying the condition of apprenticeship training of any category of apprentices undergoing such training, then the terms and conditions of every contract of apprenticeship relating to that category of apprentices and immediately before the making of such rule shall be deemed to have been modified accordingly.

It is not provided by the Apprentices Act that registration of a contract of apprenticeship is necessary as the intention of the legislation was to include only those persons in the category of apprentices who have entered into a contract of apprenticeship which has been registered. However, according to Rule 6 of the amended Apprenticeship Rules, 1991 as published in Gazette of India (Dated 1-8-1992, Part II, Section 3(i) page 1405) it is provided that every employer shall send to the Apprenticeship Adviser a contract of apprenticeship for registration within three months of the date on which it was signed.

REGISTRATION OF CONTRACT OF APPRENTICESHIP

It is not provided by the Apprentices Act that registration of a contract of apprenticeship is necessary as the intention of the legislation was to include only those persons in the category of apprentices who have entered into a contract of apprenticeship which has been registered. The word 'registered' would have used before the word 'contract'. It, therefore, becomes clear that it is the existing contract of apprenticeship that is required to be registered and not that such contract becomes a contract of apprenticeship only after it is registered as required by sub-section (4) of section 4 of the Act. Therefore, the registration of the contract of apprenticeship is not a necessary ingredient for answering the description of the expression 'apprentice' occurring in section 2(aa) of the Act.

APPRENTICE IS NOT A 'WORKMAN' OR GOVERNED BY LABOUR LAWS

Section 18 of the Apprentices Act, 1961 provides that an apprentice shall not be regarded as a worker if he is undergoing apprenticeship training in a designated trade in an establishment and that an apprentice as defined in the Act cannot claim any privilege as workman under any law including Industrial Disputes Act. The provisions of section 25F of the Industrial Disputes Act are not attracted in this respect.

APPRENTICE'S CLAIM FOR REGULAR POST

Under section 22(1) of the Act, it is not obligatory on the part of the employer to offer any employment to an apprentice who has completed his period of apprenticeship training in his establishment nor it is obligatory on the part of the apprentice to accept the employment under the employer.

OBLIGATIONS OF AN APPRENTICE TO ACCEPT EMPLOYMENT FROM EMPLOYER

Since it is not obligatory on the part of the employer to offer any employment to any apprentice who has completed his period of apprenticeship similarly an apprentice is also not bound to accept the employment under the employer.

OBLIGATIONS OF THE APPRENTICE

Every trade apprentice undergoing apprenticeship training shall have the following obligations, namely:—

- (i) to learn his trade conscientiously and diligently and endeavour to qualify himself as a skilled craftsman before the expiry of the period of training;
- (ii) to attend practical and instructional classes regularly;
- (iii) to carry out all lawful orders of his employer and superiors in the establishment; and
- (iv) to carry out his obligations under the contract of apprenticeship.

Every graduate or technician apprentice undergoing apprenticeship training shall have the following obligations, namely:—

- (i) to learn his subject field in engineering or technology conscientiously and diligently at his place of training;
- (ii) to attend the practical and instructional classes regularly;
- (iii) to carry out all lawful orders of his employer and superiors in the establishment; and
- (iv) to carry out his obligations under the contract of apprenticeship which shall include the maintenance of such records of his work as may be prescribed.

OBLIGATIONS OF EMPLOYERS TOWARDS APPRENTICES

Without prejudice to the other provisions of the Act, every employer shall have the following obligations in relation to an apprentice, namely:—

- (a) to provide the apprentice with the training in his trade in accordance with the provisions of the Act, and the rules made thereunder;
- (b) if the employer is not himself qualified in the trade, to ensure that a person who possesses the prescribed qualifications is placed in charge of the training of the apprentice; and

(c) to carry out his obligations under the contract of apprenticeship.

APPRENTICES AND BONUS

By the very definition of 'employee', the apprentices are not eligible for bonus as per section 2(13) of the Payment of Bonus Act.

APPRENTICES AND COVERAGE UNDER EMPLOYEES' PROVIDENT FUNDS ACT

An apprentice is not an 'employee' as defined by the Employees' Provident Fund and Miscellaneous Provisions Act. The amended provisions of Provident Fund and Miscellaneous Provisions Act *vide* amendment by Act 33 of 1988 defining 'employees' provides that it will include any person engaged as an apprentice, not being an apprentice engaged under Apprentices Act, 1961, or under the Industrial Employment (Standing Orders) Act, 1946.

APPRENTICES AND COVERAGE UNDER EMPLOYEES' STATE INSUR-ANCE ACT

The amending Act 29 of Employees' State Insurance Act, 1989 while defining an 'employee' under the ESI Act has provided that it does not include any person engaged as an apprentice under the Apprentices Act, 1961 or under the Standing Orders of the establishment.

HOURS OF WORK

The daily hours of work of an apprentice shall not be more than 8 hours per day and weekly hours not less than 40 hours but not more than 45 hours. A short term apprentice may however be engaged to work upto a maximum limit of 48 hours per week. The hours of training of the apprentice should not be between 10 p.m. and 6 a.m. except with the prior approval of the Apprenticeship Adviser. An apprentice is entitled to leave in accordance with the Leave Rules which exist for the workers of that establishment provided every apprentice must put in a minimum attendance of 264 days in a year of training, 1/6th of which should be devoted to related instructions and 220 days to practical training.

LEAVE

An apprentice is entitled to the following leaves:—
  (a) *Casual leave* :
      (i) Casual leave shall be admissible for a maximum period of twelve days in a year;
      (ii) Any holidays intervening during the period of casual leave shall not be counted for purpose of the limit of twelve days;

(iii) Casual leave not utilised during any year shall stand lapsed at the end of the year;

(iv) Casual leave shall not be combined with medical leave. If casual leave is preceded or followed by medical leave, the entire leave taken shall be treated either as medical or casual leave provided that it shall not be allowed to exceed the maximum period prescribed in respect of medical or casual leave, as the case may be;

(v) Except in case of extreme urgency applications for such leave shall be made to the appropriate authority and sanction obtained prior to the availing of leave.

(b) *Medical leave :*

(i) Medical leave up to fifteen days for each year of training may be granted to the apprentice who is unable to attend duty owing to illness. The unused leaves shall be allowed to accumulate up to a maximum of forty days;

(ii) Any holidays intervening during the period of medical leave shall be treated as medical leave and accounted for in the limits prescribed under clause (i);

(iii) The employer may call upon the apprentice to produce a medical certificate from a registered medical practitioner in support of his medical leave. A medical certificate shall, however, be necessary, if the leave exceeds six days;

(iv) It shall be open to the employer to arrange a special medical examination of an apprentice if he has reason to believe that the apprentice is not really ill or the illness is not of such a nature as to prevent his attendance.

(c) *Extraordinary leave :*

Extraordinary leave up to a maximum of ten days in a year may be granted to the apprentice, after he has exhausted the entire casual and medical leave, if the employer is satisfied with grounds on which the leave is applied for.

VIOLATION OF THE ACT BY AN EMPLOYER—CONSEQUENCES OF

1. The Apprentices Act provides that if any employer (a) engages as an apprentice a person who is not qualified for being so engaged; or (b) fails to carry out the terms and conditions of a contract of apprenticeship; or (c) contravenes the provisions of the Act relating to the number of apprentices which he is required to engage under those provisions, he shall be punishable with imprisonment for a term which may extend to six months or with fine or with both.

2. If any employer or any other person (a) required to furnish any information or return, refuses or neglects to furnish such information or return, or, furnishes or causes to be furnished any information or return which is false and which he either knows or believes to be false or does not believe to be true, or refuses to answer, or gives a false answer to any question necessary for obtaining any information required to be furnished by him; or (b) refuses or wilfully neglects to afford the Central or the State Apprenticeship Adviser or such other person, not below the rank of an Assistant Apprenticeship Adviser, as may be authorised by the Central or the State Apprenticeship Adviser in writing in this behalf, any reasonable facility for making any entry, inspection, examination or inquiry authorised by or under this Act; or (c) requires an apprentice to work over-time without the approval of the Apprenticeship Adviser; or (d) employs an apprentice on any work which is not connected with his training; or (e) makes payment to an apprentice on the basis of piece-work; or (f) requires an apprentice to take part in any output bonus or incentive scheme, he shall be punishable with imprisonment for a term which may extend to six months or with fine or with both.

TERMINATION OF APPRENTICESHIP CONTRACT

(i) The contract of apprenticeship shall terminate on the expiry of the period of apprenticeship training;

(ii) Either party to a contract of apprenticeship may make an application to the Apprenticeship Adviser for the termination of the contract, and when such application is made, the party shall send by post a copy thereof to the other party to the contract;

(iii) After considering the contents of the application and the objections, if any, filed by the other party, the

Apprenticeship Adviser may, by order in writing, terminate the contract, if he is satisfied that the parties to the contract or any of them have or has failed to carry out the terms and conditions of the contract and it is desirable in the interests of the parties or any of them to terminate the same.

TERMINATION OF CONTRACT—CONSEQUENCES OF

Where the contract of apprenticeship is terminated through failure on the part of any employer in carrying out the terms and conditions thereof, such employer shall be liable to pay the apprentice compensation of an amount equivalent to his three months' last drawn stipend; and when the said termination is due to failure on the part of an apprentice in the above manner then a training cost of an amount equivalent to his three months' last drawn stipend shall be made recoverable from such apprentice or from his guardian in case he is minor.

STIPEND TO THE APPRENTICES

The rates of stipend for the apprentices are revised from time to time by the authorities and as such for rates of stipend for different categories be asked from the Apprenticeship Adviser in particular State, wherein the factory or the establishment is located.

EMPLOYMENT EXCHANGE, SPONSORING NOT NECESSARY

When the petitioner had successfully completed his apprenticeship training, he is eligible to be considered for any future appointment, without being sponsored by any employment exchange.

HEALTH, SAFETY AND WELFARE OF APPRENTICES

When the apprentices are undergoing training in a factory, the provisions of Chapters III, IV and V of the Factories Act, 1948, shall apply in relation to health, safety and welfare of the apprentices, as if they are workers within the meaning of the Factories Act and when the apprentices are undergoing training in a mine, the provisions of Chapter V of the Mines Act, 1952 shall apply in relation to health and safety of the apprentices as if they were persons employed in the mine.

SETTLEMENT OF DISPUTES

Any disagreement or dispute between an employer and an apprentice arising out of the contract of apprenticeship shall be referred to Apprenticeship adviser for decision. Any person aggrieved by the decision of the said Authority, may within 30 days from the date of communication to him of such decision, prefer an appeal against such decision to the Apprenticeship Council and such appeal shall be heard and determined by a Committee of that Council appointed for the purpose. The decision of the Committee and subject only to such decision, the decision of Apprenticeship Adviser, shall be final.

The penalties can roughly be summarised as follows:—

Sec.	Action/Omission	PENALTY	
		Imprison-ment upto	Fine
30(1)	(i) Engaging as an apprentice a person who is not qualified for being so engaged;	Six months	Not specified but can be imposed
	(ii) Failure to carry out terms and conditions of apprenticeship contract;		
	(iii) Contravention of the Act relating to number of apprentices which he is required to engage.		
30(2)	(i) Refusal to furnish any information or return;	Six months	Not specified but can be imposed
	(ii) Furnishing false return;		
	(iii) Refusal to answer or giving false information;		
	(iv) Refusing to extend reasonable facility to the competent Authorities under the Act for making any entry, inspection, examination or inquiry;		
	(v) Requiring an apprentice to work overtime without approval of the Apprenticeship Adviser;		
	(vi) Employing an apprentice on work not connected with his training;		
	(vii) Making payment to an apprentice on the basis of piece rate work;		
	(viii) Requiring an apprentice to take part in any output bonus or incentive scheme.		
	Contravening the provisions of the Act for which no punishment is provided.	No	Upto Rs. 500

CHECKLIST

BONDED LABOUR SYSTEM (ABOLITION) ACT, 1976

Object of the Act

An Act to provide for the abolition of bonded labour system with a view to prevent the economic and physical exploitation of the weaker sections of the people and for matters connected therewith or incidental thereto.

Bonded labourer - Who is?

A labourer who incurs, or has, or is presumed to have, incurred a bonded debt.

Sec. 2(f)

Abolition of bonded labour system

- The bonded labour system shall stand abolished and every bonded labourer shall stand free and discharged from any obligation to render any bonded labour.
- No person shall-
  - make any advance under the bonded labour system or,
  - compel any person to render any bonded labour or other form of forced labour.

Sec. 4

Liability to Repay Bonded debt to Stand Extinguished

- No suit or proceedings shall lie in Civil Court or other authorities.
- No decree will be valid or executable.
- Property belonging to bonded labourer shall be restored.

Sec. 6

Property of Bonded Labour to be freed from Mortgage

Mortgagee will restore the property and if delayed will be liable for mesne profit.

Sec. 7

Freed Bonded Labourer not to be evicted from Homestead

- Which he was occupying either homestead or residential premises.
- The Executive Magistrate shall get the possession restored.

Sec. 8

Creditor not to accept payment against extinguished debt

Sec. 9

Vigilance Committee

To be constituted by every State Government by a Notification

Sec. 13

PENALTIES

Sec.	Offence	Punishment
Sec. 9(2)	Acceptance of payment of extinguished debt	Imprisonment upto 3 years and with fine.
Sec. 16	Compelling any person to render bonded labour	Imprisonment upto 3 years and also with fine upto Rs.2,000.
Sec. 17	For advancement of Bonded Debt	Imprisonment upto 3 years and also with fine upto Rs.2000.
Sec. 18	Extracted bonded labour under Bonded Labour System	Imprisonment 3 years and also with fine upto Rs.2,000 payable to bonded labour @Rs.5 for each day of bonded labour out of fine collected.
Sec. 19	Omission or failure to restore possession of property	Imprisonment upto one year or fine upto Rs.1,000 fine to be paid @Rs.5 for each day of possession out of fine collected.
Sec. 20	Abetment of offence	Punishment as provided for particular offence.

2. The Bonded Labour System (Abolition) Act, 1976

THE OBJECT

The object of the Bonded Labour Act is to abolish the bonded labour system and freeing and discharging every bonded labourer from any obligation to render any bonded labour. On the commencement of the Act, no person can compel any person to render any bonded labour or other form of forced labour and every obligation of a bonded labourer to repay any bonded debt or any bonded debt which may have remained unsatisfied is deemed to have been extinguished. This apart, no suit or other proceeding can lie for the recovery of any bonded debt or any part thereof before any civil court or any other authority.

It is the duty of the Government to identify, release and rehabilitate the bonded labour and it cannot repudiate its obligation.

ACT TO HAVE OVERRIDING EFFECT

The provisions of the Bonded Labour System (Abolition) Act, 1976, by virtue of section 3, have the overriding effect on any other law contained in any enactment other than this Act or in any instrument having effect by virtue of any enactment other than this Act. In other words, notwithstanding anything inconsistent contained in any enactment other than this Act, or in any instrument having effect by virtue of any enactment other than this Act, the provisions of this Act shall have effect.

AGREEMENT, CUSTOM, ETC., TO BE VOID

On the commencement of the Bonded Labour Act, any custom or tradition or any contract, agreement or other instrument, whether entered into or executed before or after its commencement, by virtue of which any person, or any member of the family or dependent of such person, is required to do any work or render any service as a bonded labourer, is deemed to be void and inoperative.

EXTINGUISHMENT OF LIABILITY TO REPAY BONDED DEBT

The Act has also extinguished the liability of the bonded labourer to repay bonded debt. The Act has the effect of treating pending suit or proceeding for recovery of any advance made to a bonded labourer as dismissed or not enforceable.

PROPERTY OF BONDED LABOURER TO BE FREED FROM MORTGAGE, ETC.

All property vested in a bonded labourer which was or is under any mortgage, charge, lien or other encumbrances in connection with any bonded debt is to stand freed and discharged from such mortgage and is to be restored to the possession of such bonded labourer.

FREED BONDED LABOURER NOT TO BE EVICTED FROM HOMESTEAD, ETC.

No person, who has been freed and discharged under this Act from any obligation to render any bonded labour, is to be evicted from any homestead or other residential premises which he was occupying immediately before the commencement of the Act as part of the consideration for the bonded labour. And if any such person has been evicted from any such homestead or other residential premises then the same is to be restored as early as practicable to the possession of such bonded labourer, on his complaint.

CREDITOR NOT TO ACCEPT PAYMENT AGAINST EXTINGUISHED DEBT

After the commencement of the Act, the creditors are also forbidden to accept any payment against any bonded debt which has been extinguished or fully satisfied by virtue of the provisions of this Act.

PUNISHMENT FOR CONTRAVENTION OF ABOVE PROVISIONS

Whoever contravenes the provisions by accepting any payment against any bonded debt which has been extinguished or fully satisfied by virtue of the provisions of this Act is punishable with imprisonment for a term which may extend to three years and also with fine.

PUNISHMENT FOR CONTRAVENTION OF OTHER PROVISIONS OF THE ACT

Any person who after the commencement of the Act, compels any person to render any bonded labour is punishable with imprisonment for a term which may extend to three years and also with fine which may extend to two thousand rupees. For advancement of bonded debt, the punishment is imprisonment which may extend to three years and also fine which may extend to two thousand rupees. The punishment prescribed for extracting bonded labour under the bonded labour system, is the same *viz.* imprisonment of three years. Further, if a person fails or omits to restore possession of property to bonded labourer, he is liable to punishment with imprisonment for a term which may extend to one year, or with fine which may extend to one thousand rupees or with both. Any person who abets any offence punishable under this Act is also punishable under the Act, and for this purpose, "abetment" has the meaning assigned to it in the Indian Penal Code.

CONTRACT LABOUR
(REGULATION & ABOLITION)
ACT, 1970

CHECKLIST

Object of the Act
To regulate the employment of contract labour in certain establishments and to provide for its abolition in certain circumstances and for matters connected therewith.

Applicability
• Every establishment in which 20 or more work men are employed or were employed on any day of the preceding 12 months as contract labour.
• Every contractor who employs or who employed on any day of the preceding twelve months 20 or more workmen.

Sec. 1

Registration of Establishment
Principal employer employing 20 or more workers through the contractor or the contractor(s) on deposit of required fee in Form 1.

Sec. 7

Prohibition of Employment of Contract Labour
Only by the appropriate Government through issue of notification after consultation with the Board (and not Courts) can order the prohibition of employment of contract labour.

Sec. 10

Revocation of Registration
When obtained by misrepresentation or suppression of material facts etc. after opportunity to the principal employer.

Sec. 9

Licensing of Contractor
• Engaging 20 or more than 20 workers and on deposit of required fee in Form IV.
• Valid for specified period.

Sec. 12. Rule 21

Revocation or Suspension & Amendment of Licences
• When obtained by misrepresentation or suppression of material facts.
• Failure of the contractor to comply with the conditions or contravention of Act or the Rules.

Sec. 14

Welfare measures to be taken by the Contractor
• Contract labour either one hundred or more employed by a contractor for one or more canteens shall be provided and maintained.
• First Aid facilities.
• Number of rest-rooms as required under the Act.
• Drinking water, latrines and washing facilities.

Secs. 16 & 17

Liability of Principal Employer
• To ensure provision for canteen, rest-rooms, sufficient supply of drinking water, latrines and urinals, washing facilities.
• Principal employer entitled to recover from the contractor for providing such amenities or to make deductions from amount payable.

Sec. 20

Responsibility of Contractor for Payment of Wages
• To pay timely and to ensure the disbursement of wages in the presence of the authorised representative of the principal employer.
• Rate of wages not less than the rates as fixed or prevailing in such employement as fixed by agreement.

Sec.21, Rule 25

Laws, Agreement or Standing Orders inconsistent with the Act - Not Permissible
Unless the privileges in the contract between the parties are more favourable than the prescribed in the Act, such contract will be invalid and the workers will continue to get more favourable benefits.

Sec.30

Muster Roll, Wages Register, Deduction Register and Overtime Register by Contractor
• Every contractor shall
  • Maintain Muster Roll and a Register of Wages in Form XVI and Form XVII respectively when combined.
  • Register or wage-cum-Muster Roll in Form XVII where the wage period is a fortnight or less.
  • Maintain a Register of Deductions for damage or loss, Register or Fines and Register of Advances in Form XX, form XXI and Form XXII respectively.
• Maintain a Register of Overtime in Form XXIII.
• To issue wage slips in Form XIX, to the workmen at least a day prior to the disbursement of wages.
• Obtain the signature or thumb impression of the worker concerned against the entries relating to him on the Register of Wages or Muster Roll-cum-Wages Register.
• When covered by Payment of Wages Act, register and records to be maintained under these rules -
  • Muster Roll, • Register of Wages, • Register of Deductions, • Register of Overtime, • Register of Fines, • Register of Advances, • Wage slip.

Rule 79

Registers of Contractors
• **Principal employer**
  • To maintain a register of contractors in respect of every establishment in Form XII.
  Rule 74
• **Contractor**
  • To maintain register of workers for each registered establishment in Form XIII.
  • To issue an employment card to each worker in Form XIV.
  • To issue service certificate to every workman on his termination in Form XV.
  Rules 75, 76 and 77

• To display an abstract of the Act and Rules in English and Hindi and in the language spoken by the majority of workers in such form as may be approved by appropriate authority.
Rule 80
• To display notices showing rates of wages, hours of work, wage period, dates of payment, names and addresses of the Inspector and to send copy to the inspector and any change forthwith.
Rule 81

Returns
Contractor to send half yearly return in Form XXIV in duplicate within 30 days Principal employer to send annual return in Form XXV in duplicate before 15th Feb. following the end of the concerned year.

Rule 82

PENALTIES

Section	Offence	Punishment
Sec. 22	Obstructions	For obstructing the inspector or failing to produce registers etc. - 3 months 'imprisonment or fine upto Rs.500, or both.
Sec. 23	Violation	For violation of the provisions of Act or the Rules, imprisonment of 3 months or fine upto Rs.1000. On continuing contravention, additional fine upto Rs.100 per day.

3. The Contract Labour (Regulation and Abolition) Act, 1970

THE OBJECT

The object of the Contract Labour (Regulation and Abolition) Act, 1970, is to regulate the employment of contract labour in certain establishments and to provide for its abolition in certain circumstances and for matters connected therewith.

APPLICABILITY OF THE ACT

This Act applies to every establishment in which 20 or more workmen are employed or were employed on any day of the preceding 12 months as contract labour and to every contractor who employs or employed on any day of the preceding 12 months 20 or more workmen. However, the appropriate Government is empowered to extend the application of the Act to any establishment or contractor employing less than 20 workmen, after giving not less than 2 months' notice of its intention so to do, by notification in Official Gazette.

The Act is not applicable to an establishment in which work only of an intermittent or casual nature is performed. Where, however, work is performed in an establishment for more than 120 days in the preceding twelve months or if it is of seasonal nature and is performed for more than 60 days in a year, it shall not be deemed to be of an intermittent nature.

ESTABLISHMENT

Section 2(1)(e) of the Act defines 'establishment'. It means any office or department of the Government or a local authority or any place where any industry, trade, business, manufacturing or occupation is carried on.

In an establishment to which the Act is applicable and where employment of contract labour has not been prohibited by the appropriate Government, employment of contract labour is not permitted if it is not registered. A contractor coming within the purview of the Act is not permitted to undertake or execute any work through contract labour until he obtains a licence from the licensing officer for execution of a specific contract.

APPROPRIATE GOVERNMENT

According to section 2(1), the 'appropriate Government' means—

   (i) in relation to an establishment under the Industrial Disputes Act, 1947, the Central Government;

   (ii) in relation to any other establishment, the Government of the State in which that other establishment is situate.

In view of the above, the Central Government has jurisdiction over the establishments in respect of which the appropriate Government under the Industrial Disputes Act, 1947, is the Central Government and for other establishments, the State Governments concerned are the appropriate Government.

WORKMAN

"Workman" has been defined under section 2(i) to mean any person employed in or in connection with the work of any establishment to do any skilled, semi-skilled or un-skilled manual, supervisory, technical or clerical work for hire or reward, whether the terms of employment be express or implied, but does not include any such person—

   (a) who is employed mainly in a managerial or administrative capacity; or

   (b) who, being employed in a supervisory capacity draws wages exceeding five hundred rupees per mensum or exercises, either by the nature of the duties attached to the office or by reason of the powers vested in him, functions mainly of a managerial nature; or

(c) who is an out-worker, that is to say, a person to whom any articles and materials are given out by or on behalf of the principal employer to be made up, cleaned, washed, altered, ornamented, finished, repaired, adapted or otherwise processed for sale for the purposes of the trade or business of the principal employer and the process is to be carried out either in the home of the out-worker or in some other premises not being premises under the control and management of the principal employer.

REGISTRATION FOR PRINCIPAL EMPLOYER

Principal Employer means the owner or occupier or the person who exercises ultimate control and supervision and manages the affairs of the establishment.

According to section 9, no principal employer of an establishment to which the Act applies shall employ contract labour without obtaining registration certificate within the prescribed time and in the case of an establishment the registration has been revoked under section 8 of the Act.

If an establishment has more than one contractor each employing less than 20 workers, the Act will not be applicable to any such contractor, though the establishment will be covered by the Act if the total number of workmen employed by such contractors is twenty or more. The number of workmen employed by a contractor should be taken into consideration to decide whether the contractor should obtain a licence under the Act or not.

LICENCE FOR CONTRACTOR

Contractor in relation to the establishment means a person who undertakes to produce a given result for the establishment other than a mere supply of goods or articles of manufacture to such establishment, through contract labour or who supplies contract labour for any work of the establishment and includes a sub-contractor.

No contractor to whom this Act applies shall undertake or execute any work through contract labour except under and in accordance with a licence issued in that behalf by the Licensing Officer.

Every contractor falling within the purview of the Act shall apply for a licence for executing any work through contract labour, in or in respect of establishment to which the Act is applicable. According to Rule 24 of the Contract Labour (Regulation and Abolition) Central Rules, 1971, before a licence is issued, an amount calculated as prescribed under the Rules for each of the workmen to be employed as contract labour in respect of which the application for licence has been made shall be deposited by the contractor for due performance of the conditions of the licence and compliance with the provisions of the Act or Rules made thereunder. Thus a contractor is required to obtain a licence for every contract and to deposit security at the rate prescribed under the said Rules for each workman employed by him for each contract.

PROHIBITION OF CONTRACT LABOUR

The employment of contract labour under the Act is permissible in different processes/operations in the industry, unless it is prohibited in accordance with the procedure laid down under the Act.

According to section 10 of the Act, the appropriate Government may, after consultation with the Central Board or, as the case may be, a State Board, prohibit by notification in the Official Gazette, employment of contract labour in any process, operation or other work in any establishment. Before issuing such notification in relation to an establishment, the appropriate Government shall have regard to the conditions of work and benefits provided for the contract labour in that establishment, and other relevant factors, such as—

(a) whether process, operation or other work is incidental to or necessary for the industry, trade, business, manufacture or occupation that is carried on in the establishment;

(b) whether it is of a perennial nature, that is to say, it is of sufficient duration having regard to the nature of industry, trade, business, manufacture or occupation carried on in that establishment;

(c) whether it is done ordinarily through regular workmen in that establishment or an establishment similar thereto; and

(d) whether it is sufficient to employ considerable number of whole time workmen.

If a question arises whether any process or operation or other work is of a perennial nature, the decision of the appropriate Government thereon shall be final.

EFFECT OF NON-REGISTRATION

The matter whether the contract workers working in an establishment of principal employer who have not obtained registration certificate will be treated as workers of the principal employer, has always remained in dispute. Earlier, the number of High Courts have held that in case the principal employer did not obtain the registration certificate under section 7 or a contractor has not obtained a licence under section 12 of the Act, the contractor's workers will be deemed to be the employees of the principal employer.

The Supreme Court in one judgment has held that if the principal employer does not get registration under section 7 and/ or the contractor does not get a licence under section 12 of the Contract Labour (Regulation and Abolition) Act, the persons so appointed by the contractor would not be deemed to be the direct employees of the principal employer.

ABSORPTION OF CONTRACT LABOUR

It has been well settled by the various judgments of the Apex Court and High Courts that the contractor's employees will not become the employees of the principal employer, even if the principal employer does not get registration and the contractor does not hold licence, though employing contract labour without obtaining registration or without obtaining licence is an offence under the Act. Also if the principal employer terminates the contract of the contractor and thus the employees of the contractor become surplus, it is not obligatory on the principal employer to absorb the employees of contractor.

NO AUTOMATIC ABSORPTION OF CONTRACT LABOUR ON PROHIBITION/ABOLITION

The Constitution Bench of the Supreme Court has set aside the earlier judgment of *Air India* by holding that on abolition or prohibition of contract labour, the employees/workers engaged through the contractor will not automatically become the employees of the principal employer.

Steel Authority of India Ltd. v. National Union, Water Front Workers, 2001 LLR 961 (SC).

APPROPRIATE GOVERNMENT AND NOT COURTS CAN ORDER FOR ABOLITION OF CONTRACT LABOUR

The Apex Court has clarified that the power of abolition/ prohibition of contract labour is vested with the appropriate Government and not with the Courts.

PAYMENT OF WAGES TO CONTRACT LABOUR

Basically a contractor is responsible for payment of wages to workmen employed by him as contract labour, before the expiry of the specified period. Every principal employer is required to nominate a representative duly authorised by him to be present at the time of disbursement of wages by the contractor and it is the duty of such representative to certify the amounts paid as wages, in such a manner as may be prescribed. In case the contractor fails to make payment of wages within the prescribed period or makes short payment, the principal employer is made liable to make payment of wages in full or the unpaid balance, as the case may be.

According to Rule 25(2)(iv) of the Contract Labour (Regulation and Abolition) Central Rules, 1971, the rates of wages payable to the workmen by the contractor shall not be less than the rates prescribed under the Minimum Wages Act for such employment where applicable and where the rates have been fixed by agreement, settlement or award, not less than the rate so fixed.

According to Rule 25(2)(v)(a), in case where the workmen employed by the contractor perform the same or similar kind of work as the workmen directly employed by the principal employer of the establishment, the wage rates, holidays, hours of work and other conditions of service of the workmen of the contractor shall be the same as applicable to the workmen directly employed by the principal employer of the establishment on the same or similar kind of work. In case of disagreement with regard to the type of work, the same shall be decided by the Chief Labour Commissioner (Central) whose decision shall be final.

LIABILITIES OF THE CONTRACTOR AND PRINCIPAL EMPLOYER

The Act stipulates to be provided and the responsibilities to be imposed for looking after the welfare and health of the contract labour, in as much as it has been made obligatory on the contractor employing contract labour to provide and maintain sufficient supply of wholesome drinking water and reasonable number of latrines, urinals and washing facilities, etc. Where such facilities and amenities are not provided by the contractor, the responsibility shifts to the principal employer to provide other suitable and adequate facilities to the contract labour. Canteen facilities are also to be provided by the contractor in the establishment wherein more than 100 workers are likely to work for six months or more. Provision and maintenance of first-aid box equipped with requisite materials and medicines is another requirement.

All expenses incurred by the principal employer in providing the amenities may be recovered by the principal employer from the contractor either by deduction from any amount payable to the contractor or as a debt payable by the contractor.

PENALTIES AND PROCEDURES

According to section 25(1) of the Act, if a person committing an offence under the Act is a company, the company as well as every person incharge of and responsible to the company for the conduct of its business at the time of commission of the offence shall be deemed to be guilty of the offence and liable to be proceeded against and punished accordingly. According to section 25(2) of the Act, notwithstanding anything contained in sub-section (1), where an offence under the Act has been committed by a company and it is proved that the offence has been committed with the consent or connivance of or that the commission of the offence is attributable to any neglect on the part of any director, manager, managing agent or such other officer shall also be liable to be proceeded against and punished accordingly.

OTHER LABOUR ACTS APPLICABLE TO CONTRACTORS' ESTABLISHMENTS/CONTRACT LABOUR

1. Factories Act, 1948:

The definition of 'worker' under the Factories Act does not make any discrimination between the person directly employed by the principal employer and person employed by or through a contractor in the defined processes and consequently the contract labour thus employed shall be entitled to all the privileges and benefits applicable to the workers in a factory, for example, weekly holidays, compensatory holidays, extra wages for overtime, leave with wages, etc., subject to such conditions as are prescribed in the relevant sections of the Act.

2. The Employees' Provident Funds and Miscellaneous Provisions Act, 1952:

The term 'employee' used in section 2(f) of the Act includes any person employed by or through a contractor in or in connection with the work of an establishment to which the said Act applies and he will thus get the advantage of the schemes framed under the Act. The prescribed contributions have to be made in respect of the contract labour in the same manner and at the same rates as applicable to the employees directly employed by the establishment. The principal employer has to pay the contributions in respect of contractor's employees as well as his own employees in the first instance but the amount paid on behalf of the contractor is recoverable from the latter.

3. The Employees' State Insurance Act, 1948:

The contract labour is entitled to the benefit conferred by the Act so long as they meet the requirement of the expression 'employee' as defined under section 2(9) of the Employees' State Insurance Act. The principal employer is liable to pay both the employer's contributions and the employees' contributions in respect of contract labour in the first instance but the amount so paid is recoverable from the contractor concerned.

4. The Payment of Wages Act, 1936:

The provisions of the Act are duly applicable to the contract labour employed by any factory or establishment if the employment in which they are engaged is otherwise covered by the said Act.

5. The Minimum Wages Act, 1948:

The provisions of the Act are applicable to the contract labour if the employment in which they are engaged is duly covered by Minimum Wages Act, 1948.

6. The Industrial Disputes Act, 1947:

The Act is applicable to deal with any dispute between the contractors and the labour employed by them.

7. The Workmen's Compensation Act, 1923:

Under section 12 of the Act the principal employer who engages a contractor for the purpose of his trade or business for the execution of whole or any part of any work, which is ordinarily part of the trade or business of the principal employer, shall be liable to pay the same compensation to the worker of the said contractor as he would have been liable to pay if the worker had been directly employed by him. However, the principal employer shall be indemnified by the contractor and it is open to a workman employed by the contractor to recover compensation from the contractor directly instead of proceeding against the principal employer.

MAINTENANCE OF PRESCRIBED REGISTERS, RECORDS AND SUBMISSION OF RETURNS

Section 29 of the Act enjoins upon every principal employer and the contractor to maintain the registers and records giving prescribed particulars of the contractor and the contract labour employed respectively, indicating the nature of work performed by the contract labour and the rate of wages paid to the contract labour. In short, the forms, registers and notices prescribed for the purpose are stated hereinafter—

    (a) Principal employer to maintain register of contractor in Form XII;

    (b) Every contractor to maintain in respect of each registered establishment where he employs contract labour a register in Form XIII;

    (c) Every contractor to issue an employment card in Form XIV to each worker and to issue a service certificate on termination of employment in Form XV;

    (d) Every contractor in respect of each work has to maintain registers like—

        (i) Muster Roll;

        (ii) Register of Wages;

        (iii) Register of Deductions;

(iv) Register of Overtime;

(v) Register of Fines;

(vi) Register of Advances; and;

(vii) Wage slips.

However, if a combined/alternative form is being maintained under any Act or Rule, which provides the above information, as required under the Contract Labour Act or Rules, the same could be done with previous approval of the competent authority;

(e) Duty to display notice in English and local languages :

Rule 81 of the rules enjoins upon the principal employer or the contractor, as the case may be, to exhibit the notices showing the rates of wages, hours of work, wage period, dates of payment of wages, names and addresses of the inspectors having jurisdiction in English and in Hindi and in the local language understood by the majority of workers at a conspicuous place and send a copy of the same to the Area Inspector;

(f) Submission of half-yearly return to the Licensing Officer:

Every contractor is under obligation to send half-yearly return in Form XXIV in duplicate so as to reach the Licensing Officer concerned not later than 30 days from the close of the half year, *i.e.*, for the period ending June and December. A principal employer has to send an annual return in Form XXV in duplicate so as to reach the authorities by 15th February following the close of the year;

(g) Welfare and other amenities for contract labour:

The contractor is required to provide suitable canteen, sufficiently lighted and ventilated rest rooms, creches (having the requisite number of employees), latrines, urinals, wholesome drinking water, washing facilities and first-aid-boxes for the use by the contract labour. If a contractor fails to provide such facilities, the principal employer shall be liable to provide the same and recover the expenses involved from the contractor.

Before concluding, we must have a look on the procedure as laid down in the rules under the Act for the purpose of registration of principal employers and licensing of the contractors.

We are aware that the Act is applicable to principal employer who has twenty persons working as contract labour through one or more contractors. While the Act is applicable to only such contractors who have 20 employees working under him in a particular establishment.

The procedure for registration and licensing is as under:

1. Application for registration as principal employer is to be made in Form I to the Registering Officer of the area to be accompanied by a Demand Draft showing payment of the prescribed fee for registration and such application is to be delivered either personally or sent by registered post. (Section 7 – Rule 17).

2. Registering Officer shall issue a registration certificate in Form II containing the name and address of the establishment, maximum number of labour to be employed as contract labour in the establishment, nature of business/trade and such other particulars as may be deemed necessary. The Registering Officer is required to maintain a register in Form III (Section 7 – Rule 18).

3. Once the establishment is registered, change if any in any of the particulars in the certificate of registration shall have to be intimated to the Registering Officer within 30 days of the change and in case of change in the number of contract labour, particularly, one has to deposit extra amount with the authorities (Rule 20).

4. Renewal application is required to be made 30 days in advance with the requisite information to be furnished in Form VII.

5. Similarly, a contractor having 20 or more employees shall have to make an application in Form IV to the Licensing Officer of the area who is usually the Registering Officer for grant of a licence, alongwith the certificate from principal employer in Form V which carries an undertaking from the latter that he

would be bound by the provisions of the Act and rules in so for as the same relate to him. The application is to be accompanied with requisite fee and security for each of the labour so engaged at the rates specified. Such a licence is valid for a period of one year from the date it is granted (Rules 21, 24, and 27). The said licence shall have to be got renewed by depositing the requisite fee after the expiry of the period from which the same had been granted.

6. The contractor shall observe the conditions appended to the licence as laid down in rule 25 which are 10 in number, but a few are quite important like the number of employees should not increase than the one for which the licence has been granted, to get the licence renewed, to pay the rate of wages to his employees at the same rate as is given to the employees doing same or similar work by the principal employer, but in no case the rate of wages can be less than the minimum rate of wages. The other conditions of service relating to working hours, weekly off, leave, etc., have also to be at par with the employees of principal employer. In case of disagreement over the type of work it is the Labour Commissioner in case of State Governments to determine whether the work done by the employees of the contractor is same or of similar nature when compared with the employees of the principal employers.

7. In case the Registration Certificate or the Licence is either not granted or not renewed, an appeal can be made within 30 days of the communication of the order to the Appellate Authority by depositing requisite fee and enclosing a copy of the order of Registering/Licensing Officer as the case may be.

It may be mentioned that no such formality as aforementioned is required in case the work is to last for less than 15 days.

GUIDELINES FOR DRAFTING AGREEMENT BETWEEN PRINCIPAL EMPLOYER AND THE CONTRACTOR

- The agreement should be drafted and executed on non-judicial stamp paper
- The agreement must disclose the names, addresses of the contractor and the principal employer.
- The agreement must disclose the place of work, time of working, rate of compensation (towards consideration) and consequences arising out of breach of contract and procedure for termination by either of the parties to the agreement.
- The agreement must carry out the objectives of statutory provisions and judicial pronouncements.
- The agreement must disclose the scope of work, deployment of manpower in number, period of validity, compensation, security deposit and terms of payment of bills.
- The agreement should be between the contractor and the principal employer and should be witnessed by two witnesses.

THE CHILD LABOUR
(PROHIBITION AND REGULATION)
ACT, 1986

CHECKLIST

Object of the Act
To regulate the conditions of the work of the children in certain employment.

The important clarifications
• 'Child' means a person who has not completed his 14 years of age.
• 'Establishment' includes a shop, commercial establishment, workshop, farm, residential hotel, restaurant, eating house, theatre or other place of public amusement or entertainment. **Sec. 2**

Prohibition of employment of children in certain occupations and processes
No child to be employed in occupation set forth in Part A of the Schedule or any workshop wherein any of the processes set-forth in Part B of the Schedule is carried on. **Sec. 3**

Hours and period of work
• Not to exceed three hours
• Interval for rest - one hour
• Spread over not more than six hours inclusive of interval and the time spent for waiting. **Sec.7**

Not permitted to work
• Between 7 pm to 8 am.
• Overtime working.
If such a child is working in another establishment. **Sec. 7**

Weekly holidays
One whole day, not to be altered more than once in three months. **Sec. β**

Notice to Inspector
Furnishing details of
• Name and situation of establishment.
• Name of the person in actual management of the establishment.
• Address for communication.
• Nature of the occupation. **Sec. 9**

Dispute as to age
In the absence of certificate of age, can be referred for decision of prescribed medical authority. **Sec. 10**

Maintenance & production of register by occupier
• The name and date of birth of every child so employed or permitted to work.
• Hours and period of work of any such child and the intervals of rest to which he is entitled.
• The nature of work of any such child.
• Such other particulars as may be prescribed. **Sec. 11**

Display of notice
To contain abstract of section 3 pertaining to prohibition of employment of children and the provisions for penalties. **Sec. 12**

Health and safety
To be notified by appropriate government in accordance with guidelines given in section 13 of the Act. **Sec. 13**

PENALTIES

Offence	Punishment
for violation of section 3	Imprisonment for not less than 3 months which may extend to one year, or fine not less than 10,000/- which may extend to Rs.20,000/- or both.
Repetition of violation	Imprisonment for a term not less than six months which may extend to two years.
For failure to : • give notice as required by section 9 • maintain a register as required by section 11 or make any false entry in any such registers; or • display a notice containing an abstract of section 3 and this section as required by section 12, or • comply with or contravene any other provisions of this Act or the Rules made thereunder.	Shall be punishable with simple imprisonment which may extend to one month or with fine which may extend to ten thousand rupees or with both. **Sec. 14**

The Supreme Court in *M.C. Mehta* v. *State of Tamil Nadu*, 1996 SCC 756 has directed the discontinuance of the employment of child labour and ordered payment of compensation of Rs.20,000 per child. The court has also laid down certain directions in relation to working hours in non-hazardous jobs and providing for education by the employer and the State.

4. The Child Labour (Prohibition and Regulation) Act, 1986

The main object of the Act is to prohibit the engagement of children who have not completed 14th year of age in certain employments and to regulate the conditions of work of children in certain other employments. Employment of children has been prohibited in occupations relating to (1) transport of passengers, goods or mails by railways, (2) sinder picking, clearing of ash pit or building operations in the railway premises, (3) catering establishments in railways, (4) construction of a railway station, (5) ports. Employment of children is also prohibited in the following industries : (1) bidi making, (2) carpet weaving, (3) cement manufacture, including bagging of cement, (4) cloth printing, dyeing and weaving, (5) manufacture of matches, explosives and fire works, (6) mega cutting and splitting, (7) shellac manufacture, (8) soap manufacture, (9) tanning, (10) wool cleaning, (11) building and construction industry. The Government has also prohibited employment of children in the following occupations or processes: (1) Abattoirs/Slaughter houses, (2) hazardous processes and dangerous operations as notified, (3) printing, as defined, (4) cashew and cashewnut descaling and processing, (5) soldering processes in electronic industry. The Act provides that no child shall be permitted to work between 7 p.m. and 8 a.m. and shall not be permitted to work over-time. No child shall work for more than 3 hours before he has an interval of one hour. Spread over has been fixed at six hours. A child cannot work in more than one establishment on any day. A weekly holiday is allowed. The Act also provides for health and safety measures for the children. The employer is required to notify the Factory Inspectors in case he engages a child for employment. Production of certificate of age is also required under the rules of the Act. For contravention of provisions of the Act, the employer will be punishable with imprisonment of not less than three months which may extend to one year or with a fine of Rs. 10,000 which may extend to Rs. 20,000 or with both. In case the offence is repeated, imprisonment shall not be less than six months which may extend to two years.

The Supreme Court in *M.C. Mehta* v. *State of Tamil Nadu*, 1996 SCC 756, has directed the discontinuance of the employment of child and ordered payment of compensation of Rs. 20,000 per child. The court has also laid down certain directions in relation to working hours in non-hazardous jobs and providing for education by the employer and the State.

It is pertinent to state that the employment of children as domestic servants in dhabas (roadside eateries), restaurants, hotels, motels, teashops, resorts, spas or in other recreational centres has been banned from October 10, 2006 not only in Delhi but all over India. The ban, notified by the labour ministry has been imposed under the Child Labour (Prohibition & Regulation) Act, 1986. The decision has been taken on the recommendation of the Technical Advisory Committee on Child Labour. The committee had stated that the occupations mentioned were hazardous for children and had recommended their inclusion in the occupations which are prohibited for persons below 14 years under the Child Labour (Prohibition & Regulation) Act, 1986.

MAINTENANCE OF REGISTER

Every occupier shall maintain in respect of children employed or permitted to work in any establishment, a register to be available for inspection by an Inspector at all times during working hours or when work is being carried on in any such establishment, showing—

(a) the name and date of birth of every child so employed or permitted to work;

(b) hours and periods of work of any such child and the intervals of rest to which he is entitled;

(c) the nature of work of any such child; and

(d) such other particulars as may be prescribed.

PENALTIES

Any employer who

- fails to give notice as required by section 9; or

- fails to maintain a register as required by section 11 or makes any false entry in any such register; or

- fails to display a notice containing an abstract of section 3 and section 12; or

- fails to comply with or contravenes any other provisions of this Act or the rules made thereunder,

shall be punishable with simple imprisonment which may extend to one month or with fine which may extend to ten thousand rupees or with both.

DISPLAY OF NOTICE

A notice containing abstracts of sections 3 and 14 of the Act, mainly provided for railway administration and port authority, shall be caused to be displayed by every occupier in a conspicuous and accessible place at every station on its railway or within the limits of a port or at the place of work, as the case may be, in the local language and in the English language.

———

EMPLOYEES' PROVIDENT FUNDS & MISC. PROVISIONS ACT & THE SCHEMES

CHECKLIST

Eligibility

Any person who is employed for work of an establishment or employed through contractor in or in connection with the work of an establishment.

Payment of Contribution

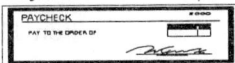

[PAYCHECK]

• The employer shall pay the contribution payable to the EPF, DLI and Employees' Pension Fund in respect of the member of the Employees' Pension Fund employed by him directly by or through a contractor.

• It shall be the responsibility of the principal employer to pay the contributions payable to the EPF, DLI and Employees' Pension Fund by himself in respect of the employees directly employed by him and also in respect of the employees employed by or through a contractor.

Clarification about Contribution

After revision in wage ceiling from Rs.5000 to **Rs.6500** w.e.f. 1-6-2001 per month, the government will continue to contribute **1.16%** upto the actual wage of maximum Rs.6500 per month towards Employees' Pension Scheme. The employer's share in the Pension Scheme will be Rs.541 w.e.f. 1-6-2001.

Under Employees' Deposit-Linked Insurance Scheme the contribution @ **0.50%** is required to be paid upto a maximum limit of Rs.6500. The employer will pay administrative charge @ **0.01%** on a maximum limit of Rs.6500.

The employer will also pay administrative charges @ **0.01%** on maximum limit of Rs.6500 whereas an exempted establishment will pay inspection charges @ **0.005%** on the total wages paid.

Notes:

(1) The above clarification is given by taking wages upto a maximum of Rs.6500 towards wage (basic + DA).

(2) Since an excluded employee *i.e.* drawing wages more than Rs.6500 can also become member of the Fund and the Schemes on joint request and if, for instance, such an employee is getting Rs.10,000 per month, his share towards provident fund contribution will be Rs.1200 *e.g.* 12% and employer's share towards provident fund contribution will be Rs.659 and Rs.541 towards Employees' Pension Fund.

Applicability

• Every establishment which is a factory engaged in any industry specified in Schedule 1 and in which 20 or more persons are employed.

• Any other establishment employing 20 or more persons which Central Government may, by notification, specify in this behalf.

• Any establishment employing even less than 20 persons can be covered voluntarily u/s 1(4) of the Act.

Benefits

Employees covered enjoy a benefit of Social Security in the form of an unattachable and unwithdrawable (except in severely restricted circumstances like buying house, marriage/ education, etc.) financial nest egg to which employees and employers contribute equally throughout the covered persons' employment.

This sum is payable normally on retirement or death. Other Benefits include Employees' Pension Scheme and Employees' Deposit Linked Insurance Scheme.

Rates of Contribution

SCHEME	EMPLOYEE'S	EMPLOYER'S	CENTRAL GOVT.'S
Provident Fund Scheme	12%	Amount > 8.33% (in case where contribution is 12% or 10%) 10% (in case of certain Establishments as per details given earlier)	NIL
Insurance Scheme	NIL	0.5%	NIL
Pension Scheme	NIL	8.33% (Diverted out of Provident Fund Contributions)	1.16%

Damages

• Less than 2 months	.... @17% per annum
• Two months and above but less than four months	.... @22% per annum
• Four months and above but less than six months	.... @27% per annum
• Six months and above	..... @37% per annum

Penal Provision

Liable to be arrested without warrant being a cognisable offence. Defaults by employer in paying contributions or inspection/administrative charges attract imprisonment upto 3 years and fine upto Rs.10,000 (S.14). For any retrospective application, all dues have to be paid by employer with damages upto 100% of arrears.

5. The Employees' Provident Funds and Miscellaneous Provisions Act, 1952

THE OBJECT

Among the social security legislations, the Employees' Provident Funds and Miscellaneous Provisions Act occupies the most important position. The Act came into existence in 1952 to ensure compulsory Provident Fund, Employees Pension Scheme and Deposit Linked Insurance in factories and other establishments for the benefits of employees.

APPLICABILITY OF THE ACT

It is a Central Act and extends to whole of India except the State of Jammu and Kashmir. It applies to those factories which employ twenty or more persons and are engaged in the manufacturing of the items as mentioned in Schedule I of the Act. Apart from factories, the Act also applies to other establishments wherein twenty or more persons are employed and also that the Central Government has issued notification for coverage of establishments under section 1(3) of the Act. The infancy benefit for first three years from setting up of the factory or an establishment about the applicability of the Act, hitherto available stands withdrawn w.e.f. 23-9-1997 by Amendment Act 10 of 1998.

The Employees' Pension Scheme (EPS), 1995 applies w.e.f. 16-11-1995 to all establishments to which the Employees' Provident Funds and Miscellaneous Provisions Act, 1952 is applicable and on its introduction the Family Pension Scheme, 1971 ceases to exist.

Rate of Contributions

An employer has to make a matching contribution of 10% and 12% (as revised w.e.f. 22-9-1997) of employees' pay to Provident Fund Account. The rate of contribution towards the Employees' Pension Fund is 8.33% of pay, *i.e.*, basic wages with dearness allowance, retaining allowance and cash value of food concession admissible, if any.

Payment of Contribution

1. The employer shall pay the contribution payable to the Employees' Pension Fund in respect of the member of the Employees' Pension Fund employed by him directly or by or through a contractor.

2. It shall be the responsibility of the principal employer to pay the contributions payable to the Employees' Pension Fund by himself in respect of the employees directly employed by him and also in respect of the employees employed by or through a contractor.

LEVY OF DAMAGES WHEN THE PAYMENT OF CONTRIBUTION IS DELAYED

The employer of an establishment to which the provisions of the Employees' Provident Funds and Miscellaneous Provisions Act, 1952 apply must pay the contributions payable under the E.P.F. & M.P. Act, Family Pension Fund or Insurance Fund, both the employees' contribution as well as his own every month within the time specified in Para 38(1) of the Employees'Provident Funds Scheme, 1952, *i.e.*, before 15th of the following month. On failure to do so, the Central Provident Commissioner or such officer as may be authorised by the Central Government may recover from the employer by way of penalty such damages, not exceeding the amount of arrears, as may be specified in the Scheme. However, the Central Board is empowered to reduce or waive the damages in relation to an establishment which is a sick industrial company and in respect of which a scheme for rehabilitation has been sanctioned by Board of Industrial and Financial Reconstruction established under section 4 of the Sick Industrial Companies (Special Provisions) Act, 1985 subject to such terms and conditions as may be specified in the Scheme.

RECOVERY OF DAMAGES FOR DEFAULT IN PAYMENT OF ANY CONTRIBUTIONS:

1. Where an employer makes default in the payment of any contribution to the Employees' Pension Fund, or in the payment of any charges payable under any other provisions of the Act or the Scheme, the Central Provident Fund Commissioner or such officer as may be authorised by the Central Government, by notification in the Official Gazette, in this behalf, may recover from the employer by way of penalty, damages at the rates given below:—

Period of default	Rate of damages (Percentage of arrears per annum)
(a) Less than two months	Seventeen
(b) Two months and above but less than four months	Twenty-Two
(c) Four months and above but less than six months	Twenty-Seven.
(d) Six months and above	Thirty-Seven.

2. The damages shall be calculated to the nearest rupee, 50 paise or more to be counted as the nearest higher rupee and fraction of a rupee less than 50 paise to be ignored.

WAGES ETC., OF THE EMPLOYEES CANNOT BE REDUCED

No employer in relation to an establishment to which any Scheme or the Insurance Scheme applies shall, by reason only of his liability for the payment of any contribution to the Fund or the Insurance Fund or any charges under this Act or the Scheme or the Insurance Scheme, reduce whether directly or indirectly, the wages of any employee to whom the Scheme or the Insurance Scheme applies or the total quantum of benefits in the nature of old age pension, gratuity, Provident Fund or Life Insurance to which the employee is entitled under the terms of his employment, express or implied.

PAYMENT OF CONTRIBUTION ALSO FOR THE EMPLOYEES OF A CONTRACTOR

(1) The employer shall, in the first instance, pay both the contribution payable by himself (in the scheme referred to as the employer's contribution) and also on behalf of the member employed by him directly or by or through a contractor, the contribution payable by such member in the Scheme referred to as the member's contribution.

(2) In respect of employees employed by or through a contractor, the contractor shall recover the contribution payable by such employee (in the Scheme referred to as the member's contribution) and shall pay to the principal employer the amount of member's contribution so deducted together with an equal amount of contribution in this Scheme referred to as the employer's contribution and also administrative charges.

(3) It shall be the responsibility of the principal employer to pay both the contributions payable by himself in respect of the employees directly employed by him and also in respect of the employees employed by or through a contractor and also administrative charges.

Explanation.—For the purposes of this paragraph the expression "administrative charges" means such percentage of the pay (basic wages, dearness allowance, retaining allowance, if any and cash value of food concessions admissible thereon) for the time being payable to the employees other than an excluded employee, and in respect of which Provident Fund contributions are payable as the Central Government may, in consultation with the Central Board and having regard to the resources of the Fund for meeting its normal administrative expenses fix.

(4) An employer shall not be entitled to deduct the employer's contribution from the wages of a member or otherwise to recover it from him.

DECLARATION BY PERSON TAKING UP EMPLOYMENT

The employer in relation to a factory or other establishment shall before taking any person into employment, ask him to state in writing whether or not he is a member of the Fund and if he is, ask for the Account Number and/or the name and particulars of the last employer, if he is unable to furnish the Account Number.

He shall require such person to furnish and such person shall, on demand, furnish to him for communication to the Commissioner particulars regarding himself and his nominee required for the Declaration Form. Such employer shall enter the particulars in the Declaration Form and obtain the signature or thumb impression of the person concerned:

> *Declaration by persons taking up employment after the Fund had been established.*

The employer shall before taking any person into employment, ask him/her to state in writing whether or not he is a member of the Employees' Pension Fund and, if he/she is, also ask him/her to furnish a copy of the scheme certificate issued by the Commissioner to him/her in respect of the past employment in terms of paragraph 12 as the case may be. If the person concerned was not in employment previously or had availed of return of contribution in respect of his/her previous employment, he/she shall, on demand by the employer, furnish to him, for communication to the Commissioner particulars concerning him/herself and his/her family in the Form prescribed by the Central Provident Fund Commissioner.

PREPARATION OF CONTRIBUTION CARDS

The employer shall prepare a contribution card in Form 3 or Form 3A as may be appropriate, in respect of every employee in his employment at the commencement of the Scheme or who is taken into employment after that date and who is required or entitled to become or is a member of the Fund including those who produce an Account Number and in respect of whom no fresh Declaration Form is prepared :

Provided that in the case of any such employee who has become a member of the Family Pension Fund under the Employees' Family Pension Scheme, 1971, the aforesaid Forms shall also contain such particulars as are necessary to comply with the requirements of that Scheme.

PREPARATION OF CONTRIBUTION CARDS FOR EMPLOYEES' PENSION SCHEME

The employer shall prepare as Employees' Pension Fund Contribution Card, in respect of each employee who has become a member of the Employees' Pension Fund.

DUTIES OF EMPLOYERS UNDER EMPLOYEES' PROVIDENT FUNDS SCHEME

(1) Every employer shall send to the Commissioner, within fifteen days of the commencement of this Scheme, a consolidated return in such form as the Commissioner may specify, of the employees required or entitled to become members of the Fund showing the basic wage, retaining allowance (if any) and dearness allowance including the cash value of any food concession paid to each of such employees:

Provided that if there is no employee who is required or entitled to become a member of the Fund, the employer shall send a 'Nil' return.

(2) Every employer shall send to the Commissioner within fifteen days of the close of each month a return—

(a) in Form 5, of the employees qualifying to become members of the Fund for the first time during the preceding month together with the declarations in Form 2 furnished by such qualifying employees; and

(b) in such form as the Commissioner may specify, of the employees leaving service of the employer during the preceding month:

Provided that if there is no employee qualifying to become a member of the Fund for the first time or there is no employee leaving service of the employer during the preceding month, the employer shall send a 'Nil' return.

(3) Every employer shall maintain an inspection note book in such form as the Commissioner may specify, for an Inspector to record his observations on his visit to the establishment.

(4) Every employer shall maintain such accounts in relation to the amounts contributed to the Fund by him and by his employees as the Central Board may, from time to time, direct and it shall be the duty of every employer to assist the Central Board in making such payments from the Fund to his employees as are sanctioned by or under the authority of the Central Board.

EMPLOYER TO FURNISH PARTICULARS OF OWNERSHIP

Every employer in relation to a factory or other establishment to which the Act applies or is applied hereafter shall furnish to the Commissioner particulars of all the branches and departments, owners, occupiers, directors, partners, managers or any other person or persons who have the ultimate control over the affairs of such factory or establishment and also send intimation of any change in such particulars, within fifteen days of such change, to the Commissioner by registered post.

DUTIES OF THE EMPLOYER UNDER EMPLOYEES' PENSION SCHEME

(a) Every employer shall send to the Regional Provident Fund Commissioner (RPFC) within three months of the commencement of this scheme, a consolidated return of the employees entitled to become members of the Employees' Pension Scheme with their wages. If no employee is entitled, then a 'NIL' return should be sent to RPFC.

(b) Every employer shall send to the RPFC within fifteen days of the close of each month a return in respect of the employees leaving service during the preceding month.

(c) The principal employer shall ensure that every contractor submits to him within seven days of the close of every month, a statement showing the particulars in respect of his employees for its further submission to the RPFC.

(d) The employer shall prepare an Employees' Pension Fund Contribution Card in respect of each employee who has become a member of the Employees' Pension Fund.

(e) The employer shall ensure the collection of particulars concerning the member and his family in the prescribed form.

(f) Every employer shall furnish to the RPFC particulars of all the branches and departments, owners, occupiers, directors, partners, managers or any other person or persons who have ultimate control of the establishment and shall also send intimation of any change within 15 days by a registered post.

(g) The employer shall before taking any person into employment, ask him/her to state in writing whether or not he/she is a member of the Employees' Pension Fund and, if he/she is, also ask him/her to furnish a copy of the scheme certificate issued by the RPFC to him/her in respect of the past employment in terms of paragraph 12, as the case may be. If the person concerned was not in employment previously or had availed of return of contribution in respect of his/her previous employment, he/she shall, on demand by the employer, furnish to him, for communication to the RPFC, particulars concerning him/herself and his/her family in the prescribed form.

MODE OF PAYMENT OF CONTRIBUTIONS—SUBMISSION OF RETURNS/FORMS

(1) The employer shall, before paying the member his wages in respect of any period or part of period for which contributions are payable, deduct the employee's contribution from his wages which together with his own contribution as well as an administrative charges of such percentage of the pay, basic wages, dearness allowance, retaining allowance, if any, and cash value of food concessions admissible thereon for the time being payable to the employees other than an excluded employee, and in respect of which Provident Fund contributions are payable as the Central Government may fix, he shall within fifteen days of the close of every month pay the same to the Fund by separate bank drafts or cheques on account of contributions and administrative charges:

Provided that if payment is made by a cheque on an outstation bank, the actual bank collection charges in respect of both the contributions and the administrative charges shall be included in the amount for which the cheque is drawn in respect of the administrative charges :

Provided further that where there is no branch of the Reserve Bank or the State Bank of India at the station where the factory or other establishment is situated, the employer shall pay to the Fund the amount mentioned above by means of Reserve Bank of India (Government) Drafts at par, separately on account of contributions and administrative charges.

(2) The employer shall forward to the Commissioner, within twenty-five days of the close of the month, a monthly consolidated statement, in such form as the Commissioner may specify, showing recoveries made from the wages of each employee and the amount contributed by the employer in respect of each such employee:

Provided that an employer shall send a 'NIL' return, if no such recoveries have been made from the employees:

Provided that in the case of any such employee who has become a member of the Family Pension Fund under the Employees' Family Pension Scheme, 1971, the aforesaid Form shall also contain such particulars as are necessary to comply with the requirements of that Scheme.

(3) Notwithstanding anything contained in sub-paragraph (2), in respect of such establishments as are notified by the Commissioner to be annually posted establishments, the employer shall forward to the Commissioner within twenty-five days of the close of each month, a monthly abstract in such form as the Commissioner may specify showing, *inter alia,* the aggregate amount of recoveries made from the wages of all the members and the aggregate amount contributed by the employer in respect of all such members for the month. The employer shall also send to the Commissioner, within one month of the close of the period of currency, a Consolidated Annual Contribution Statement in Form 6A, showing the total amount of recoveries made during the period of currency from the wages of each member and total amount contributed by the employer in respect of each such member for the said period. The employer shall maintain on his record duplicate copies of the aforesaid monthly abstract and Consolidated Annual Contribution Statement for production at the time of inspection by an Inspector.

TO MAKE ENTRY OF CONTRIBUTIONS IN THE CONTRIBUTION CARD

The amount recovered every month from the wages of an employee as well as the contribution made by the employer in respect of each such employee shall be entered by the employer every month in the contribution card opened in the name of each member under this Scheme.

RENEWAL OF CONTRIBUTION CARDS

An employer shall, on or before the expiration of the period of currency of the contribution card prepare in respect of each member employed by him a card in Form 3 or Form 3A as may be appropriate, for the next period of currency:

Provided that in the case of any such employee who has become a member of the Family Pension Fund under the

Employees' Family Pension Scheme, 1971, the aforesaid form shall also contain such particulars as are necessary to comply with the requirements of that Scheme.

SUBMISSION OF CONTRIBUTION CARDS TO THE COMMISSIONER

Every employer shall, within one month from the date of expiration of the period of currency of the contribution cards in respect of members employed by him, send the contribution cards to the Commissioner together with a statement in Form 6:

Provided that where a member leaves service, the employer shall send the contribution card in respect of such member before the twentieth day of the month following that in which the member left the service :

Provided further that in the case of any such employee who has become a member of the Family Pension Fund under the Employees' Family Pension Scheme, 1971, the aforesaid Form shall also contain such particulars as are necessary to comply with the requirements of that Scheme.

CUSTODY OF CONTRIBUTION CARDS

The employer shall retain in his custody the contribution cards in respect of each member employed by him and shall take every precaution against loss or damage of the contribution cards.

INSPECTION OF CARDS BY MEMBERS

Any member making a request in this behalf to the employer shall be permitted to inspect his cards himself or to have the same inspected by any person duly authorised by him in writing to do so within 72 hours of making such request provided that no such request shall be entertained more than once in every two calendar months.

PRODUCTION OF CARDS AND RECORDS FOR INSPECTION BY THE COMMISSIONER OR INSPECTOR

Every employer shall, whenever the Commissioner or any other officer authorised by him in this behalf or an Inspector so requests, either in person or by notice in writing, produce before the Commissioner, Officer or Inspector, as the case may be, the records of any member employed by him and any card then in his possession, and if so required by the said Commissioner, Officer or Inspector, shall deliver such record to the said Commissioner.

OBLIGATION OF EMPLOYERS PERTAINING TO RETURNS AND TO CARRY OUT DIRECTIONS

1. Every employer shall send to the Commissioner within three months of the commencement of this Scheme, a consolidated return of the employees entitled to become members of the Employees' Pension Fund showing the basic wage, retaining allowance, if any, and dearness allowance including the cash value of any food concession paid to each of such employees:

Provided that if there is no employee who is entitled to become a member of the Employees' Pension Fund, the employer shall send a 'NIL' return.

2. Every employer shall send to the Commissioner within fifteen days of the close of each month a return in respect of the employees leaving service of the employer during the preceding month:

Provided that if there is no employee leaving service of the employer during the preceding month the employer shall send a 'NIL' return.

3. Every employer shall maintain such accounts in relation to the amounts contributed by him to the Employees' Pension Fund as the Central Board may, from time to time direct and it shall be the duty of every employer to assist the Central Board in making such payments from the Employees' Pension Fund to his employees as are sanctioned by or under the authority of the Central Board.

4. Notwithstanding anything contained in this paragraph, the Central Board may issue such directions to the employers generally, as it may consider necessary or expedient, for the purpose of implementing the scheme, and it shall be the duty of every employer to carry out such directions.

ADVANCES/WITHDRAWALS

An employee can avail of his non-refundable withdrawals/ advances for construction of house, sickness, marriage of self/ dependents and higher education of his children etc.

SCALE OF BENEFITS PAYABLE UNDER EDLI SCHEME

DEATH CASES OCCURRING DURING THE PERIOD	QUANTUM OF BENEFIT PAYABLE
1. August, 1976 to February, 1990	Equal to the average balance in Provident Fund A/c of the member subject to maximum Rs. 10,000
2. March, 1990 to March, 1993	Equal to the average balance in Provident Fund A/c of the member subject to maximum Rs. 25,000
3. April, 1993 to June, 2000	Equal to the average balance upto Rs.25,000 in the Provident Fund A/c of the member plus 25% of the remaining balance, if any, subject to Rs. 35,000 maximum
4. July, 2000 onwards	Equal to the average balance upto Rs. 35,000 plus 25% of the balance amount, if any, subject to Rs. 60,000 maximum

SCALES OF BENEFITS UNDER EMPLOYEES' DEPOSIT LINKED INSURANCE SCHEME, 1976

Salary Slab (upper limit), Rate of Contribution, Administrative Charges and Inspection Charges to be Borne by Employer

Salary Slab	Rate of Contribution	Adm. Charges	Inspection Charges
Rs. 1,000 from 1-8-1976 to 28-2-1983	0.5% from 1-8-1976 till date	0.1% from 1-8-1976 to 30-9-1987	0.02% from 1-8-1976 to 31-12-1988
Rs. 1,600 from 1-3-1983 to 31-8-1985	0.5% from 1-8-1976 till date	0.01% from 1-10-1987 till date (min. Rs. 2 w.e.f. 1-1-89)	0.005% from 1-10-1989 till date (min. Rs. 2 w.e.f. 1-6-89)
Rs. 2,500 from 1-9-1985 to 31-10-1990	—do—	—do—	—do—
Rs. 3,500 from 1-11-1990 to 30-9-1994	—do—	—do—	—do—
Rs. 5,000 from 1-10-1994 to 31-5-01	—do—	—do—	—do—
Rs. 6,500 from 1-6-2001 till date	—do—	—do—	—do—

BENEFITS

On the death while in service of the member, the nominee of the deceased shall in addition to PF/EPS accumulation, be paid an amount equal to the average balance in the PF accumulation of the deceased for the preceding twelve months and if the average balance exceeds Rs. 35,000 then the amount payable shall be Rs. 35,000 plus 25% in excess of Rs. 35,000 subject to a maximum of Rs. 60,000 (Revised rates w.e.f. 1-6-2000).

WITHDRAWAL OF ADVANCES AND THE CONDITIONS THERETO

TYPE OF WITHDRAWAL	CONDITION	AMOUNT RECEIVABLE	DOCUMENT REQUIRED
1. Withdrawal from the fund for (Para 68-B)			(Available once in lifetime)
(a) The purchase of site for construction of house	5 yrs. of membership of the Fund	(i) 24 months wages (Basic + D.A)	Original of Allotment Order (in case the purchase is through agency) with copy.
		OR	Original to be returned after verification.
	(Min.balance in member's a/c should be Rs.1000)	Member's own share of contributions + Co's share of contribution with interest thereon	Original Title-Deed (if purchase is from individual) with copy. Original to be returned after verification. Photocopy of the Registered Agreement with Seller alongwith the receipt of advance paid alongwith Original copy for verification & return.
(b) The construction of house	—do—	(i) 36 months wages (Basic + D.A.) OR Member's own share of contributions + Co's share of	Same as per Col.(a) Photocopy of the plan approved by the Collector's

TYPE OF WITHDRAWAL	CONDITION	AMOUNT RECEIVABLE	DOCUMENT REQUIRED
		contribution with interest thereon.	Office or Municipal Corporation or the Local Bodies, Gram Panchayat as the case may be.
(c) The purchase of dwelling flat	—do—	—do—	(i) Original Allotment Order (if purchase is through Agency) with copy. (ii) Copy of the Agreement with seller, duly registered under the Indian Registration Act, 1908 (photocopy + Original) for verification and return. (iii) Non-encumbrance declaration from the member and seller. (iv) Receipt of Advance Payment towards Flat. (v) If purchase is in the Co-op. Housing Society, then Registration No. of the Society.
2nd Advance (d) Additions, Alterations or	5 yrs. from the date of	12 months basic or member's own	(i) Proof of ownership

TYPE OF WITHDRAWAL	CONDITION	AMOUNT RECEIVABLE	DOCUMENT REQUIRED
improvements to the dwelling house	completion of dwelling house	share of contributions with interest thereon.	(ii) Details of addition/ alteration to be carried out alongwith permission to carry out additions etc. (iii) Estimate from the appropriate authority
3rd Advance (e) —do—	10 yrs. from the date of completion of the dwelling house	—do—	—do—
2. Withdrawal from the fund for repayment of loan in special cases to State Govt., Registered Co-op. Societies, State Housing Board, Nationalised Banks, Public Financial institutions, Municipal Corp. or Secular Bodies.	10 yrs. membership of the fund and should have Rs.1000 as employee's share of contributions + Co's share of contributions with interest thereon.	36 months wages (Basic + D.A.) OR Member's own share	A certificate from the leading authority furnishing the details of loan and outstanding amount and if they are ready to accept premature payment.
3. Advance from the fund for illness *viz.*, hospitalisation for more than a month, major surgical operation or suffering from T.B., Leprosy, Paralysis, Cancer, Heart ailment etc., (for member of family and self)		6 months wages (Basic + D.A.) or his share of PF whichever is less.	(i) A certificate from the Regd. Medical Practitioner, Govt. Doctor for hospitalisation or operation. In case of serious diseases, of the specialist. (ii) Certificate from employer that ESI benefits

TYPE OF WITHDRAWAL	CONDITION	AMOUNT RECEIVABLE	DOCUMENT REQUIRED
			are not available to the member.
4. Advance form the fund for Marriage of self/son/ daughter/sister/ brother etc.	7 yrs. membership of the fund and min. balance of member's a/c should be Rs. 1,000	50% of member's own share of contribution (Max.advances allowed: 3)	Marriage Invitation Card/declaration of member.
5. Advance from the fund for education of son/daughter	—do—	50% of member's own share of contribution (Max. advances allowed: 3)	Certificate from the Institution regarding the course of study and anticipated expenditure.
6. Grant of advance in abnormal condition (para 68L) Natural calamities etc.	(i) Certificate of damage (ii) State Government Declaration	Rs.5000 or 50% of member's own share of contributions	Certificate from the appropriate authority within the State Government (To apply within 4 months)
7. Withdrawal within one year before retirement	(i) He should have attained the age of 54 years (ii) to retire within ensuing year	90% of both contributions	Certificate by employer to this effect
8. Option for withdrawal for investment in Pension Beema Yojana	(i) More than 55 years of age (ii) LIC Policy for Pension Beema Yojana	(i) 90% of both contributions (ii) Payment to be made to LIC directly	Proposal from LIC duly accepted and passed

PUNISHMENT FOR CONTRAVENTION OF CERTAIN PROVISIONS OF THE ACT

An employer who contravenes, or makes default in complying with the provisions of section 6 or clause (a) of sub-section (3) of section 17 insofar as it relates to the payment of inspection charges, or paragraph 48 of the Scheme in so far as it relates to the payment of administrative charges, shall be punishable with imprisonment for a term which may extend to three years—

    (a) which shall not be less than one year and fine of ten thousand rupees in case of default in payment of the employees' contribution which has been deducted by the employer from the employees' wages;

    (b) which shall not be less than six months and fine of five thousand rupees, in any other case :

Provided that the court may, for any adequate and special reasons to be recorded in the judgment, impose a sentence of imprisonment for a lesser term.

An employer who contravenes, or makes default in complying with the provisions of section 6C, or clause (a) of sub-section (3A) of section 17 insofar as it relates to the payment of inspection charges, shall be punishable with imprisonment for a term which may extend to one year but which shall not be less than six months and shall also be liable to fine which may extend to five thousand rupees :

Provided that the court may, for any adequate and special reasons to be recorded in the judgment, impose a sentence of imprisonment for a lesser term.

OFFENCES BY COMPANIES

(1) If the person committing an offence under the E.P.F & M.P. Act, the Scheme or the Family Pension Scheme or the Insurance Scheme is a company, every person, who at the time the offence was committed was in charge of, and was responsible to, the company for the conduct of the business of the company as well as the company, shall be deemed to be guilty of the offence and shall be liable to be proceeded against and punished accordingly.

Punishment for failure to submit return, etc., under Employees' Pension Scheme

If any person,—

    (a) deducts or attempts to deduct from the wages or other remuneration of the member, the whole or any part of the employer's contribution, or

    (b) fails or refuses to submit any return, statement or other documents required by this Scheme or submits a false return, statement or other documents, or makes a false declaration, or

(c) obstructs any Inspector or other official appointed under the Act or this Scheme in the discharge of his duties or fails to produce any record for inspection by such Inspector or other officials, or

(d) is guilty of contravention of or non-compliance with any other requirement of this Scheme,

he shall be punishable with imprisonment which may extend to one year or with fine which may extend to five thousand rupees or with both:

Provided that nothing contained in the above sub-section shall render any such person liable to any punishment, if he proves that the offence was committed without his knowledge or that he exercised all due diligence to prevent the commission of such offence.

(2) Notwithstanding anything contained above, where an offence under this Act, the Scheme or the Family Pension Scheme or the Insurance Scheme has been committed by a company and it is proved that the offence has been committed with the consent or connivance of, or is attributable to any neglect on the part of any director or manager, secretary or other officer of the company, such director, manager, secretary or other officer shall be deemed to be guilty of that offence and shall be liable to be proceeded against and punished accordingly.

Explanation.—For the purposes of above provisions—

(a) "company" means any body corporate and includes a firm and other association of individuals; and

(b) "director" in relation to a firm, means a partner in the firm.

ENHANCED PUNISHMENT IN CERTAIN CASES AFTER PREVIOUS CONVICTION

Whoever, having been convicted by a court of an offence punishable under the E.P.F. & M.P. Act, the Scheme of the Family Pension Scheme or the Insurance Scheme, commits the same offence shall be subject for every such subsequent offence to imprisonment for a term which may extend to five years but which shall not be less than two years and shall also be liable to fine which may extend to twenty-five thousand rupees.

5A. THE EMPLOYEES' PENSION SCHEME, 1995

1. APPLICABILITY

The Scheme is applicable to all factories and other establishments to which the Employees' Provident Funds and Miscellaneous Provisions Act, 1952 applies. The Scheme is meant for members of the Provident Funds subscribing to Employees' Provident Fund Scheme, 1952 or any scheme exempted thereunder.

2. MEMBERSHIP ELIGIBILITY

(i) Membership of the scheme is compulsory for
- All Provident Fund subscribers including those employed in Exempted Establishments contributing to the Employees' Family Pension Scheme, 1971; and
- All New entrants to the Provident Funds Scheme, 1952 from 16-11-1995 onwards, automatically become members of the Employees' Pension Scheme, 1995.

(ii) Membership is available on Optional basis for
- Existing members of Exempted and Un-exempted Provident Fund Scheme as on 15-11-1995 who are not members of the Family Pension Scheme, 1971.
- Members of the Family Pension Scheme, 1971 who left employment between 1-4-1993 – 15-11-1995 whether they have withdrawn their benefits or not.

– Beneficiaries of Family Pension Scheme, 1971 who have died on or after 1-4-1993.

3. FUNDING OF THE SCHEME

– No separate/additional contribution is payable for Employees' Pension Scheme.
– 8.33% of subscribers 'Pay' is being diverted from employers' share of Provident Fund contributions; and
– 1.1/6% of subscribers' pay shall be paid by the Government as Government contribution.
– Existing assets and liabilities of the ceased Family Pension Fund, 1971 as on 16-11-1995 will form the corpus of the Scheme.
– Provident Fund accumulations upto 15-11-1995 (both shares with interest will remain available to members in toto. Likewise the balance of 1.67%/3.67% employer's share of contribution in case of 10%/12% contribution rate will continue to remain in Provident Fund a/c of the member.

4. BENEFIT PACKAGE

The Employees' Pension Scheme, 1995 provides for following benefit package.

I. For Member
    (i) Pension Payment for life on Retirement/ Superannuation.
    (ii) Pension Payment for life on invalidation during employment.
    (iii) Lump sum payment to the member by way of commutation of Pension upto one third pension amount on optional basis.
    (iv) Capital return on option formula basis upon cessation of members pension payment.

II. Pension Payment to Family Members upon Death of the Member
    (i) To spouse for life or until remarriage.
    (ii) To children (two at a time) till they attain the age of 25 years additionally along with pension payment to spouse:
    For total and permanently disabled children pension for life.

(iii) Orphan Pension to Children at higher rate upon cessation of Pension Payment to Spouse,

(iv) To Nominee/Dependent parents for life in case member is unmarried or having no eligible family member.

The Scheme covers members death risk unconditionally - *i.e.* irrespective of whether such death occurs

(i) while in service;

(ii) away from employment and not contributing to the fund; or

(iii) after retirement as a pensioner.

The family members shall remain entitled for pensionary support uniformly.

– The scheme, in its benefit package precisely covers as under:

(i) Pension Payment to the member against contribution component diverted-permitting communication/ return of capital on option formula basis; and

(ii) Complete security coverage to the family members for pensionary support in the event of members death. delinking contribution component altogether on a Social Insurance Pattern.

5. SPECIAL PROVISIONS MADE IN THE SCHEME TO FACILITATE BENEFIT AVAILABILITY/DELIVERY FOR SEASONAL/CASUAL EMPLOYEES

– Employees engaged seasonally in any establishment, the period of "actual service" in any year, notwithstanding that such service is less than a year, shall be treated as full year.

– Pensionable salary will be worked out "Notionally" for full month in the event of drawal of salary for a part of the month.

– Pensionary benefits shall be extended to the members without co-relating compliance by the employer of the establishment.

SALIENT FEATURES

In the scheme three scales of pensionary benefits have been offered according to the length of service.

- **For service below 10 years**

  Return of contribution on exit from employment - Table - D

  Example: Suppose a member exits from employment after four years of service his wage on exit is Rs. 4,000. Return of contribution will be calculated as Rs. 4,000 x 4.18 of wages on exit *i.e.*, Rs. 16,720.

- **Service above 10 years but below 20 years**

  In the first instance pension will be calculated by applying the formula, *i.e.*—

  Pensionable Salary *x* Pensionable service

  70

  Say, a member has done 18 years of pensionable Service. Pensionable Salary determined as Rs. 4,000. Pension payable to him will be Rs. 1029.

- **Service over 20 years**

  Full pension according to the formula stated above. It is to be noted here that for rendering 20 years of pensionable service or more, member's pensionable service shall in all cases be increased by adding 2 years. In other words, 20 years actual pensionable service will be treated as 22 years of pensionable service for calculation of pension.

- **Special provisions for existing members**

  Special provisions have been made for calculation of pension in case of member who was a member of the ceased Family Pension Scheme 1971 and who has attained the age of 48 years in the 16th November, 1995 or a member who has attained the age of 48 years but is less than 53 years on 16th November, 1995, member who has attained the age of 53 years of more on the 16th November, 1995. In the aforesaid cases the formula for calculating pension will be as follows:—

  A member who has not attained the age of 48 years on 16-11-1995

  Pension is determined by the above formula *i.e.*—

  Pensionable Salary *x* Pensionable service

For the period of pensionable service rendered from the
16th November 1995 or Rs. 635 whichever is more plus
past service benefits as under:—

Sr. No.	Year of past service	*The past service benefit payable on completion of 58 years of age on 16-11-95	
		Salary upto Rs 2,500 p.m	Salary more than Rs. 2,500 p.m.
(1)		(2)	(3)
(i)	Upto 11 yrs.	80	85
(ii)	More than 11 yrs. but up to 15 yrs.	95	105
(iii)	More than 15 yrs.	120	135
(iv)	Beyond 20 yrs.	150	170

* To arrive at past service benefit, payable on the
completion of 58 years of age on 16-11-1995 under
column (2) & (3) above shall be multiplied by the factor
given in Table B corresponding to the period between
16-11-1995 and date of attainment of age 58.

Subject to a minimum of Rs. 800 per month provided the
past service is 24 years. If the members aggregate service
is less than 24 years, Pension and the benefits computed
as above will be reduced proportionately to a minimum
of Rs. 450 per month.

*A member who has attained the age of 48 years but less
than 53 years on 16-11-1995*

Pension as determined by the above mentioned formula
i.e.:—

$$\frac{\text{Pensionable Salary} \times \text{Pensionable service}}{70}$$

for the period of service rendered from 16-11-1995 or
Rs. 438 per month whichever is more **plus** past service
benefit as laid down in Para 12(3) subject to a minimum
of Rs. 5,00 per month, in case the past service is 24 years.
If it is less than 24 years, pension payable and the past
service benefit taken together shall be proportionately
less subject to a minimum of Rs. 325 p.m.

*A member who has attained the age of 53 years or more
on 16-11-1995*

Pension as determined by the above mentioned formula i.e.:—

$$\frac{\text{Pensionable Salary} \times \text{Pensionable service}}{70}$$

for the period of service rendered from 16-11-1995 till the date of exit or Rs. 335 p.m. whichever is more **plus** past service benefit as provided in para 12(3) subject to a minimum of Rs. 500 p.m. (both together) in case past service period is 24 years. If it is less than 24 years pension payable and the past service benefit shall be proportionately lesser subject to a minimum of Rs. 265 p.m.

EARLY PENSION ON CESSATION OF EMPLOYMENT

Old age pension on account of superannuation/retirement is normally payable on attaining the age of 58 years. However, member cannot opt for taking earlier than 58 years on his exit from employment but under no circumstances pension will be payable before the age of 50 years. A member who desires to draw monthly pension from a date earlier than 58 years of age will be allowed to draw a monthly reduced pension. The amount of pension in such a case shall be reduced at the rate of 3% for every year the age falls short of 58 years.

SCHEME CERTIFICATE

There are occasions when a member may leave employment and or may move from a covered establishment to an uncovered establishment before he reaches the date of superannuation, he may opt for a Scheme Certificate. The certificate will indicate his pensionable salary and the amount of pension due on the date of exit from employment. If the member is subsequently employed in a covered establishment, his pensionable service in the scheme certificate will be taken into account for working out his full pensionable service.

WIDOW PENSION

Widow pension is of three categories (i) on the death of the member during service, (ii) on the death of the member after leaving service but before attaining the age of 58 years, and (iii) in case of death of the member after commencement of payment of monthly members pension.

Widow pension on death of the member during the service is equal to monthly members pension.

The essential conditions for grant of widow pension are as follows:—

    (a) The death of the member occurred while in service.

    (b) The member has contributed at least one month's contribution.

    (c) The member had not attained the age of 58 years.

    (d) The death of the member had taken place before the commencement of monthly members pension.

Example 1: Mr. X, a worker in an establishment, became member of the Employees Pension Scheme on 2nd January, 1996. He died in February, 1996 after a short illness. His wages at the time of death was Rs. 1,500 p.m. He left behind his widow aged 22 years and a child aged 1 year. What will be the widow pension in this case?

It is confirmed that pension contribution for Mr. X was paid by the employer for the month of January, 1996. Widow Pension entitlement.

    (i) Pensionable service One month

         Pensionable salary Rs. 1500

Either

    (ii) Pension according to the formula:

$$\frac{\text{Pensionable service} \times \text{Pensionable Salary}}{70} \quad i.e.$$

$$\frac{1}{12} \quad \times \quad \frac{1500}{70} \quad = \quad \text{Rs. 1.78}$$

Or (ii) Minimum pension payable as per para 16(2)(a)(i) of the Scheme Rs. 450 p.m.

Or (iii) The amount indicated in table 'C' Rs. 718 per month – whichever is more.

        Since (iii) is more than (i) & (ii), Widow pension will be fixed at Rs. 718 per month for life or remarriage of the widow, whichever is earlier.

    (iv) For the child, 25% of the widow pension will be granted as monthly pension i.e., 25% of Rs. 718 = Rs. 179.50 or Rs. 180 p.m., till 25 years of age.

Example 2: Mr. 'Y' Joined Family Pension Scheme in January 1972. He died while in service, say, on 30th March 1998. He was drawing a salary of Rs. 2,500 p.m. from January 97 till death.

He had attained the age of 48 years at the time of his death. He left behind the widow, two sons–one aged 16 years, one 7 years and one daughter aged 20 years. What would be the widows pension and children pension, payable?

   (i) Mr. 'Y' had done 26 years 3 months of pensionable service at the time of his death. In calculation of eligible service for pension, fraction of three months will be ignored as per explanation to para 9(a) of the Scheme and thus eligible service will be taken as 26 years only. The average 12 months' salary at the time of his death was Rs. 2,500. Hence members monthly pension will be:

Either

$$\frac{\text{Pensionable service } x \text{ Pensionable Salary}}{70} \; i.e.$$

   (i) 26 x 2500/70 = Rs. 928.57 or Rs. 929 p.m.

Or   (ii) In terms of para 16(2)(a)(ii) - Rs. 250 p.m.

Or   (iii) Table 'C' - Rs. 1087 - Whichever is more.

   The amount at (iii) being more than (i) & (ii), the widow pension payable will be Rs. 1087 for life or remarriage of the widow, whichever is earlier.

Children Pension

   (i) The member left behind three children one daughter aged 20 years, one son aged 16 years and the other son age 7 years. To start with, only the elder two, the daughter and the elder son will get pension. The daughter will get pension for 5 years by which time she will be 25 years of age after 5 years of the vesting of pension. After the daughter ceases to be the beneficiary, the youngest child, then aged 12 years, will start receiving pension till the age of 25 years.

   (ii) The amount of children pension will be @ 25% of widow pension for each of the two children, *viz.*

   25% + 25% of Rs. 1087 or Rs. 272 + Rs. 272 for two children.

WIDOW PENSION AFTER COMMENCEMENT OF MONTHLY PENSION

In case of death of the member after vesting of pension, the amount of widow pension is payable @ 50% of the monthly members pension subject to a minimum of Rs. 250 p.m. for example. Mr. 'Z' a pensioner, dies at the age of 66 years leaving behind his widow aged 62 years.

Mr. Z drawing pension @ Rs. 1000 p.m. The widow pension in this case will be Rs. 500 p.m.

In case the member leaves behind any child less than 25 years of age, children pension is payable for each equal to 25% of the widow pension subject to a minimum of Rs. 115 p.m.

OPTION FOR RETURN OF CAPITAL

The member may opt to draw revised pension and avail of return of capital under any one of the three alternatives as per the table shown u/p 13 of the scheme.

SUMMARY OF BENEFITS TO EXISTING MEMBERS

Vide Para of E.P.S. 1995	Age of employees as on 16-11-95	Pension amount for serviceAfter 16-11-95 till date		Past service till Benefit 15-11-95		If aggregate service less than 24 yrs. then the minimum MMP payable
		Amount as per calculation	Minimum Pension Payable	Min. Past Service benefit Payable for 24 years Past service	If PSB is less than 24 yrs	
12 (3)	Upto 47yrs	Do	Rs. 635	Rs. 800	On proportionate basis of the mm. PSB payable or as per calculation whichever is more	Rs. 450
12 (4)	48 yrs to 52 yrs	Do	Rs. 438	Rs. 600		Rs. 325
12 (5)	53 yrs and	Do	Rs. 335	Rs. 500		Rs. 265

WITHDRAWAL BENEFIT

If the member renders less than 10 years pensionable service on the date of exit or on attaining the age of 58 years, whichever is earlier, he is entitle for withdrawal benefit as per Table 'D' or he may opt for scheme certificate.

The existing member, *i.e.* member of E.P.F. shall receive additional benefit for his past service under the E.P.F Scheme 1971, as per Table 'A' multiplied by factor given in Table 'B'.

PAYMENT OF PENSION THROUGH BANKS

The pension is disbursed through Nationalised Banks of the respective state. The member/pensioner are required to open an account in the Bank where pension is desired and indicate the option in the application in Form 10-D. The Statewise list of Banks, where pension can be opted is given below.

REGION	NOMINATED BANK	REGION	NOMINATED BANK
Andhra Pradesh	Andhra Bank & SBI	Maharashtra	Bank of India, PNB & SBI
Bihar	Punjab National Bank	North East Region (Assam)	Punjab National Bank & SBI
Delhi	Punjab National Bank & SBI	Orissa	Bank of India & SBI
Gujarat	Dena Bank & SBI	Punjab	Punjab National Bank & SBI
Haryana	Punjab National Bank & SBI	Rajasthan	State Bank of Bikaner & Jaipur, Punjab National Bank
Karnataka	Canara Bank	Tamil Nadu	Indian Bank & SBI
Kerala	Canara Bank & SBI	Uttar Pradesh	PNB & SBI
Madhya Pradesh	Punjab National Bank & SBI	West Bengal	Punjab National Bank & Union Bank of India
Himachal Pradesh	Punjab National Bank & SBI	In addition to above	HDFC, UTI & ICICI Bank for all Regions

WITHDRAWAL BENEFIT (AS PER PARA 14 OF THE SCHEME)

No. of full year's Contribution paid (1)	Proportion of pay payable at cessation of membership (2)	No. of full year's Contribution paid (1)	Proportion of pay payable at cessation of membership (2)	No. of full year's Contribution paid (1)	Proportion of pay payable at cessation of membership (2)	No. of full year's Contribution paid (1)	Proportion of pay payable at cessation of membership (2)
1	0.20	11	2.47	21	5.21	31	8.52
2	0.41	12	2.72	22	5.52	32	8.89
3	0.62	13	2.98	23	5.83	33	9.26
4	0.84	14	3.24	24	6.14	34	9.64
5	1.06	15	3.51	25	6.46	35	10.33
6	1.29	16	3.78	26	6.79	36	10.43
7	1.51	17	4.05	27	7.12	37	10.83
8	1.75	18	4.34	28	7.46	38	11.24
9	1.98	19	4.62	29	7.81	39	11.66
10	2.23	20	4.92	30	8.16	40	12.08

FACTOR FOR COMPUTATION OF PAST SERVICE BENEFIT UNDER THE CEASED FAMILY PENSION SCHEME FOR EXISTING MEMBERS ON EXIT FROM THE EMPLOYMENT (AS PER PARA 14 OF THE SCHEME)

(1) years	(2) Factor	(1) years	(2) Factor	(1) years	(2) Factor	(1) years	(2) Factor
Less than 1	1.049	Less than 7	1.858	Less than 13	3.292	Less than 19	5.810
Less than 2	1.154	Less than 8	2.044	Less than 14	3.621	Less than 20	6.414
Less than 3	1.269	Less than 9	2.248	Less than 15	3.983	Less than 21	7.056
Less than 4	1.396	Less than 10	2.473	Less than 16	4.381	Less than 22	7.761
Less than 5	1.536	Less than 11	2.720	Less than 17	4.819	Less than 23	8.537
Less than 6	1.689	Less than 12	2.992	Less than 18	5.301	Less than 24	9.390

EQUIVALENT WIDOW PENSION (AS PER PARAGRAPH 16 OF THE SCHEME)

Salaray at day of death not more than	Equivalent widow pension	Salaray at day of death not more than	Equivalent widow pension	Salaray at day of death not more than	Equivalent widow pension	Salaray at day of death not more than	Equivalent widow pension
(1)	(2)	(3)	(4)	(5)	(6)	(7)	(8)
Rs.	Rs.	1100	578	1950	880	2800	1201
Upto 300	250	1150	595	2000	898	2850	1221
350	327	1200	612	2050	916	2900	1241
400	343	1250	629	2100	935	2950	1261
450	359	1300	646	2150	954	3000	1281
500	375	1350	664	2200	973	3050	1301
550	391	1400	682	2250	992	3100	1321
600	408	1450	700	2300	1011	3150	1341
650	425	1500	718	2350	1030	3200	1561
700	442	1550	736	2400	1049	3250	1381
750	459	1600	754	2450	1068	3300	1401
800	476	1650	772	2500	1087	3350	1421
850	493	1700	797	2550	1106	3400	1441
900	510	1750	808	2600	1125	3450	1461
950	527	1800	826	2650	1144	3500	1481
1000	544	1850	844	2700	1163	3550	1501
1050	561	1900	862	2750	1182	3600	1521

EMPLOYEES' STATE INSURANCE

ACT & the SCHEME

CHECKLIST

Applicability
of the Act & Scheme

Is extended area-wise to factories using power and employing 10 or more persons and to non-power using manufacturing units and establishments employing 20 or more persons upto Rs. 6500/- per month. It has also been extended upon shops, hotels, restaurants, road motor transport undertakings, equipment maintenance staff in the hospitals.

Coverage
of employees

Drawing wages (w.e.f. 1-10-2006) upto **Rs. 10,000/- per** month engaged either directly or thru' contractor.

Rate of Contribution
of the wages

Employers' **4.75%**
Employees' **1.75%**

THE ESI SCHEME TODAY

No. of implemented Centres	677
No. of Employers covered	2.38 lacs
No. of Insured Persons	85 lacs
No. of Beneficiaries	330 lacs
No. of Regional Offices/SRO's	26
No. of ESI Hospitals/Annexes	183
No. of ESI Dispensaries	1453
No. of Panel Clinics	2950

Manner and Time Limit
for making payment of contribution

The total amount of contribution (employee's share and employer's share) is to be deposited with the authorised bank through a challan in the prescribed Form in quadruplicate on or before 21st of month following the calendar month in which the wages fall due.

Benefits
to the employees under the Act

Medical sickness, extended sickness for certain diseases, enhanced sickness, dependants, maternity, besides funeral expenses, rehabilitation allowance, medical benefit to insured person and his or her spouse.

WAGES FOR ESI CONTRIBUTIONS
Registers/files to be maintained by the employers.

Contribution period

1st April to 30th September

1st October to 31st March

Benefit period

If the person joined insurable employment for the first time, say on 5th January, his first contribution period will be from 5th January to 31st March and his corresponding first benefit will be from 5th October to 31st December.

To be deemed as wages

- Basic pay
- Dearness allowance
- House rent allowance
- City compensatory allowance
- Overtime wages (but not to be taken into account for determining the coverage of an employee)
- Payment for day of rest
- Production incentive
- Bonus other than statutory bonus
- Night shift allowance
- Heat, Gas & Dust allowance
- Payment for unsubstituted holidays
- Meal/food allowance
- Suspension allowance
- Lay off compensation
- Children education allowance (not being reimbursement for actual tuition fee)
- Conveyance

NOT to be deemed as wages

- Contribution paid by the employer to any pension/provident fund or under ESI Act
- Sum paid to defray special expenses entailed by the nature of employment - Daily allowance paid for the period spent on tour.
- Gratuity payable on discharge
- Pay in lieu of notice of retrenchment compensation
- Benefits paid under the ESI Scheme
- Encashment of leave
- Payment of Inam which does not form part of the terms of employment
- Washing allowance
- Amount towards reimbursement for duty related journey.

Penalties

Different punishments have been prescribed for different types of offences in terms of section 85 : (i) (six months imprisonment and fine Rs.5,000), (ii) (one year imprisonment and fine), and 85-A : (five years imprisonment and not less to 2 years) and 85-C(2) of the ESI Act, which are self-explanatory. Besides these provisions, action also can be taken under section 406 of the IPC in cases where an employer deducts contributions from the wages of his employees but does not pay the same to the corporation which amounts to criminal breach of trust.

numberof factories and establishments that come under the ESI The

6. The Employees' State Insurance Act, 1948

THE OBJECT

The Employees' State Insurance Act is the first major legislation on social security for industrial workers in India. The Scheme, as per provisions of the Act, is devised so as to provide social protection to workers in contingencies such as illness, long term sickness or any other health risks due to exposure to employment injury or occupational hazards. Under the provisions of the scheme, medical facilities are also made available to the legal dependents of insured persons. Medical facility has also now been introduced for retired insured persons and permanently disabled workers and their spouses at a nominal contribution of Rs. 10 per month.

The Act applies in the first instance to non-seasonal factories using power and employing 20 or more persons. After enforcement of the provisions of the Employees' State Insurance (Amendment) Act, 1989, the Act is now applicable, in the first instance, to non-seasonal factories using power and employing 10 or more persons and non-power using factories and establishments employing 20 or more persons. As of now employees of the covered factories and establishments earning wages upto Rs. 10,000 (w.e.f. 1-10-2006) per month come under the purview of the scheme.

Over the last 41 years the scheme has been implemented at 625 centres in the country in 21 States and Union Territories. The number of factories and establishments that come under the purview of the scheme at present has reached a new high of 1.5 lakh units. At an average the scheme is implemented at 15 new centres each year under the programme of continued extension.

CONTINUOUS APPLICABILITY OF THE ACT

By an amendment of the ESI Act in 1989, it has been provided that a factory or an establishment shall continue to be governed by this Act notwithstanding that the number of persons employed therein at any time falls below the limit specified by or under this Act or the manufacturing process therein ceases to be carried on with the aid of power.

APPRENTICES/TRAINEES

Under section 2(9) of the ESI Act *inter alia* providing that any person engaged as apprentice, not being an apprentice engaged under the Apprentices Act, 1961, or under the standing orders of the establishment will be covered under the Act. Even unpaid trainees provided with boarding and lodging will also be covered under the ESI.

EMPLOYEES ENGAGED BY A CONTRACTOR

The employees engaged by a contractor are squarely to be covered under ESI Act and the Scheme thereto.

PARTNER OF A FIRM

The Supreme Court has held that a partner engaged for the work of the factory or establishment and being paid monthly will not come within the Purview of an 'employee' as defined in section 2(9) of the ESI Act.

MANAGING DIRECTOR

Managing Director of a Company will be covered under the Act if his salary is below prescribed ceiling.

CASUAL/TEMPORARY EMPLOYEE

Casual or temporary employees will be liable to be covered under the Act from the date of their joining the service.

COMMISSION AGENTS

The commission agents are not coverable under the ESI Act. But they are employed as representatives and incurring other expenses besides commission, such persons are coverable under the provisions of ESI Act.

LOADERS AND UNLOADERS

Merely because the loaders and unloaders have not been able to get the benefit, it will not be a ground for non coverage under ESI Act.

CONTRIBUTIONS

The amount of contribution for a wage period shall be as follows:—

 (i) employer's contribution, a sum (rounded off to the next of five paise) equal to four and three-fourth per cent of the wages payable to an employee; and

 (ii) employees' contribution, a sum (rounded off to the next higher multiple of five paise) equal to one and three-fourth per cent of the wages payable to an employee.

REGISTRATION OF FACTORIES OR ESTABLISHMENTS

Section 2A of the ESI Act and Regulation 10B framed under the Act requires the employer to which the Act applies for the first time and to which an Employer's Code Number is not yet allotted and the employer in respect of a factory or an establishment to which the Act previously applied but has ceased to apply for the time being, to furnish to the appropriate Regional Office not later than 15 days after the Act becomes applicable, as the case may be, to the factory or establishment, a declaration of registration in writing in Form 10 called the Employer Registration Form. The correctness of all the particulars and information required for and furnished on the Employer Registration Form is the responsibility of the employer. It is also the responsibility of the employer to enter the Employer's Code Number on all documents prepared and completed by him in connection with the Act, the Rules and the Regulations and in all correspondence with the appropriate office.

DUTY TO COMPLETE DECLARATION FORM

It is the duty of every employer in respect of a factory or an establishment to require every employee in such factory or establishment to furnish on the appointed day correct particulars required for the purpose of Form 1, i.e., "Declaration Form" and to enter the same in the Declaration Form including the Temporary Identification Certificate and to obtain the signature or thumb-impression of such employee and also to complete the form as indicated thereon. Where, however, an Identity Card is produced, the employer shall make relevant entries thereon.

SUBMISSION OF DECLARATION FORM AND RETURN IN FORM 3

Regulation 14 requires the employer to send to the appropriate office by Registered Post or messenger, all Declaration Forms without detaching the Temporary Identification Certificate together with a return in duplicate in Form 3 within ten days of the date on which the particulars for the Declaration Forms were furnished.

PROCEDURE FOR ALLOTMENT OF INSURANCE NUMBER

On receipt of the return required under Regulation 14, the appropriate office is required to allot an Insurance Number to each person in respect of whom the Declaration Form has been received unless it finds that the person had already been allotted an Insurance Number. The Temporary Identification Certificate with Insurance Numbers marked thereon is then detached and returned to the employer along with one copy of Form 3. Thereafter, the employer is required to deliver the Temporary Identification Certificate to the employee to whom it relates after obtaining his signature or thumb-impression thereon except in the case of an employee to whom a certificate of employment has been issued under Regulation 17A. The Insurance Number allotted by the Regional/Local Office to an employee and indicated in the copy of Form 3 returned to the employer, shall then be entered by the employer in the prescribed register.

PROCEDURE FOR REGISTRATION OF FAMILIES

On the issue of a notification under Regulation 95A by the Government, specifying the date from which the family of an insured person shall also be entitled to medical benefit under the Act, every insured person who has not furnished the particulars of his family at the time of his registration under the Act is required to furnish to his employer correct particulars in respect of his family in Form 1A. Thereafter, the employer is required to enter the particulars in the form and obtain the signature or the thumb-impression of such person and complete the form as indicated thereon and send it to the appropriate office within ten days of the date on which the particulars were furnished to him by the employee.

REGISTRATION OF CHANGES IN THE FAMILY

After an insured person is registered, it is obligatory on his part to intimate all changes in the membership of his family, which includes the spouse and minor legitimate and adopted children dependent upon the insured person and his dependent parents, to the employer within fifteen days of such change having occurred and thereafter it is the duty of the employer to make entries of such particulars in Form 1B and forward it to the appropriate office within ten days of the date on which the particular of the changes were furnished to him by the insured person.

DUTY TO ASSIST THE CORPORATION

Regulation 16 makes it obligatory on the part of every employer to whom this Act applies to render all necessary assistance required by the Corporation in connection with the registration of his factory or establishment and the registration of his employees and specially for photographing such employees and affixing the photographs to the Identity Cards.

IDENTITY CARDS

It is the duty of every employer to obtain the signature or thumb-impression of the employee on the Identity Cards prepared by the Corporation in Form 4 if the employee has been in his service for 13 weeks and deliver the Identity Card to the employee after obtaining a receipt. However, if the employee has not been in his service for 13 weeks then such a card should not be issued to him and be returned to the appropriate office from whom it was received. In this connection, reference may be made to Regulation 17.

ISSUE OF CERTIFICATE OF EMPLOYMENT

If an insured person happens to need medical care before the Temporary Identification Certificate is issued to him or if issued he loses his Temporary Identification Certificate, it is obligatory on the part of the employer to issue a Certificate of Employment to him on demand.

CONTINGENCIES IN WHICH CONTRIBUTION CARDS BE SENT TO REGIONAL OFFICE

It is obligatory on the part of every employer being in possession of a Contribution Card in respect of any person to send it by Registered Post or messenger together with a return in duplicate in Form 6 to the appropriate office—(a) within seven days of the date on which he comes to know of the death of such person; (b) within seven days of the date of receipt of a requisition in that behalf from the appropriate office; (c) within 42 days of the termination of the contribution period to which it relates; and (d) within 28 days of the date of permanent closure of the factory and for this purpose, the due date by which the evidence of contributions having been paid must reach the Corporation shall be the last of the days respectively specified in clauses (a), (b), (c) and (d) above.

DUTY TO ISSUE CERTIFICATE OF CONTRIBUTION RATE ON LEAVING EMPLOYMENT

Where an insured person leaves employment during currency of a contribution period, it is the duty of the employer to issue a certificate of rate of contributions to such person and where such a person to whom the certificate specified above has been issued is employed during the currency of the contribution period and he furnishes the said certificate to the new employer then the latter is required to calculate the contributions in respect of that insured person for the balance of the contribution period at the rate indicated in such certificate.

DUTY TO PAY INTEREST ON CONTRIBUTION DUE BUT NOT PAID IN TIME

An employer who fails to pay contribution within the stipulated period is liable to pay interest at the rate of fifteen per cent per annum in respect of each day of default or delay in payment of contribution.

DUTY TO MAINTAIN REGISTER OF EMPLOYEES

Regulation 32, which deals with the maintenance of a register of employees, requires every employer to maintain a register in respect of each wage period for every employee in his factory or establishment showing: (a) Name; (b) Insurance No.; (c) Name of Dispensary; (d) Occupation; (e) Department and shift, if any; (f) Wage group in Schedule I to the Act to which the employee belongs in respect of that wage period; (g) Number of contribution days for which contribution fell due in the wage period; (h) Total contribution under the Act for the wage period; and (i) Employee's share of the contribution. However, an employer is deemed to have complied with this requirement if in any register maintained by him additional particulars stated above are also shown.

Note: The register referred to above is required to be preserved after it is filled, for a period of five years from the date of the last entry therein.

MODE FOR PAYMENT OF CONTRIBUTION WHEN EMPLOYMENT IS BY TWO OR MORE EMPLOYERS

Where an employee is employed by two or more employers successively in any week, the first employer employing him in that week is treated as his employer for the purposes of the provisions of the Act and the regulations relating to contributions and the contributions, in respect of such week shall fall due on the last day of employment by the first employer during that week.

SCHEME BY JOINT EMPLOYERS

Where an employee is ordinarily employed by two or more employers in a week, the employers of such an employee are entitled to frame and submit to the Corporation a scheme for the payment of contributions in respect of such employee for approval and if the same is approved then contribution in respect of such an employee shall be payable according to that scheme.

RECKONING OF WAGES OF AN EMPLOYEE IN CASE OF TWO OR MORE EMPLOYERS

Regulation 38, which deals with reckoning of wages in respect of an employee employed by two or more employers in the same period lays down that where an employee is employed by an employer for only a part of the period or where he is employed by two or more employers in a period, only the wages payable to him for the days upto and including the day on which the contribution falls due for that period shall be taken into account in reckoning wages for the purposes of determining the average daily wages of the employee for that period.

DUTY TO FURNISH PARTICULARS IN RESPECT OF ABSTENTION OF AN INSURED PERSON

Regulation 52A casts a duty on every employer to furnish to the appropriate office such information and particulars in respect of the abstention of an insured person from work for which sickness benefit or maternity benefit or disablement benefit for temporary disablement, as provided under the Act have been claimed or paid, in Form 25 and within such time as the said office may in writing require in the said form.

DUTY TO MAINTAIN ACCIDENT BOOK

Regulation 66 enjoins upon every employer to (i) keep an Accident Book in Form 15 readily accessible for entering the appropriate particulars of any accident causing personal injury to an insured person; and (ii) preserve the same when it is completed for a period of five years from the date of the last entry made therein. Regulation 67 further enjoins upon the employer when notice of an employment injury is given otherwise than by an entry in the Accident Book to make appropriate entry in the book in respect of the accident to which the notice relates immediately after such notice is received and where the notice is received otherwise than in writing, read over the particulars to the person who gives the notice and obtain his signature or thumb-impression on the Accident Book.

DUTY TO REPORT ACCIDENT TO THE NEAREST LOCAL OFFICE

It is obligatory on the part of every employer to send a report of the accident in Form 16 to the nearest Local Office and to the nearest Medical Officer: (i) immediately if the injury is serious, *i.e.*, it is likely to cause death or permanent disablement or loss of a member; and (ii) in any other case within 24 hours after the receipt of the notice or of time when the accident came to his notice or to his foreman or other official under whose supervision the insured person was employed at the time of the accident or any other person designated for the purpose by the employer. If the injury results in death at the place of employment, the report to the Insurance Medical Officer and the Local Office should be sent through a special messenger, or otherwise, as speedily as may be practicable under the circumstances. In case such a report is made under the Factories Act, 1948 then it may be made in the same Form, of course, after giving all the additional information required under Form 16. Further if the injury is caused by an occupational disease specified in Schedule III to the Workmen's Compensation Act then it shall not be necessary for the employer to send the report in Form 15 but the employer in such a case is required to furnish on demand to the appropriate Local Office, within the specified time such information and particulars as may be required of the nature of and other relevant circumstances relating to any employment specified in Schedule III to the Workmen's Compensation Act.

DUTY TO ARRANGE FIRST-AID

It is the duty of every employer to arrange for such first-aid and medical care and transport for obtaining such aid and care as the circumstances of the accident may require till the injured person is seen by the Insurance Medical Officer and thereafter to get reimbursements in respect of such expenses from the Corporation.

EMPLOYER TO FURNISH FURTHER PARTICULARS OF ACCIDENT

Every employer is required to furnish to the appropriate office such further information and particulars of an accident as may be required and within such time as the said office may, in writing, require.

DUTY TO REPORT DEATH IF IT IS BY EMPLOYMENT INJURY

In case of death of an insured person as a result of an employment injury, it is incumbent upon every employer to immediately report the same to the nearest Local Office and to the nearest dispensary, hospital, clinic or other institution where medical benefit under the Act is available—(a) if the death occurs at the place of employment; but (b) if the death occurs at any other place, a dependent intending to claim dependent's benefit or any other person present at such time is required to report the same. The position is the same with regard to the report of death of insured person under Regulation 95B.

DUTY TO MAINTAIN INSPECTION BOOK

Every principal employer is required by Regulation 120A to maintain a bound inspection book and be responsible for its production on demand by an Inspector irrespective of the fact whether the principal employer is present in the factory or establishment or not during the inspection. A note of all irregularities and illegalities discovered at the time of inspection indicating therein the action, if any, proposed to be taken against the principal employer together with the orders for their remedy or removal is required to be sent to the principal employer by the Inspector and thereafter it is the duty of the principal employer to enter the note and orders in the inspection book and to maintain such book for a period of five years from the date of the last entry therein.

BAR TO PUNITIVE ACTION DURING SICKNESS PERIOD

Section 73(1) of the Act provides that no employer shall dismiss, discharge, or reduce or otherwise punish an employee during the period the employee is in receipt of sickness benefit or maternity benefit, nor shall he, except as provided under the regulations, dismiss, discharge or reduce or otherwise punish an employee during the period he is in receipt of disablement benefit for temporary disablement or is under medical treatment for sickness or is absent from work as a result of illness duly certified in accordance with the regulations to arise out of the pregnancy or confinement rendering the employee unfit for work. Sub-section (2) thereof provides that no notice of dismissal or discharge or reduction given to an employee during the period specified in sub-section (1) shall be valid or operative. The important words in the section are "during the period the employee is in receipt of sickness benefit or maternity benefit." Though the clause is not very happily worded, it seems that the plain object of the clause is to put a sort of a moratorium against all punitive action during the pendency of the employee's illness. If the employee is ill and if it appears that he has received sickness benefit for such illness, during that period of illness, no punitive action can be taken after the sickness period is over. Regulation 98 framed under the Act provides that if the conditions of service of any employee so allow, an employer may discharge or reduce on due notice an employee—(i) who has been in receipt of disablement benefit for temporary disablement, after he has been in receipt of such benefit or for a continuous period of six months or more; (ii) who has been under medical treatment for sickness or has been absent from work as a result of illness duly certified in accordance with these regulations to arise out of the pregnancy or confinement rendering the employee unfit for work, after the employee has been under such treatment or has been absent from work for a continuous period of six months or more; and (iii) who has been under medical treatment for any of the following diseases, duly certified in accordance with these regulations after the employee has been under such treatment for a continuous period of 18 months or more, notwithstanding provisions of clauses (i) and (ii):

1. Tuberculosis
2. Leprosy
3. Chronic Empyema
4. Bronchiactesis
5. Intersistial Lung Disease
6. HIV/AIDS
7. Malignant Diseases
8. Diabetes Mellitus with proliferative ratinopathy/ diabetic foot/Nephropathy
9. Monoplegia
10. Hemiplegia
11. Paraplegia
12. Hemiparesis
13. Intracranial space occupying lession
14. Spinal Cord Compression
15. Parkinson's disease

16. Myaesthenia Gravis/Neuromuscular Dystrophies
17. Immature Cataract with vision 6/60 or less
18. Detachment of Retina
19. Glaucoma
20. Coronary Artery Disease
    (a) Unstable Angina
    (b) Myocardial Infarction with ejection less than 45%
21. Congestive Heart Failure Left/Right
22. Cardiac Valvular Diseases with failure complications
23. Cardimyopathies
24. Heart Disease with Surgical Intervention alongwith complications
25. Chronic Obstructive Lung Disease (COPD) with congestivem heart failure (Cor Pulmonale)
26. Cirrhosis of liver with ascitie/chronic active hepatitis
27. Dislocation of vertebra/prolapse of intervertebral disc
28. Non union or delayed union of fracture
29. Post Traumatic Surgical amputation of lower extremity
30. Compound Fracture with chronic ostemyelitis
31. Psychosis – the following sub-groups:—
    (a) Schizophrenia
    (b) Endogenous depression
    (c) Manic Depressive Psychosis (MDP)
    (d) Dementia
32. More than 20% burns with infection/complication
33. Chronic Renal Failure
34. Reynaud's disease/Burger's disease

FORMS AND RETURNS

Certain forms including returns are required to be filled and submitted by the employers to the ESI authorities. Forms generally required to be filled in by the employers are as under :

Revised Form No.	Purpose
Form-01 and Form-01-A or Regulation 10-B(a)	Registration of factories establishment
Form-1 Regulation 11 & 12	Declaration by person in employment on/after appointed day
Form-2 Regulation 15B	Changes in family
Form-5 Reuglation 26	Return of contributions to be sent to appropriate Office
Form-5A Regulation 31 (Second proviso)	Statement of contribution
Form-6 Regulation 32(1)(a)	Register of employees
Form-7 Regulations 57, 58, 59, 89B	Medical Certificate
Form-10 Regulations 52A(1) & (2)	Abstention verification
Form-8 Regulations 61 & 89B	Intermediate medical certificate
Form-9 Regulations 63 & 89B	Claim for sickness or Temporary disablement
Form-11 Regulation 66	Accident book
Form-12 Regulation 68	Report of accident by an employer
Form-14 Regulation 76A	Submission of claims for permanent disablement
Form-13 Regulations 79 & 95C	Issue of death certificate
Form-15 Regulation 80	Submission of claim for dependants benefit
Form-16 Regulation 83A	Submission of claims for periodical payments of dependents
Form-17 Regulation 87	Notice of pregnancy
Form-18 Regulation 88(i)(iii) & 89	Claim for maternity benefit
Form-19 Regulation 88(ii), 89 & 91	—do—
Form-20 Regulation 89A	Claim for maternity benefit after the death of an insured woman leaving behind the child
Form-21 Regulation 89A	—do—
Form-22 Regulation 95E	Claim for funeral expenses
Form-23 Regulation 107	Certificate in respect of a person claiming permanent disablement
Form-24 Regulation 107A	Declaration by and certificate in respect of a person claiming dependants' benefit

Note: Forms are supplied free of cost by the Local Offices of ESIC. However, the employers have to make an intent for required number of Forms to the appropriate Local Office indicating therein the number of employees as covered under the Act.

PUNISHMENT FOR FALSE STATEMENT

Whoever, for the purpose of causing any payment or benefit to be made where no payment or benefit is authorised by or under this Act, or for the purpose of avoiding any payment to be made by himself under this Act or enabling any other person to avoid any such payment, knowingly makes or causes to be made any false statement or false representation, shall be punishable with imprisonment for a term which may extend to six months, or with fine not exceeding two thousand rupees, or with both.

PUNISHMENT FOR FAILURE TO PAY CONTRIBUTIONS, ETC.

If any person—

(a) fails to pay any contribution which under this Act he is liable to pay, or

(b) deducts or attempts to deduct from the wages of an employee the whole or any part of the employer's contribution, or

(c) in contravention of section 72 reduces the wages or any privileges or benefits admissible to an employee, or

(d) in contravention of section 73 or any regulation dismisses, discharges, reduces or otherwise punishes an employee, or

(e) fails or refuses to submit any return required by the regulations, or makes a false return, or

(f) obstructs any Inspector or other official of the Corporation in the discharge of his duties, or

(g) is guilty of any contravention of or non-compliance with any of the requirements of this Act or the rules or the regulations in respect of which no special penalty is provided,

he shall be punishable—

(i) where he commits an offence under clause (a), with imprisonment for a term which may extend to six months but—

    (a) which shall not be less than three months, in case of failure to pay the employees' contribution which has been deducted by him from the employees' wages;

    (b) which shall not be less than one month, in any other

case, and shall also be liable to fine which may extend to two thousand rupees:

Provided that the court may, for any adequate and special reasons to be recorded in the judgment, impose a sentence of imprisonment for a lesser term or of fine only in lieu of imprisonment;

(ii) where he commits an offence under any of the clauses (b) to (g) (both inclusive), with imprisonment for a term which may extend to one year, or with fine which may extend to four thousand rupees, or with both.

ENHANCED PUNISHMENT IN CERTAIN CASES AFTER PREVIOUS CONVICTION

Whoever, having been convicted by a court of an offence punishable under this Act, commits the same offence shall, for every such subsequent offence, be punishable with imprisonment for a term which may extend to two years, or with fine which may extend to five thousand rupees:

Provided that where such subsequent offence is for failure by the employer to pay any contribution which under this Act he is liable to pay, he shall, for every such subsequent offence, be punishable with imprisonment for a term which may extend to five years, but which shall not be less than two years and shall also be liable to fine of twenty thousand rupees.

POWER TO RECOVER DAMAGES

(1) Where an employer fails to pay the amount due in respect of any contribution or any other amount payable under this Act, the Corporation may recover from the employer such damages not exceeding the amount of arrears as it may think fit to impose:

Provided that before recovering such damages, the employer shall be given a reasonable opportunity of being heard.

(2) Any damages recoverable under sub-section (1) may be recovered as an arrear of land revenue.

The Corporation is empowered to recover damages as under:—

Period of Delay in Payment of Contribution	Rate of Damages on amount due
upto less than 2 months	5%
2 months and above but less than 4 months	10%
4 months and above but less than 6 months	15%
6 months and above	25%

BENEFITS TO INSURED PERSONS UNDER ESI SCHEME

Since employees' State Insurance Act was enacted in 1948 to provide certain benefits, it claims that there are to more than 4 crore benefices. The benefits which are being provided to the benefices under its scheme are presently as under:—

1. Medical treatment without any charges is offered to an insured person and his family from the day he enters into insurable employment.

2. About 7/12th of employees normal wage will be payable to him by ESI during sickness.

3. Maternity benefit for 12 weeks of which not more than 6 weeks should be preceding confinement.

4. Injury during/in course of employment resulting in temporary/permanent disablement entitles the covered employee to a regular payment to substitute his lost wages.

5. Death during course of employment entitles specified dependants to a regular payment.

6. One time payment of Rs. 3,000 to help meet funeral expenses of the insured person.

TABLE OF STANDARD BENEFITS

Sr. No.	Average Daily Wages are	Standard Benefit Rate (in Rs.)
1.	Below Rs. 28.00	14 or Full average daily wage whichever is less
2.	Rs. 28.00 & above but below Rs. 32.00	Rs. 16.00
3.	Rs. 32.00 & above but below Rs. 36.00	Rs. 18.00
4.	Rs. 36.00 & above but below Rs. 40.00	Rs. 20.00
5.	Rs. 40.00 & above but below Rs. 48.00	Rs. 24.00
6.	Rs. 48.00 & above but below Rs. 56.00	Rs. 28.00
7.	Rs. 56.00 & above but below Rs. 60.00	Rs. 30.00
8.	Rs. 60.00 & above but below Rs. 64.00	Rs. 32.00
9.	Rs. 64.00 & above but below Rs. 72.00	Rs. 36.00
10.	Rs. 72.00 & above but below Rs. 76.00	Rs. 38.00
11.	Rs. 76.00 & above but below Rs. 80.00	Rs. 40.00
12.	Rs. 80.00 & above but below Rs. 88.00	Rs. 44.00
13.	Rs. 88.00 & above but below Rs. 96.00	Rs. 48.00
14.	Rs. 96.00 & above but below Rs. 106.00	Rs. 53.00
15.	Rs. 106.00 & above but below Rs. 116.00	Rs. 58.00

Sr. No.	Average Daily Wages	Standard Benefit Rate (in Rs.)
16.	Rs. 116.00 & above but below Rs. 126.00	Rs. 63.00
17.	Rs. 126.00 & above but below Rs. 136.00	Rs. 68.00
18.	Rs. 136.00 & above but below Rs. 146.00	Rs. 73.00
19.	Rs. 146.00 & above but below Rs. 156.00	Rs. 78.00
20.	Rs. 156.00 & above but below Rs. 166.00	Rs. 83.00
21.	Rs. 166.00 & above but below Rs. 176.00	Rs. 88.00
22.	Rs. 176.00 & above but below Rs. 186.00	Rs. 93.00
23.	Rs. 186.00 & above but below Rs. 196.00	Rs. 98.00
24.	Rs. 196.00 & above but below Rs. 206.00	Rs. 103.00
25.	Rs. 206.00 & above but below Rs. 216.00	Rs. 108.00
26.	Rs. 216.00 & above but below Rs. 226.00	Rs. 113.00
27.	Rs. 226.00 & above but below Rs. 236.00	Rs. 118.00
28.	Rs. 236.00 & above but below Rs. 250.00	Rs. 125.00
29.	Rs. 250.00 & above but below Rs. 260.00	Rs. 130.00
30.	Rs. 260.00 & above but below Rs. 270.00	Rs. 136.00
31.	Rs. 270.00 & above but below Rs. 280.00	Rs. 140.00
32.	Rs. 280.00 & above but below Rs. 290.00	Rs. 145.00
33.	Rs. 290.00 & above but below Rs. 300.00	Rs. 150.00
34.	Rs. 300.00 & above but below Rs. 310.00	Rs. 155.00
35.	Rs. 310.00 & above but below Rs. 320.00	Rs. 160.00
36.	Rs. 320.00 & above but below Rs. 330.00	Rs. 165.00
37.	Rs. 330.00 & above but below Rs. 340.00	Rs. 170.00
38.	Rs. 340.00 & above but below Rs. 350.00	Rs. 175.00
39.	Rs. 350.00 & above but below Rs. 360.00	Rs. 180.00
40.	Rs. 360.00 & above but below Rs. 370.00	Rs. 185.00
41.	Rs. 370.00 & above but below Rs. 380.00	Rs. 190.00
42.	Rs. 380.00 & above	Rs. 195.00

EXEMPTION FROM PAYMENT OF ESI CONTRIBUTIONS TO LOWER INCOME EMPLOYEES

The employees, who are in receipt of daily wages up to and inclusive of Rs. 70 will not be required to pay employees share of contribution. However, employer's share of contribution would continue to be paid.

Temporary Disablement Benefit & Dependent Benefit Rate	40% more than the Standard Benefit Rate
Maternity Benefit Rate	Twice the Standard Benefit Rate

BENEFITS, CONTRIBUTIONS CONDITIONS

Benefits	Contributory Conditions	Duration	Rate	To Whom Payable
1.(a) Sickness Benefit	Insured Person should work for wages for 78 no. days in the corresponding C.P. (W.e.f. 19-9-1998)	91 days in any two consecutive B.P.	As per S.B.R.	Only to the insured Person.
(b) Extended Sickness benefit for specified long term diseases like TB, Leprosy, etc.	In insurable employment for at least two years. Should pay contribution for minimum of 156 days in the preceding 4 C.P's.	309 days duration has been extended beyond 400 days (91 days S.B. plus 309 days (E.S.B.) to two years in deserving cases.	40% above S.B.R.	Only to the insured person.
(c) Enhanced Sickness Benefit (for undergoing sterilization operation for family Planning	Same as for Sickness Benefit at (a) above	7 days for vasectomy & 14 days for tubectomy extended in cases of post-operative complications etc.	Twice the S.B.R.	Only to the Insured Person.
2. Disablement Benefit (employment injury)	No condition	In case of temp. disablement: as long as incapacity lasts & in case of permanent disablement: for life time.	(a) For - temporary disablement 40% above S.B.R.	Only to the Insured Person.

Note.—Where more injuries than one are caused by the same accident, the rate of benefit payable under clauses (c) & (d) shall be aggregated but not so in any case as to exceed the FULL RATE and in cases of disablement not covered by clauses (a), (b), (c) & (d) at such rate, not exceeding the FULL RATE, as may be provided in the regulations.

(b) For Permanent Total Disablement specified in PART-1 of 2nd Schedule at the FULL RATE of TDB

(c) For permanent partial Disablement resulting from an injury specified in Part-II of the 2nd Schedule at such %age of the FULL RATE as specified in the said schedule as being the %age of the loss of earning capacity caused by the injury.

(d) For permanent partial Disablement resulting from an injury not specified in Part-II of the 2nd schedule at such

Benefit	Contributory Conditions	Duration	Rate	To Whom Payable
			%age of the FULL RATE payable in the case of Permanent Total Disablement as is proportionate to the loss of earning capacity permanently caused by the injury.	
3. Dependent's Benefit (employment injury)	No Condition	1. To the widow/s during life time until remarriage. 2. To the widowed mother	3/5 of the FULL RATE, if there are 2 or more widows, the amount payable to the widow shall be divided equally between the widows.	
		To the legitimate or adopted SON/S until he attains the age of 18 yrs.	2/5 of the FULL RATE, if there are 2 or more sons, the amount payable to the son shall be divided equally between the sons. Subject to min. of Rs. 14	
		To the legitimate or adopted unmarried Daughter/s until she attains the age of 18 yrs. or until marriage, whichever is earlier.	—Do—	
		(in case the deceased person does not leave a widow or legitimate or adopted child. D.B. shall be payable to......		
		(a) Parent or grand parent, for a life	3/10 of the FULL RATE	
		(b) Any other male dependent, until he attains the age of 18 yrs.	2/10 of the FULL RATE	
		(c) Any other female dependent, until she attains the age of 18 yrs. or until marriage whichever is earlier	—Do—	

Note.—An insured person whose PERMANENT DISABLEMENT has been assessed as final and who has been awarded permanent disablement benefit at a rate not exceeding Rs. 1.50 per day may apply for a lump-sum payment and such amount shall be determined by multiplying the daily rate of permanent disablement benefit by the figure indicated in Col. 2 of the Schedule III of the Regulations.

Benefit	Contributory Conditions	Duration	Rate	To Whom Payable
4. Maternity Benefit	Payment of contribution for 70 days in one or two consecutive periods.	12 weeks of which not more than the 6 weeks can precede the expected date of confinement.	Twice the S.B.R. subject to min of Rs. 20 p.d.	Only to the Insured person.
		6 weeks for miscarriage or for medical termination of pregnancy. Additional payment for one month for Complications (pre or post) arising out of Pregnancy	Medical bonus of Rs. 1,000 where ESI hospital facility is not availed for child delivery	to insured woman or in r/o wife of I.P.
5. Medical Benefit	No condition	From the date of entry of an employee into an insurable employment so long as he remains in insurable employment and there after for certain additional period.	Full Medical care including hospitalisation	Person as well as his/her family Members as defined u/s 2(11) of the Act.
6. Funeral Expenses	No condition (*i.e.* merely by virtue of being an insured person	One time lumpsum payment	Not more than Rs. 25,000 w.e.f. 1-10-2000	To the eldest surviving member of the family of the deceased I.P. or to the person who actually incurs the expenditure on the Funeral of an I.P.
7. Rehabilitation Allowance	No condition	For each day of which I.P. remains admitted in Artifical Limb Centre for fixation, repair or replacement of artificial limb.	Double the Standard Sickness Benfit Rate but not less than full wages.	Only to the I.P.
8. Medical Benefit to insured persons who ceases insurable employment on account of permanent disablement	No condition but an I.P. has to pay Rs. 10 pm in lumpsum for one year in advance every year.	Till the date on which an I.P. would have attained the age of superannuation	—	Medical Benefit to I.P. and spouse.
9. Medical Benefit to retired	(1) Insurable employment for a period of 5 years	Till the time yearly contribution is paid to the Concerned	—	Insured person and his spouse.

Benefit	Contributory Conditions	Duration	Rate	To Whom Payable
Insured period.	and (2) Payment of Contribution @ Rs. 10 pm in lump-sum for one year in advance, each year	Office of the Corporation.		

OTHER BENEFITS

Supply of special aids: Insured persons and members of their families are provided artificial limbs, hearing aids, artificial dentures, spectacles (for insured person only) & artificial appliances like spinal supports, cervical collars, walking callopers, crutches, wheel chairs and cardiac pace makers, dialysis/dialysis with kidney transplant etc., as part of medical care under the ESI Scheme.

AVAILABILITY OF BENEFITS-WHEN CONTRIBUTIONS ARE NOT PAID

Non-payment of contributions won't affect for availing of ESI benefits by an employee.

DEPOSIT OF ESI CONTRIBUTION DOES NOT DEPEND ON DISBURSEMENT OF WAGES

Timely payment of ESI's contributions is the responsibility of the employer and does not depend upon actual disbursement of wages and, as such, an employer cannot escape its obligation by taking the plea that the Company has become sick and the scheme for its rehabilitation has been sanctioned by BIFR.

I. Aids to ESI record keeping

Rubber Stamps

(i) Rubber stamp of about 1" size for employer's Code Number	For affixing in all correspondence, returns, forms and documents.
(ii) Rubber stamp showing the name and designation of the officer who has to countersign the various documents.	To be affixed on the Declaration Forms, Temporary Identification Certificates, Return of Declaration Forms, Return of Contributions, Accident Reports.
(iii) Rubber stamp showing name, address and Code No. of the employer.	To be affixed on the Declaration Forms, Temporary Identification Certificates, Return of Declaration Forms, Return of Contributions, Accident Reports etc.

(iv) A rubber stamp with the word 'FEMALE'	For affixing on Declaration Forms, Return of Declaration Forms and other documents in respect of female employees.

II. Registers/Files to be maintained by Employers

    (i) Register of Employees under Regulation 32.

    (ii) Accident Book under Regulation 66.

    (iii) Inspection Book under Regulation 102A in one quire leather bound register.

    (iv) File for copies of Return of Declaration Forms.

    (v) File for copies of Return of Contributions, Challans, etc.

    (vi) File for general correspondence with the Regional Office regarding coverage, inspection, etc., and other important circulars.

    (vii) File for copies of Accident Reports and correspondence in connection therewith.

DESIRABLE ACTION PLAN

(i) To furnish any requisite information promptly as and when asked for by the Regional Office/Local Office/any other office of the Corporation/Scheme.

(ii) To facilitate proper inspection of factory/establishment by any authorized officer of the Corporation and produce before him all relevant records on demand.

(iii) To intimate the date of closure or shifting (temporary or permanent) of the factory/establishment, to the Regional Office/ Local Office within seven days of its closure or shifting.

(iv) To report any change in the business activity, ownership of the concern or its management.

(v) To ascertain the liability towards ESI dues, while taking over the ownership of any factory/establishment by purchase, gift, lease or licence or in any other manner whatsoever as new owner is liable to discharge the past liabilities if any.

(vi) Maintain proper sanitation for a hygienic and healthy environment within the workplace and in residential quarters if allotted to the insured persons.

EMPLOYMENT EXCHANGES
(COMPULSORY NOTIFICATION OF VACANCIES)
ACT, 1959

CHECKLIST

Object of the Act
To provide for the compulsory notification of vacancies to employment exchanges.

Applicability of the Act
By notification in the Official Gazette, appoint in this behalf for such State and different dates may be appointed for different States or for different areas of a State

When Act is not applicable
- Any employment in agriculture, horticulture etc.
- Any employment in domestic service.
- Any employment, the total duration of which is less than three months.
- Any employment to do unskilled office work.
- Any employment connected with the staff of Parliament.

Sec. 3

Notification of vacancies to Employment Exchanges
- Before filling up any vacancy as prescribed.
- Employer not obliged to recruit the person through employment exchange.
- To notify the vacancies to such employment exchanges as may be prescribed.

Sec. 4

Furnishing information and returns
The employer in every establishment in public sector in that State or area shall furnish such information or return as may be prescribed in relation to vacancies that have occurred or are about to occur in that establishment, to such employment exchanges as may be prescribed.

Sec. 5

Time limit for notification of vacancies and selection
- At least 15 days before the applicants will be interviewed or tested.
- Employer to furnish the result of selection within 15 days.

Rule 5

Submission of Returns
- **Quarterly** in Form ER-I
- **Biennial** Return in Form ER-II
- Within 30 days by 30th **June**, 31st **March**, 30th **September** & 31st **December**.

Rule 6

PENALTIES
- An employer contravening the provisions of Sec. 4(1) or (2).
- Fine upto Rs.500 for first offence and for every subsequent offence fine Rs.1000.
- If any person -
  - required to furnish any information or return -
    - refuses or neglects to furnish such information or return, or
    - furnishes or causes to be furnished any information or return which he knows to be false, or
    - refuses to answer, or gives a false answer to any question necessary for obtaining any information required to be furnished under section 5; or
  - impedes the right of access to relevant records or documents or the right of entry conferred by section 6; he shall be punishable for the first offence with fine upto Rs.250 and for every subsequent offence with fine upto Rs.500.

Sec. 7

7. The Employment Exchanges (Compulsory Notification of Vacancies) Act, 1959

THE OBJECT

This Act has been enacted on the recommendations of the Training and Employment Services Organisation Committee, 1952.

Compulsory notification of all vacancies to the employment exchanges is now required under the law. No doubt the notification of vacancies is compulsory but selection of workmen and employees still rests with the employers, who are free to call on other sources also.

The Act stipulates that every establishment in public sector in that State or area shall, before filling up any vacancy in any employment in the establishment, notify that vacancy to such employment exchanges as may be prescribed.

The appropriate Government may by notification in the Official Gazette, require that from such date as may be specified in the notification, the employer in every establishment in private sector or every establishment pertaining to any class or category of establishments in private sector shall, furnish such information or return as may be prescribed in relation to vacancies that have occurred or are about to occur in that establishment to such employment exchanges as may be prescribed, and the employer shall thereupon comply with such requisition.

The manner in which the vacancies referred to in sub-section (1) or sub-section (2) shall be notified to the employment exchanges and the particulars of employments in which such vacancies have occurred or are about to occur shall be such as may be prescribed.

Nothing in sub-sections (1) and (2) shall be deemed to impose any obligation upon any employer to recruit any person through the employment exchange to fill any vacancy merely because that vacancy has been notified under any of those sub-sections.

However, the Act does not apply in relation to vacancies—

(a) in any employment in agriculture (including horticulture) in any establishment in private sector other than employment as agricultural or farm machinery operative;

(b) in any employment in domestic services;

(c) in any employment the total duration of which is less than three months;

(d) in any employment to do unskilled office work;

(e) in any employment connected with the staff of Parliament.

UNLESS THE CENTRAL GOVERNMENT OTHERWISE DIRECTS BY NOTIFICATION IN THE OFFICIAL GAZETTE IN THIS BEHALF, THIS ACT SHALL ALSO NOT APPLY IN RELATION TO:

(a) Vacancies which are proposed to be filled through promotion or by absorption of surplus staff of any branch or department of the same establishment or on the result of any examination conducted or interview held by, or on the recommendation of, any independent agency, such as the Union or a State Public Service Commission and the like;

(b) Vacancies in any employment which carries a remuneration of less than sixty rupees in a month.

OFFENCES AND PENALTIES

	Offences	Penalties
(i)	Failure to notify vacancies	1st Offence...Fine upto Rs. 500, subsequent offence... Fine upto Rs. 1000.
(ii)	Refusing or neglecting to: (a) furnish the information or returns	1st offence...Fine upto Rs. 250, subsequent offence...Fine upto Rs. 500
	(b) furnish or cause to furnish any information/return, knowing it to be false	—Do—
	(c) refusing to answer or giving false answer, in relation to any information sought for	—Do—
	(d) impeding the right of access to relevant records/documents or right of entry to officers entitled to inspect	—Do—

EMPLOYMENT EXCHANGES TO WHICH VACANCIES ARE TO BE NOTIFIED

The following vacancies, namely:—

    (a) Vacancies carrying total monthly emoluments of Rs. 200 per month or more occurring in establishment in respect of which the Central Government is the appropriate Government under the Act, and

    (b) Vacancies which an employer may desire to be circulated to the employment exchanges outside the State or Union Territory in which the establishment is situated,

shall be notified to the Central Employment Exchange.

Vacancies other than those specified in sub-rule (1) shall be notified to the local employment exchange concerned.

FORM AND MANNER OF NOTIFICATION OF VACANCIES

The vacancies shall be notified in writing to the appropriate employment exchange and the following particulars shall be furnished, where practicable, in respect of each type of vacancy:—

1. Name and address of the employer.

2. Telephone number of the employer, if any :

3. Name of vacancy—

   (a) Type of work required (Designation);

   (b) Description of duties;

   (c) Qualifications required—

      (i) Essential,

      (ii) Desirable;

   (d) Age-limits, if any;

   (e) Whether women are eligible?

4. Number of vacancies—

   (a) Regular,

   (b) Temporary.

5. Pay and allowances.

6. Place of work (name of town/village and district in which it is situated).

7. Probable date by which the vacancy will be filled.

8. Particulars regarding interview/test of applicants—

   (a) Date of interview/test;

   (b) Time of interview/test;

   (c) Place of interview/test;

   (d) Designation and address of the person to whom applicants should report.

9. Whether there is any obligation or arrangement for giving preference to any category of persons in filling up the vacancies.

10. Any other relevant information.

TIME LIMIT FOR THE NOTIFICATION OF VACANCIES

Vacancies, required to be notified to the Local Employment Exchange, shall be notified at least one week before the date on which applicants will be interviewed or tested, where interviews or tests are held, or the date on which vacancies are intended to be filled, if no interviews or tests are held.

Vacancies required to be notified to the Central Employment Exchange, shall be notified at least three weeks before the date on which applicants will be interviewed or tested where interviews or tests are held, or the date on which vacancies are intended to be filled, if no interviews or tests are held.

SUBMISSION OF RETURN

An employer shall furnish to the Local Employment Exchange, Quarterly returns in Form ER-I and Biennial returns in Form ER-II. Quarterly returns shall be furnished within thirty days of the due dates, namely 31st March, 30th June, 30th September and 31st December. Biennial returns shall be furnished within thirty days of the due date as notified in the Official Gazette.

CHECKLIST

EMPLOYERS' LIABILITY ACT, 1938

Object of the Act
The Employers' Liability Act was passed with the primary object of prohibiting certain defences as pleaded in suits for damages in respect of injuries sustained by workmen under common law.

Extension of the Act
The Employers' Liability Act extends to the whole of India.

Sec. 1(2)

Close proximity with ESI Act & Workmen's Compensation Act
The Employers' Liability Act is closely related to Chapters IV, V and VA of the Employees' State Insurance Act 1948 and to section 3 of the Workmen's Compensation Act, 1923.

Defences of the Employers
• **The doctrine of common employment**
By this doctrine an employer is not normally liable to pay damages to a workman for an injury resulting from the default of another workman.
• **The doctrine of assumed risk**
By this doctrine an employee is presumed to have accepted a risk if it is such that he ought to have known it to be part of the risks of his occupation.

Definitions
• **Workman :** A workman is a person who has entered into or works under a contract of service or apprenticeship with an employer. This contract of service or apprenticeship is for manual labour or clerical work or for any other purpose. This contract may be made expressly or by implication or orally or in writing.

Sec.2(a)

Bar on contracting out
In a suit for damages, the strong presumption shall be that the workman has undertaken any risk attaching to the employment without full knowledge. But this presumption may be rebutted only when the employer proves that the risk was fully explained to and understood by the workman and that the workman voluntarily undertook the same with full knowledge. The doctrine of contracting out has been inserted in the Act so as to exclude the provisions of the Contract Act, 1872.

Sec. 3A

• **Employer :** Employer is generally a person who gives employment and directs the manner in which the work is to be done and exercises control and supervision over the work done or to be done. The definition of employer includes (i) any body of persons, whether incorporated or not, (ii) the legal representatives of a deceased employer. Where the services of a workman are temporarily lent or let on hire to another person by the person with whom the workman has entered into a contract of service or apprenticeship, the employer means such person to whom the services of the workman are lent or let on hire.

Sec.2(b)

Risk not to be deemed to have been assumed without full knowledge
In any such suit for damages, the workman shall not be deemed to have undertaken any risk attaching to the employment unless the employer proves that the risk was fully explained to and understood by the workman and the workman voluntarily undertook the same.

Sec. 4

Saving
This Act shall not affect the validity of any decree or order of a civil court passed before the commencement of this Act in any such suit for damages.

Sec. 5

8. The Employers' Liability Act, 1938

THE OBJECT

The Act provides that certain defences shall not be raised in suits for damages in respect of injuries sustained by workmen.

IMPORTANT WORDS AND PHRASES

"Workman" means any person who has entered into or works under a contract of, service or apprenticeship with an employer whether by way of manual labour, clerical work or otherwise, and whether the contract is expressed or implied, oral or in writing; and

"Employer" includes any body of persons whether incorporated or not, any managing agent of an employer, and the legal representatives of a deceased employer, and, where the services of a workman are temporarily lent or let on hire to another person by the person or apprenticeship, means such other person while the workman is working for him.

DEFENCE OF COMMON EMPLOYMENT BARRED IN CERTAIN CASES

Where personal injury is caused to a workman—

(a) by reason of the omission of the employer to maintain in good and safe condition any way, works, machinery or plant connected with or used in his trade or business, or by reason of any like omission on the part of any person in service of the employer who has been entrusted by the

74

employer with the duty of seeing that such way, works, machinery or plant are in good and safe condition; or

(b) by reason of the negligence of any person in the service of the employer who has any superintendence entrusted to him, whilst in the exercise of such superintendence; or

(c) by reason of the negligence of any person in the service of the employer to whose orders or directions the workman at the time injury resulted from his having so conformed; or

(d) by reason of the act or omission of any person in the service of the employer done or made—

    (i) in the normal performance of the duties of that person; or

    (ii) in obedience to any rule or bye-law of the employer (not being a rule or bye-law which is required by or under any authority and which has been so approved); or

    (iii) in obedience to particular instruction given by any other person to whom the employer has delegated authority in that behalf;

    a suit for damages in respect of the injury instituted by the workman or by any person entitled in case of his death shall not fail by reason only of the fact that the workman was at the time of the injury a workman of, or in the service of, or engaged in the work of, the employer.

PROHIBITION FOR CONTRACTING OUT

Any provision contained in a contract of service or apprenticeship, or in an agreement collateral thereto, shall be void in so far as it would have the effect of excluding or limiting any liability to the employer in respect of personal injuries caused to the person employed or apprenticed by the negligence of persons in common employment with him.

EQUAL REMUNERATION ACT, 1976

Object of the Act

To provide for the payment of equal remuneration to men and women workers and for the prevention of discrimination, on the ground of sex, against women, in the matter of employment and for connected or incidental matters.

Act to have overriding effect

The provisions of this Act shall have effect notwithstanding anything inconsistent therewith contained in any other law or in the terms of any award, agreement or contract of service, whether made before or after this Act. **Sec. 3**

No discrimination to be made while recruiting men and women workers

• No discrimination on promotion, training or transfer except where employment of women is restricted.

• These provisions not applicable when priority is to be given to scheduled castes or scheduled tribes, ex-servicemen or retrenched employees. **Sec. 5**

Duty of employer to pay equal remuneration to men and women workers for same work or work of a similar nature

• No employer shall pay to any worker, employed by him in an establishment or employment, remuneration, cash or in kind, at rates less favourable than those at which remuneration is paid by him to the workers of the opposite sex for performing the same work or work of a similar nature.

• No employer shall reduce the rate of remuneration.

• Where the rates or remuneration payable before the commencement of this Act for men and women workers for the same work or work of a similar nature are different only on the ground of sex, then the higher or the highest rate at which remuneration to be paid. **Sec. 4**

Maintaining of register

Upto date for all workers employed in Form D at the place where the workers are employed. **Sec. 8, Rule 6**

PENALTIES   Sec. 10

• When any employer
  • omits or fails to maintain any register or other document in relation to workers.
  • omits or fails to produce any register, muster-roll or other document.
  • omits or refuses to give any evidence or prevents his agent, servant, etc. from giving evidence, or
  • omits or refuses to give any information.
	Simple imprisonment upto one month or fine upto Rs.10,000 or both.

• If any employer
  • makes any recruitment in contravention to the provisions of the Act, or
  • makes any payment of remuneration at unequal rates to men and women workers, for the same work or work of a similar nature, or
  • makes any discrimination between men and women workers in contravention of the provisions of the Act, or
  • omits or fails to carry out any direction made by the appropriate Government under sub-section (5) of section 6.
	Fine not less than Rs.10,000 which may extend to Rs.20,000 or imprisonment not less than 3 months which may extend upto one year for 1st offence, and upto two years for second and subsequent offences.

• On omission or failure to produce any register or record.	Fine upto Rs.500.

9. The Equal Remuneration Act, 1976

■

THE OBJECT

The Equal Remuneration Act provides for payment of equal remuneration to men and women workers and for the prevention of discrimination, on the ground of sex, against women in the matter of employment and for matters connected therewith or incidental thereto. Article 39 of the Constitution envisages that the State shall direct its policy, among other things, towards securing that there is equal pay for equal work for both men and women. To give effect to this constitutional provision the President promulgated on 26th September, 1975, the Equal Remuneration Ordinance, 1975 so that the provision of the Article 39 of the Constitution may be implemented in the year which was being celebrated as the International Women's Year. The Act was passed on 11th January, 1976.

IMPORTANT WORDS AND PHRASES

"Men" and "Women" mean male and female human beings respectively, of any age.

"Remuneration" means the basic wage or salary, and any additional emoluments whatsoever payable, either in cash or in kind, to person employed in respect of employment or work done in such employment, if the terms of the contract of employment, express or implied, were fulfilled.

"Same work or work of a similar nature" means work in respect of which the skill, effort and responsibility required are the same, when performed under similar working conditions, by a man or a woman and the differences, if any, between the skill, effort and responsibility required of a man and those required of a woman is not of practical importance in relation to the terms and conditions of employment.

"Worker" means a worker in any establishment or employment in respect of which this Act has come into force.

DUTY OF EMPLOYER TO PAY EQUAL REMUNERATION TO MEN AND WOMEN WORKERS FOR SAME WORK OF A REGULAR NATURE

(a) The employer shall pay to any worker, employed by him in an establishment or employment, remuneration, whether payable in cash or in kind, at rates less favourable than those at which remuneration is paid by him to the workers of the opposite sex in such establishment or employment for performing the same work or work of a similar nature.

(b) No employer shall, for the purpose of complying with the provisions of the above reduce the rate of remuneration of any worker.

(c) Where, in an establishment or employment, the rates of remuneration payable before the commencement of this Act for men and women workers for the same work or work of a similar nature are different only on the ground of sex, then the higher (in cases where there are only two rates), or, as the case may be, the highest (in cases where there are more than two rates), or such rates shall be the rate at which remuneration shall be payable, on and from such commencement, to such men and women workers:

Provided that nothing above shall be deemed to entitle a worker to the revision of the rate of remuneration payable to him or her with reference to service rendered by him or her before the commencement of this Act.

NO DISCRIMINATION TO BE MADE WHILE RECRUITING MEN AND WOMEN WORKERS

On and from the commencement of this Act, no employer shall, while making recruitment for the same work or work of a similar nature, make any discrimination against women except where the employment of women in such work is prohibited or restricted by or under any law for the time being in force :

Provided that the above provisions shall not affect any priority or reservation for scheduled castes or scheduled tribes, ex-servicemen, retrenched employees or any other class or category of persons in the matter of recruitment to the posts in an establishment or employment.

DUTY OF EMPLOYERS TO MAINTAIN REGISTERS

On and from the commencement of this Act, every employer shall maintain such registers and other documents in relation to the workers employed by him as may be prescribed. Rule 6 of the Equal Remunerations Rules provides that every employer shall maintain a register in relation to the workers employed by him in Form D.

PENALTIES

(1) If after the commencement of this Act, any employer, being required by or under the Act, so to do—

(a) omits or fails to maintain any register or other document in relation to workers employed by him, or

(b) omits or fails to produce any register, muster-roll or other document relating to the employment of workers, or

(c) omits or refuses to give any evidence or prevents his agent, servant, or any other person in charge of the establishment, or any worker, from giving evidence, or

(d) omits or refuses to give any information,

he shall be punishable with fine which may extend to one thousand rupees.

(2) If, after commencement of this Act, any employer—

(a) makes any recruitment in contravention of the provisions of this Act; or

(b) makes any payment of remuneration at unequal rates to men and women workers, for the same work or work of a similar nature; or

(c) makes any discrimination between men and women workers in contravention of the provisions of this Act; or

(d) omits or fails to carry out any direction made by the appropriate Government under sub-section (5) of section 6, pertaining to issue of directions by the appropriate Government in respect of employment of women workers,

he shall be punishable with fine which may extend to five thousand rupees.

(3) If any person being required so to do, omits or refuses to produce to an Inspector any register or other document or to give any information, he shall be punishable with fine which may extend to five hundred rupees.

OFFENCES BY COMPANIES

(1) Where an offence under this Act has been committed by a company, every person who, at the time the offence was committed, was in charge of, and was responsible to, the company, for the conduct of the business of the company, as well as the company, shall be deemed to be guilty of the offence and shall be liable to be proceeded against and punished accordingly:

Provided that nothing contained in this sub-section shall render any such person liable to any punishment, if he proves that the offence was committed without his knowledge or that he had exercised all due diligence to prevent the commission of such offence.

(2) Notwithstanding anything contained in sub-section (1), where any offence under this Act has been committed with the consent or connivance of, or is attributable to, any neglect on the part of any director, manager, secretary or other officer of the company, such director, manager, secretary or other officer shall be deemed to be guilty of that offence and shall be liable to be proceeded against and punished accordingly.

Explanation.—For the purposes of this section—

(a) "company" means any body corporate and includes a firm or other association of individuals; and

(b) "director" in relation to a firm, means a partner in the firm.

FACTORIES ACT, 1948

CHECKLIST

Applicability of the Act
Any premises whereon 10 or more persons with the aid of power or 20 or more workers are/were without aid of power working on any day preceding 12 months, wherein Manufacturing process is being carried on.
Sec.2(ii)

Employer to ensure health of workers pertaining to
• Cleanliness • Disposal of wastes and effluents • Ventilation and temperature • Dust and fume • Overcrowding • Artificial humidification • Lighting • Drinking water • Spittoons
Secs. 11 to 20

Registration & Renewal of Factories
To be granted by Chief Inspector of Factories on submission of prescribed form, fee and plan.
Sec.6

Safety Measures
• Fencing of machinery
• Work on or near machinery in motion.
• Employment prohibition of young persons on dangerous machines.
• Striking gear and devices for cutting off power.
• Self-acting machines.
• Casing of new machinery.
• Prohibition of employment of women and children near cotton-openers.
• Hoists and lifts.
Secs. 21 to 28

Welfare Measures
• Washing facilities
• Facilities for storing and drying clothing.
• Facilities for sitting
• First-aid appliances - one first aid box (not less than one) for every 150 workers.
• Canteens when there are 250 or more workers.
• Shelters, rest rooms and lunch rooms when there are 150 or more workers.
• Creches when there are 30 or more women workers.
• Welfare office when there are 500 or more workers.
Secs. 42 to 49

Working Hours, Spread Over and Overtime of Adults
• Weekly hours not more than 48.
• Daily hours, not more than 9 hours.
• Intervals for rest at least ½ hour on working for 5 hours.
• Spreadover not more than 10½ hours.
• Overlapping shifts prohibited.
• Extra wages for overtime double than normal rate of wages.
• Restrictions on employment of women before 6 A.M. and beyond 7 P.M.
Secs.51,54 to 56,59 & 60

Employment of Young Persons
• Prohibition of employment of young children e.g. 14 years.
• Non-adult workers to carry tokens e.g. certificate of fitness.
• Working hours for children not more than 4½ hrs. and not permitted to work during night shift.
Secs. 67, 68 & 71

Annual Leave with Wages
A worker having worked for 240 days @ one day for every 20 days and for a child one day for working of 15 days.
• Accumulation of leave for 30 days.
Sec. 79

OFFENCE	PENALTIES Secs. 92 to 106A
• For contravention of the provisions of the Act or Rules.	• Imprisonment upto 2 years or fine upto Rs.1,00,000 or both.
• On continuation of contravention	• Rs.1000 per day.
• On contravention of Chapter IV pertaining to safety or dangerous operations.	• Not less than Rs.25,000 in case of death. • Not less than Rs.5,000 in case of serious injuries.
• Subsequent contravention of some provisions.	• Imprisonment upto 3 years or fine not less than Rs.10,000 which may extend to Rs.2,00,000.
• Obstructing Inspectors	• Imprisonment upto 6 months or fine upto Rs.10,000 or both.
• Wrongful disclosing result pertaining to results of analysis.	• Imprisonment of 6 months or fine upto Rs.10,000 or both.
• For contravention of the provisions of Secs.41B, 41C and 41H pertaining to compulsory disclosure of information by occupier, specific responsibility of occupier or right of workers to work imminent danger.	• Imprisonment upto 7 years with fine upto Rs.2,00,000 and on continuation fine @ Rs.5,000 per day. • Imprisonment of 10 years when contravention continues for one year.

even if the employment is less than that given in the definition

10. The Factories Act, 1948

THE OBJECT

The Factories Act, 1948, has been promulgated, primarily to provide safety measures and to promote the health and welfare of workers employed in factories. The object, thus brings this Act, within the competence of the Central Legislature to enact. Thus State Governments/Union Territory Administrations, have been empowered under certain provisions of this Act, to make rules, to give effect to the objects and the scheme of the Act.

This Act was first enacted in 1934. Since then, it has been amended from time to time. The Factories (Amendment) Act, 1986 has brought in some drastic changes in the Factories Act, 1948 and has given it a new complexion. Its primary object is to protect workers employed in factories against industrial and occupational hazards. For that purpose, it seeks to impose upon the owners or the occupiers certain obligations to protect workers unwary as well as negligent and to secure for them, employment in conditions condusive to their health and safety from accidents. Besides, certain incidental provisions have been made for securing information to ensure that the objects of the Act are carried out.

APPLICABILITY

This Act applies to factories, which qualify the definition of "Factory", under section 2(m) of the Act or to those industrial establishments, to whom section 85 have been made applicable by the State Government, by a notification in the Official Gazette, even if the employment is less than that given in the definition under section 2(m).

This Act is applicable to all factories, including those belonging to the Central Government or any State Government, unless otherwise provided and is enforceable by the State Governments/ UTs Administrations, through its Directorate/Inspectorate of Factories.

OBLIGATIONS OF AN EMPLOYER

An employer is under statutory obligation to safeguard the health and safety of workers and extends to providing adequate plant, machinery and appliances, supervision over workers, to provide healthy and safe environment, proper system of working and extends to giving reasonable instructions. The detailed provisions, are therefore, made in diverse chapters of this Act, imposing obligations upon the owners of the factories to employ staff and for maintenance of health, cleanliness, prevention of over-crowding and provisions for amenities such as lighting, drinking water, creches, etc. Provisions are also made for welfare of the workers, such as restrictions on working hours and on employment of young persons and females and grant of annual leave with wages.

Undoubtedly, the Factories Act imposes numerous restrictions upon the employers to secure to the workers adequate safeguards, for their health and physical well being. But imposition of these restrictions cannot be regarded as unreasonable, in context of modern out-look on industrial relations.

The salient features of this Act have been summarised as under, which may be used merely as a guideline and for proper and fair interpretation, it would be desirable to refer to the Act and the rules in case any point requires further clarification.

CHAPTER I (PRELIMINARY)

(i) This Act extends to the whole of India and has come into force w.e.f. 1-4-1949.

(ii) Section 2 of this Act, defines "adult", "adolescent", "child", "competent person", "hazardous process", "factory", "manufacturing process", "worker", "power", "occupier", "week", etc.

(iii) Section 6 of the Act, requires prior approval of the CIF or the State Government, to be taken by the occupier of the factory before its construction/extension. After the construction, the management is required to obtain licence to run the factory. This licence is granted on payment of prescribed fees and submission of details prescribed under section 7 of this Act. This licence is to be renewed and the annual renewal fees is same as for grant thereof.

CHAPTER II (THE INSPECTING STAFF)

(i) *Section 7A:* General duties of the occupier, in so far as, is reasonably practicable and relates to health, safety and welfare of workers, have been detailed in section 7A of the Factories Act, 1948, which has been inserted *vide* the Factories (Amendment) Act, 1987 and is applicable w.e.f. 1-12-1987. These duties include providing information, instruction, training and supervision, necessary for health and safety of workers. It also includes provisions for monitoring of work environment.

(ii) *Section 7B:* This section prescribes general duties of designer, manufacturer, importer or supplier, as regards articles and substances for use in factories. This section is made applicable w.e.f. 1-6-1988.

(iii) *Sections 8 and 9:* Deal with the appointment of Inspectors, under this Act and define their powers. The Chief Inspector of Factories, to be assisted by other functionaries such as Joint Chief Inspector, Dy. Chief Inspector and Inspectors.

(iv) *Section 11 (Certifying Surgeons):* The State Government, may appoint qualified medical practitioners to be Certifying Surgeons. Their duties are:—

(a) examination and certification of young persons,

(b) examination of persons engaged in factories in specified dangerous operations,

(c) medical surveillence on factory workers.

CHAPTER III (HEALTH)

This Chapter, *inter alia*, requires proper cleanliness, frequency and mode of cleaning, arrangement for disposal of trade waste and affluents, provision of proper ventilation and temperature conditions of reasonable comfort of worker, control of dust and fumes, so as to prevent its inhalation by the workers. There should be no overcrowding in the factory, to an extent, it may be injurious to their health. It is the responsibility of the occupier/manager of the factory to provide adequate latrines, urinals, washing points, drinking water points, etc.

CHAPTER IV (SAFETY)

To ensure safety of workers working on or around the machines, it is essential that all dangerous parts of machinery should be properly fenced with safe-guards of substantial construction, which shall be maintained and kept in position, while the machinery is in motion (section 21). This section also prohibits examination and lubrication of machinery while in motion, unless it is carried out by a trained, male adult worker, whose name has been recorded in the register prescribed for this purpose. Section 23 of this Act prohibits employment of young persons on dangerous machines such as presses, wood working machines, etc. The other sections of this Chapter deal with the safety of self-acting machines, casing of new machinery, prohibition on employment of women and children under cotton openers, maintenance and testing of hoists and lifts, lifting machines, chains, ropes, etc., revolving machines, pressure plants. The maintenance of floors, stairs, pits, sumps, excessive weights, protection of eyes, precautions against dangerous fumes, precautions regarding use of portable electric lights, explosive and flammable dusts, precautions in case of fire, are the other areas where safety measures to be taken, have been detailed. The safety requirements also extend to maintenance and safety of buildings. In addition to these requirements, all factories ordinarily employing 1000 workers or more are required to employ such of safety officers, as may be prescribed in the State rules. The duties, qualifications and conditions of service of safety officers, have been prescribed under the State Factory Rules.

CHAPTER IVA (PROVISIONS RELATING TO HAZARDOUS PROCESSES)

This Chapter exclusively deals with the safety and work-environment in hazardous process industries. The provisions of this Chapter and definition of "Hazardous Process", under section 2(cb), were inserted, *vide* the Factories (Amendment) Act, 1987. All these amendments except section 41F and the Second Schedule are applicable w.e.f. 1-12-1987, whereas section 41F and the Second Schedule are applicable w.e.f. 1-6-1988. The salient features of this Chapter are:—

(a) *Section 41A:* Constitution of a Site Appraisal Committee to consider applications for grant of permission for the initial location of a factory, involving hazardous process or an expansion of any such factory.

(b) *Section 41B:* Compulsory disclosure of information by the occupier.—

It shall be the duty of the occupier to—

(i) disclose information regarding dangers, including health hazards and measures to overcome such hazards arising out of hazardous substances, to the Chief Inspector of Factories, local authority and the general public in the vicinity;

(ii) prepare health and safety policy. It also applies to non-hazardous and non-dangerous operations of factories employing 100 or more workers, without the aid of power or 50 or more workers, with the aid of power;

(iii) furnish information on hazardous waste;

(iv) prepare on-site emergency plan, detailing safety measures to be taken in the event of an accident taking place;

(v) assist the District Emergency Office, in preparation of off-site Emergency Plan and preparation of information to be furnished to general public;

(vi) collection, development and dissemination of information in the form of Material Safety Data Sheet (MSDS) and labelling of containers of hazardous substances.

(c) *Section 41C:* Specific responsibility of the occupier in relation to hazardous processes:—

(i) to maintain accurate and upto date medical record of the workers;

(ii) to appoint qualified, experienced and competent supervisors to supervise handling of hazardous substances;

(iii) pre-employment and post-employment medical examination of workers, at regular intervals.

(d) *Sections 41D and 41E:* These sections empower the Central Government to appoint an Enquiry Committee, in extraordinary situations and to prescribe safety standards, wherever the same have not been prescribed.

(e) *Section 41F:* Permissible limits of exposure of chemical and toxic substances have been prescribed under the Second Schedule. These limits are applicable, whether the industry is hazardous or not.

(f) *Section 41G:* Workers participation in Safety Management.—

"Safety Committees", are required to be set up, comprising of representatives of management and workers, to promote better co-operation. This requirement also applies to non-hazardous, non-dangerous operation factories employing more than 250 workers in factories in Delhi.

(g) *Section 41H:* Right of workers to warn about imminent danger.—

This section empowers workers to bring to the notice of the occupier, manager or incharge, directly or through the Safety Committee, any situation where there is a likelihood of imminent danger to human life and to simultaneously bring to the notice of the Inspector of Factories.

CHAPTER V (WELFARE)

The prominent requirements of this Chapter are to provide—

(i) Separate and adequate washing facilities for male and female;

(ii) Facilities for storing and drying of wet clothes;

(iii) Facilities for sitting for workers obliged to work normally in standing position;

(iv) First-Aid Box under the charge of a trained first-aider;

   (v) Ambulance Room for factory ordinarily employing more
         than 500 workers;

  (vi) Canteen of prescribed standards, in factories ordinarily
         employing more than 250 workers, to be run on no-profit
         basis by a duly constituted Canteen Managing
         Committee;

 (vii) Suitable and adequate Rest Shelter or a Rest Room and
         Lunch Room to be provided in factories, ordinarily
         employing more than 150 workers. However, this
         provision shall not be required, if canteen according to
         section 46 has been provided;

(viii) Creche of prescribed standards for use of children below 6
         years of age of women workers, employed in factories
         ordinarily employing more than 30 women workers. Such
         creche should be under the charge of a trained woman;

  (ix) Factories ordinarily employing 500 or more workers, are
         required to appoint a Welfare Officer, whose duties,
         qualifications and conditions of service are prescribed
         under the State Factory Rules.

CHAPTER VI (WORKING HOURS OF ADULT)

An "adult" has been defined under section 2(a) of the Factories
Act and would mean a person, who has completed 18 years of
age. The salient provisions relating to adult workers, are given
here as under:

   (i) Weekly holiday on the first day of the week, which is
         Sunday or may be any other day, as may be approved in
         writing by the Chief Inspector of Factories, for a particular
         area. There is a provision for substitution of weekly
         holiday, under section 52, so that by complying with the
         requirements of this section, workers may be permitted to
         work on the day of weekly holiday. Also provision for
         allowing compensatory holiday, in lieu of unavailed
         weekly holiday;

  (ii) Work for not more than 48 hours a week and not more
         than 9 hours a day. The spread-over should not exceed
         10-1/2 hours, unless exempted by the Chief Inspector. A
         rest interval of at least half an hour should be provided, in
         such a way that no period of work shall exceed 5-1/2
         hours. (Reference sections 51, 53, 54, 55 and 56);

(iii) Overlapping of shifts is not permitted, unless exemption obtained from the Chief Inspector of Factories;

(iv) A worker, who works in a factory for more than 9 hours on any day or more than 48 hours in a week, is entitled, for the overtime work, wages at the rate twice the ordinary rate of wages, in accordance with section 59;

(v) Double employment of a worker is prohibited under section 60;

(vi) The notice of period of work, fixed in accordance with the provisions of this Chapter is required to be displayed in the factory. Any proposed change should be notified to the Inspector, before the change is made. Prior permission of the Inspector is required, if the last change was less than a week old and if a factory works in more than one shift, in groups according to their nature of work. For further details, reference may be made to section 61;

(vii) It is statutorily required under section 62 to maintain a Register of adult workers, in accordance with this section. This register should be available at all the times, on demand by the Inspector. No adult worker is required or allowed to work in the factory, unless his name and particulars have been recorded in the register. The hours of work should correspond with the notice of period of work, fixed under section 61 and register of adult workers maintained under section 62;

(viii) Section 64 gives powers to the State Government to declare persons holding position of supervision or management or employed in confidential position. Such persons are exempted from provisions of Chapter VI, relating to working hours, except section 66(l)(b), which prohibits employment of women between 7.00 p.m. to 6.00 a.m.;

(ix) Section 64 empowers the State Governments to make rules for adult workers providing for exemptions to an extent and subject to such conditions as may be prescribed in the rules under this section. These rules are to be framed within the frame work given under this section;

(x) Section 65 gives powers to the State Government to grant exemptions to deal with the exceptional pressure of work, within the parameters detailed in this section;

(xi) Section 66 imposes further restrictions on employment of women, such as, not permitted to work between 7.00 p.m. to 6.00 a.m. However, the Chief Inspector is empowered to grant relaxation, but in that case women are not permitted to work between 10.00 p.m. to 5.00 a.m. Also women workers cannot be exempted from the provisions of section 54 relating to daily hours of work.

CHAPTER VII (EMPLOYMENT OF YOUNG PERSONS)

The young persons have been defined as "child" or "adolescent". A child is one, who has not completed 15 years of age and an adolescent is one, who has completed 15 years, but not completed 18 years of age.

The following are the prominent requirements of this Chapter:—

(i) A child worker, who has not completed 14 years of age is not permitted to work in a factory (section 67);

(ii) Non-adult workers are required to carry certificate of fitness granted by the Certifying Surgeon which should be in the custody of the factory manager, declaring the person fit to work as an adult or child worker, with token (giving reference to such a certificate) to such young person. The Certifying Surgeon, after examination may grant a certificate to work as a child, if completed 14 years of age and attained prescribed physical standards, and fit for such work. But if the young person has completed 15 years and is fit for full day's work in the factory, he may be granted certificate of fitness to work as an adult. The validity of certificate is 12 months and renewal thereafter, and can be revoked, in certain circumstances. The fees for grant of certificate is payable by the occupier and is not recoverable from the worker (sections 68 and 69);

(iii) An adolescent, who has been granted the certificate of fitness to work as an adult, shall be deemed to be an "adult", for all purposes of the Chapters VI and VII, except that such adolescent, who has not completed 17 years of age is permitted to work between 7.00 p.m. and 6.00 a.m. But an adolescent, who has not been granted a certificate of fitness, shall be deemed to be a child for all purposes of the Act (section 70);

(iv) The working hours of child workers are limited to 4 $\frac{1}{2}$ hours a day, with prohibition to work during night (10.00 p.m. to 6.00 a.m.). The spread-over should not exceed 5 hours, without any overlapping of shifts, restricted to two shifts only. Female child workers are prohibited to work between 7.00 p.m. and 8.00 a.m. (section 71);

(v) The requirements of (a) display of notice of period of work, (b) maintenance of register of child workers, and (c) working hours to correspond with the notice of period of work are also applicable to child workers, similar to those applicable to adult workers (sections 72, 73 and 74);

(vi) If an Inspector is of the opinion that either the young person is working in a factory without certificate of fitness or is not fit to work in the capacity stated therein, he may direct the manager to get him examined from the Certifying Surgeon, whose decision shall be final (section 75).

CHAPTER VIII (ANNUAL LEAVE WITH WAGES)

(i) The provisions of this Chapter do not apply, if a worker, under any award, agreement (including settlement) or contract of service, is entitled to leave with wages, which are more favourable. It also does not apply to workers of the factories of Railways and the Government, who are governed by leave rules approved by the Central Government (section 78).

(ii) An adult worker is entitled to leave with wages, in the subsequent calendar year, if he has worked for 240 days or more in a calendar year. Such leave is calculatable as under:

(a) One leave for 20 days actual working, in case of an adult;

(b) One leave for 15 days actual working, in case of a child;

(c) The period of lay off, maternity leave in case of female and the leave earned in the year prior to which it is enjoyed shall be deemed to be days on which the worker has worked, for the purposes of computation of 240 days, to become eligible for leave with wages, but shall not earn leave for those days;

(d) For a worker, whose services commence, otherwise than 1st of January, the person shall be entitled to leave, if he has worked for more than 2/3rd of number of days in the remainder of calendar year, even if it is less than 240 days;

(e) In case of discharge, dismissal, superannuation, death or any other mode of quitting service, the person is entitled to leave, even if he has not worked for a minimum of 240 days or a minimum of 2/3rd of the remainder of calender year, which is the eligibility criteria, as laid down and detailed above. The payment in lieu of such leave, should be paid within 2 months, from the date of superannuation or death or on the next working day, in other cases of discharge;

(f) While calculating the days of leave, Sundays and holidays should be excluded, whether occurring during or at the end of leave period.

(iii) A fraction of leave of 1/2 day or more, is to be treated as one leave.

(iv) The unavailed leave in a calendar year can be carried forward in the next year, but such a carryforward should not exceed 30 days for adult or 40 days for child worker. However, leave refused in accordance with this Chapter, can be carried forward without any limit.

(v) A notice of minimum 15 days is required to be given, from the date of commencement of leave in non-public utility services. However, for public-utility services, it shall be a minimum of 30 days. The notice period is not necessary, in case it is availed to cover period of sickness.

(vi) Leave cannot be taken for more than 3 times in a year.

(vii) There is a provision under which a scheme may be drawn up in agreement, with the Works Committee or workers representatives, regulating the manner of grant of leave with a view to ensure continuity of work. Such a scheme may be lodged in writing with the Chief Inspector, with a copy displayed on the Notice Board and shall remain in force for 12 months from the date of applicability. There is a provision for renewal with or without modifications.

(viii) An application for leave, which does not contravene the provisions of this Chapter, cannot be refused.

(ix) The unavailed leave cannot be taken into consideration, while calculating notice period, in case of discharge or dismissal.

(x) The rate of leave with wages shall be calculated on the basis of his average earning during the month, preceding the month, in which leave has been allowed. The rate of wages shall be exclusive of any overtime or bonus. If leave is for 4 or more days for adult or 5 days or more for child, there is provision of payment of leave in advance (sections 80 and 81).

(xi) The leave due but not paid, is recoverable as delayed wages, under the Payment of Wages Act, 1936.

CHAPTER IX (SPECIAL PROVISIONS)

The special provisions pertain to the following matters:—

(1) Powers to the State Government to apply any or all provisions of the Act to any place, even if the number of workers is less than 10 with power or 20 without power, in the manufacturing process (section 85).

(2) Powers to exempt Public Institutions maintained for the purposes of education, training, research, etc. (section 86).

(3) Powers to State Government, to declare certain processes, as dangerous processes, which are likely to expose any worker to serious risk of bodily injury, poisoning or disease and to frame rules, prescribing additional welfare facilities, supply of personal protective employment, periodical medical examination of workers, special safety laws, in such processes (section 87).

(4) An accident in a factory, which causes death or bodily injury, resulting in absence from place of work for 48 hours or more, is a reportable accident under the Act and should be reported to the Inspector, in the manner prescribed in the State Factory Rules (section 88).

(5) All dangerous occurrences of the nature prescribed in the State Factory Rules, such as failure of a lifting machine, etc. are required to be reported (section 88A).

(6) The cases of workers attracting occupational diseases specified in the Third Schedule, are required to be notified to the prescribed authorities (section 89).

(7) Section 90 gives powers to the State Governments to order an enquiry in cases of accidents or workers attracting occupational diseases.

(8) The procedure for taking of sample by an Inspector has been detailed in section 91.

(9) Section 91A empowers the expert organisations such as DGFASLI (Directorate General of Factory Advice Services and Labour Institutes), besides the Chief Inspector of Factories to carry out occupational health surveys.

REGISTERS, NOTICES, RETURNS AND REPORTS UNDER THE FACTORIES ACT, 1948

REGISTERS REQUIRED TO BE MAINTAINED UNDER THE FACTORIES ACT, 1948

1.	Form 6	Register of Hygrometer (Humidity Register)
2.	Form 7	Register of White Washing
3.	Form 7A	Register of Tight Cloths provided
4.	Form 9	Register of Compensatory Holidays
5.	Form 10	Register of Overtime for exempted workers
6.	Form 12	Register of Adult Workers
7.	Form 14	Register of Child Labour
8.	Form 15	Register of Leave with Wages
9.	Forms 24 & 25	Muster Roll-9
10.	Form 26	Register of Accident & Dangerous Occurrence

ACTS TO BE DONE OR MAINTAINED

1.	Form 3	Change of Name of Manager/Occupier as and when required
2.	Form 8	Report of Examination of Vessels.
3.	Form 11	Notice of Periods of Work for Adult Workers
4.	Form 13	Notice of Periods of Work for Child Labour
5.	Form 18	Notice of Accident and Dangerous Occurrence to be submitted within 24 hours by Registered Post.

6.	Form 18A	Notice of Accident and Dangerous Occurrence not resulting in bodily injury.
7.	Form 19	Notice of Accident and Dangerous Occurrence (Poisoning or Disease).
8.	Form 21	Annual Return ending 31st December.
9.	Form 22	Half yearly return by 30th June.
10.	Form 31	Accident Annual Return by 1st Week of February – Rule 107(4).
11.	Form 34	Monthly Return only for Hazardous Happenings.
12.	Form 37	Report of Hoist of Lifts.
13.	Form 2	Renewal of Annual Fees to Reach to the prescribed office.

CHAPTER X (PENALTIES AND PROCEDURES)

(1) General penalty for offences under the Act is provided under section 92, according to which save as is otherwise expressly provided in the Act, the occupier and manager shall be guilty of an offence, which is punishable with imprisonment upto 2 years or fine upto One Lakh Rupees or both. In case the contravention is continued, after conviction, it may extend to Rs. 1,000 per day. In case of contravention of Chapter IV or section 87 or rules made thereunder, the minimum fine is Rs. 25,000, in case of death or Rs. 5,000 in case of accident, causing serious bodily injury.

(2) Enhanced penalty after previous conviction has been prescribed under section 94, which provides for imprisonment upto 3 years or with a fine upto Rupees Two lakhs or both, with a minimum fine of Rs. 10,000. In case of death or accidents causing serious bodily injury, the minimum fine shall be Rs. 35,000 and Rs. 10,000 respectively.

(3) Penalty for obstructing an Inspector, has been prescribed under section 95, which may extend to imprisonment upto 6 months or a fine upto Rs. 10,000 or both.

(4) Penalty for contravention of provisions of sections 41B, 41C, and 41H, may extend to an imprisonment upto seven years, fine upto Rupees 2 lakhs or both. In case of

continued offences, the fine may extend upto Rs. 5,000 per day.

(5) Penalties for (a) wrongful disclosure of results of analysis, (b) offences by workers, (c) penalty for using false certificate of fitness, and (d) penalty for permitting double employment of child, have been prescribed under sections 96, 97, 98, and 99 of the Act.

(6) The liabilities of the owner of the building for certain common facilities, have been detailed under section 93.

(7) Limitation of Prosecution is 6 months for not obeying a written order of the Inspector and in other cases, it is 3 months.

(8) The presumption as to employment, onus as to age and onus of proving limits of what is practicable, etc., have been detailed under sections 103, 104 and 104A respectively.

(9) The procedure for bringing to the court, another person, whom the occupier/manager, charges to be the actual offender, has been detailed under section 101 of the Act. In case the charge is proved, such a person shall be convicted of the offence.

CHAPTER XI (SUPPLEMENTAL)

The supplementary provisions have been listed and briefly described as under:

(1) Appeals	-Section 107	
(2) Display of notices	-Section 108	
(3) Service of Notices	-Section 109	
(4) Submission of annual and Half-yearly returns	-Section 110	
(5) Obligations and rights of workers	-Sections 111 and 111A	
(6) No charge for facilities and convenience	-Section 114	
(7) Protection of persons acting under this Act	-Section 117	
(8) Restriction of disclosure of information on manufacturing process by Inspector	-Section 118	

INDUSTRIAL DISPUTES ACT, 1947

CHECKLIST

Object of the Act
Provisions for investigation and settlement of industrial disputes and for certain other purposes.

Important Clarifications
• **Industry** - has attained wider meaning than defined except for domestic employment, covers from barber shops to big steel companies. **Sec.2(j)**
• **Works Committee** - Joint Committee with equal number of employers and employees' representatives for discussion of certain common problems. **Sec.3**
• **Conciliation** - is an attempt by a third party in helping to settle the disputes. **Sec.4**
• **Adjudication** - Labour Court, Industrial Tribunal or National Tribunal to hear and decide the dispute. **Secs.7, 7A & 7B**

Power of Labour Court to give Appropriate Relief
Labour Court/Industrial Tribunal can modify the punishment of dismissal or discharge of workmen and give appropriate relief including reinstatement. **Sec.11A**

Right of a Workman during Pendency of Proceedings in High Court
Employer to pay last drawn wages to reinstated workman when proceedings challenging the award of his reinstatement are pending in the higher Courts. **Sec.17B**

Persons Bound By Settlement
• When in the course of conciliation proceedings etc., all persons working and joining subsequently.
• Otherwise than in course of settlement upon the parties to the settlement. **Sec. 18**

Period of Operation of Settlements and Awards
• A settlement for a period as agreed by the parties, or
• Period of six months on signing of settlement.
• An award for one year after its enforcement. **Sec.19**

Lay off and Payment of Compensation -
Conditions for Laying off
Failure, refusal or inability of an employer to provide work due to
• Shortage of coal, power or raw material.
• Accumulation of stocks.
• Breakdown of machinery.
• Natural calamity. **Sec. 2(kkk)**

Lay off Compensation
Payment of wages except for intervening weekly holiday compensation 50% of total or basic wages and DA for a period of lay off upto maximum 45 days in a year. **Sec.25-C**

Notice of Change
21 days by an employer to workmen about changing the conditions of service as provided in IV Schedule. **Sec.9A**

Prior Permission for Lay off
When there are more than 100 workmen during preceding 12 months. **Sec.25-M**

Prohibition of Strikes and Lock Outs
• Without giving to the employer notice of strike, as hereinafter provided, within six weeks before striking.
• Within fourteen days of giving such notice.
• Before the expiry of the date of strike specified in any such notice as aforesaid.
• During the pendency of any conciliation proceedings before a conciliation officer and seven days after the conclusion of such proceedings.
• During the pendency of conciliation proceedings before a Board and seven days after the conclusion of such proceedings.
• During the pendency of proceedings before a Labour Court, Tribunal or National Tribunal and two months, after the conclusion of such proceedings.
• During the pendency of arbitration proceedings before an arbitrator and two months after the conclusion of such proceedings, where a notification has been issued under sub-section (3A) of section 10A.
• During any period in which a settlement or award is in operation, in respect of any of the matters covered by the settlement or award. **Secs. 22 & 23**

Conditions of service etc. to remain unchanged under certain circumstances during pendency of proceedings
• Not to alter to the prejudice of workmen concerned the condition of service.
• To seek express permission of the concerned authority by paying one month's wages on dismissal, discharge or punish a protected workman connected with the dispute.
• To seek approval of the authority by paying one month's wages before altering condition of service, dismissing or discharging or punishing a workman. **Sec. 33**

Recognition of Protected Workman
One percent of the total number of workmen employed therein subject to a minimum number of five and maximum of 100 workmen. **Sec. 33(4)**

Retrenchment of Workmen Compensation and Conditions
• Workman must have worked for 240 days.
• Retrenchment compensation @15' wages for every completed year to be calculated at last drawn wages
• One month's notice or wages in lieu thereof.
• Reasons for retrenchment
• Complying with principle of 'last come first go'.
• Sending Form P to Labour Authorities **Secs. 25F & 25G**

Prior Permission by the Government for Retrenchment
• When there are more than 100 (in UP 300 or more) workmen during preceding 12 months.
• Three months' notice or wages thereto.
• Form QA
• Compensation @15 days' wages. **Sec. 25-N**

Prohibition of unfair labour practice either by employer or workman or a trade union as stipulated in Fifth Schedule
Both the employer and the Union can be punished. **Sec. 25-T**

Closure of an Undertaking
• 60 days' notice to the labour authorities for intended closure in Form QA. **Sec.25FFA**
• Prior permission at least 90 days before in Form O by the Government when there are 100 or more workmen during preceding 12 months (in UP 300 or more workmen) **Sec.25-O**

PENALTIES

Offence > < Punishment

Section	Offence	Punishment
Sec. 25-U	Committing unfair labour practices	Imprisonment upto 6 months or with fine upto Rs.3,000.
Sec. 26	Illegal strike and lock-outs	Imprisonment upto one month or with fine upto Rs.50 (Rs.1000 for lock-out) or with both.
Sec. 27	Instigation etc. for illegal strike or lock-outs	Imprisonment upto 6 months or with fine upto Rs.1,000
Sec. 28	Giving financial aid to illegal strikes and lock-outs	Imprisonment for 6 months or with fine upto Rs.1,000
Sec. 29	Breach of settlement or award	Imprisonment upto 6 months or with fine. On continuity of offence fine upto Rs. 200 per day.
Sec. 30	Disclosing confidential information pertaining to Sec.21	Imprisonment upto 6 months or with fine upto Rs.1,000
Sec. 31A	Closure without 60 days' notice under Sec.25FFA	Imprisonment upto 6 months or with fine upto Rs.5,000
Sec. 31	Contravention of Sec.33 pertaining to change of conditions of service during pendency of dispute etc.	Imprisonment upto 6 months or fine upto Rs.1,000
	When no penalty is provided for contravention.	Fine upto Rs.100.

11. The Industrial Disputes Act, 1947

THE OBJECT

The Preamble of the Act states that it aims at bringing in conflicts between employer and employee to an amicable settlement and at the same time it makes provisions for some of the other problems that may arise from time to time in an industrial or commercial undertaking which came within the purview of the definition of 'industry' as defined by section 2(j) of the Act. The Act does not discourage collective bargaining so long as the industrial peace is not disturbed or normal working is not disrupted. Notwithstanding that, should there be any difficulty or any problem arises under the provisions of the Act, the machinery set up may be approached so that industrial peace may be maintained and sustained without any one having to resort to illegal strike or lock-outs. The Act provides for payment of compensation to the workmen on account of retrenchment or lay off and closure. It also lays down the procedure for prior permission of the appropriate Government for laying off or retrenching the workers or closing down an industrial establishment in which not less than one hundred workmen were employed on an average per day for the preceding twelve months. Furthermore, the amended Act lays down unfair labour practices on the part of an employer or a trade union or the workers.

The Industrial Disputes Act is a benign measure which seeks to pre-empt industrial tensions, provide the mechanics of dispute-resolutions and set up the necessary infrastructure so that the energies of partners in production may not be dissipated in counter-productive battles and assurance of industrial justice may create a congenial climate.

IMPORTANT DEFINITIONS

    i. "closure" means the permanent closing down of a place of employment or part thereof [section 2(cc)].

It is only "the permanent closing down" of a place of employment that can be taken to be closure. However, closure may be partial also. Therefore, it is not necessary that the whole establishment is closed for the purposes of the definition.

    ii. "Conciliation Officer" means a conciliation officer appointed under this Act [section 2(d)].

A Conciliation Officer is appointed under section 4 of the Industrial Disputes Act. Conciliation Officers are charged with the duty of mediating in and promoting the settlement of industrial disputes.

    iii. "industry" means any business, trade, undertaking, manufacture or calling of employers and includes any calling, service, employment, handicraft, or industrial occupation or avocation of workmen [section 2 (j)].

The definition of industry is exhaustive and comprehensive. The Supreme Court in its landmark judgment of *Bangalore Water Supply and Sewerage Board* v. *Rajappa*, 1978 Lab & 1C 467: AIR 1978 SC 548: 36 FLR 266: 1978 (1) LLJ 349, has widened the scope of the definition and broad principles are given below:—

    (a) *Establishments Run Without Profit Motive*

        Absence of profit motive or gainful objective is irrelevant, be the venture in the public, private or other sector.

    (b) *Undertakings Governed by a No-profit-no-loss Rule, Statutorily or otherwise Fastened*

        Section 2(j) of the Act uses words of very wise denotation, a line would have to be drawn in a fair and just manner so as to exclude some callings, services or undertakings.

    (c) *Clubs or Other Organisations Whose General Emphasis is Not on Profit-making But Fellowship and Self-service*

   (i) Professions (ii) Clubs (iii) Educational institutions (iv) Co-operatives (v) Research institutes (vi) Charitable Projects and (vii) other kindred adventures, if they fulfil the triple tests listed above, cannot be exempted from the scope of section 2(j) of the Act.

  iv. "Industrial Dispute" means any dispute or difference between employer and employees, or between employers and workmen, or between workmen and workmen, which is connected with the employment or non-employment or the terms of employment or with the conditions of labour, of any person [section 2 (k)].

The scope of definition of 'industrial dispute' is very wide. The words 'employment and non-employment' in the definition are of widest amplitude and have been put in juxtaposition to make the definition comprehensive. Any dispute connected with 'employment or non-employment' constitutes the subject matter of one class of industrial disputes. The matters which can form subject matter of industrial dispute are enumerated in Second, Third and Fourth Schedule given at the end of the Act.

   v. "Lock-out" means the temporary closing of a place of employment or the suspension of work, or the refusal by an employer to continue to employ and number of persons employed by him [section 2 (1)].

  vi. "Retrenchment" means the termination by the employer of the service of a workman for any reason whatsoever, otherwise than as a punishment inflicted by way of disciplinary action, but does not include—

     (a) voluntary retirement of the workman; or

     (b) retirement of the workman on reaching the age of superannuation if the contract of employment between the employer and the workman concerned contains a stipulation in that behalf; or

    (bb) termination of the service of the workman as a result of the non-renewal of the contract of employment between the employer and the workman concerned on its expiry or of such contract being terminated under a stipulation in that behalf contained therein; or

    (c) termination of the service of a workman on the ground of continued ill-health [section 2(o)].

vii. "Settlement" means a settlement arrived at in the course of conciliation proceeding and includes a written agreement between the employer and workmen arrived at otherwise than in the course of conciliation proceedings where such agreement has been signed by the parties thereto in such manner as may be prescribed and a copy thereof has been sent to an officer authorised in this behalf by the appropriate Government and the conciliation officer [section 2(p)].

There are two categories of a settlement, one is arrived at in the course of conciliation proceedings and the other is a written agreement between the employer and the workman arrived at otherwise than the course of conciliation proceeding. The legal implications of these settlements are different. A settlement arrived at in the course of conciliation binds all the present and future workmen as specified in section 18(3) of the Act. The other kind of settlement binds only the actual parties to the agreement as per provisions of section 18(1) of the Act.

viii. "Strike" means a cessation of work by a body of persons employed in any industry, acting in combination or a concerted refusal, or a refusal under a common understanding, or any number of persons who are or have been so employed to continue to work or to accept employment [section 2(q)].

The word "strike" has been going constant transformation around the basic concept of stoppage of work or quitting of work by employees in their economic struggle with capital. In order to constitute strike in its technical sense it is necessary that there should be cessation of work but it is not necessary that there must be total suspension of work because even partial stoppage of work would be strike. Thus cessation of work for short duration will also be strike. The term "concert" as used in the definition means "to accord together". Thus an individual who absents himself to enforce a demand for higher wages shall not constitute "strike".

The term "strike" postulates three main ingredients, namely— (i) plurality of workmen, (ii) cessation of work or refusal to do work, and (iii) combined or concerted action. 'Go-slow' would not technically be a "strike" though go-slow tactics also are generally resorted to by the workers for compelling the employer to yield to their demands. The workers have got the right to strike but there is no such right to adopt 'go-slow' tactics which are more reprehensible in character than strike.

    ix. "Workmen" means any person (including an apprentice) employed in any industry to do any manual, unskilled, skilled, technical, operational, clerical or supervisory work for hire or reward, whether the terms of employment be express or implied, and for the purpose of any proceeding under this Act in relation to an industrial dispute, includes any such person who has been dismissed, discharged or retrenched in connection with, or as a consequence of, that dispute, or whose dismissal, discharge or retrenchment has led to that dispute, but does not include any such person—

    (i) who is subject to the Air Force Act, 1950, or the Army Act, 1950, or the Navy Act, 1957, or

    (ii) who is employed in the Police service or as an officer or other employee of a prison, or

    (iii) who is employed mainly in a managerial or administrative capacity, or

    (iv) who, being employed in a supervisory capacity draws wages exceeding one thousand six hundred rupees per mensem or exercises, whether by the nature of the duties attached to the office or by reason of the powers vested in him, functions mainly of a managerial nature [section 2 (s)].

Whether an employee of an industry is a 'workman' or not the designation given to him is not decisive. What determines the status is the consideration of the nature of duties or the functions assigned to him.

The first part of the definition gives the statutory meaning of 'workman', and includes an apprentice or any person employed in an 'industry' to do any manual, unskilled, skilled, technical, operational, clerical or supervisory work for hire or reward. The second part is designed to include something more in what the term primarily denotes. By this part of the definition persons

(i) who have been dismissed, discharged or retrenched in connection with an industrial dispute; or (ii) whose dismissal, discharge or retrenchment has led to an industrial dispute; for the purposes of any proceedings under the Act in relation to such industrial dispute, have been included in the definition of 'workman' by section 2(s) of the Industrial Disputes Act.

AUTHORITIES UNDER THE ACT FOR INVESTIGATION AND SETTLEMENT OF INDUSTRIAL DISPUTES

The Act provides following statutory authorities and vests in them necessary powers to investigate the disputes and to bring about settlement of such disputes arising between the employees and employers:—

   (i) Works Committee;

   (ii) Conciliation Officers;

   (iii) Boards of Conciliation;

   (iv) Courts of Inquiry;

   (v) Labour Courts;

   (vi) Industrial Tribunals;

   (vii) National Tribunals.

WORKS COMMITTEE

The Act provides for setting up of Works Committees in factories employing 100 or more workers. The composition of Works Committees is to be bipartite—consisting of equal number of workers' representatives as well as the employers' representatives. The representatives of the workers shall be elected from the various groups, categories and classes of workmen in consultation with their registered union, if any, but they are to be elected departmentally by workers. It will be an obligation of an employer to enquire from registered Trade Unions of the workers employed in the industry, the number of its/their total membership and its distribution in departments. The Works Committee will promote measures for securing and preserving unity and good relations between the employers and workmen and to that end to comment upon matters of their common interest or concern and to endeavour to compose any material difference of opinion in respect of such matters.

BOARD OF CONCILIATION

The Board of Conciliation is to consist of an independent Chairman and two or four other members representing the parties in equal number.

ADJUDICATION OF INDUSTRIAL DISPUTES

If despite efforts of the Conciliation Officer, no settlement is arrived at between the employer and the workmen, the Act provides for a three-tier system of adjudication, *viz.* Labour Court, Industrial Tribunal and National Tribunal, each having its own sphere of functions as allocated to each.

Schedule II of the Act refers specifically to section 7 of the Act. That section lays down that the appropriate Government may, by notification in the Official Gazette, constitute one or more Labour Courts for adjudication of industrial disputes relating to any matter specified in the Second Schedule and for performing such other functions as may be assigned to them under this Act.

INDUSTRIAL TRIBUNALS

The Industrial Tribunals may be constituted by appropriate Government as and when necessary for adjudication of industrial disputes relating to any matter, whether specified in the Second or Third Schedule. Thus the Industrial Tribunals have jurisdiction over the matters over which the Labour Courts have jurisdiction and specifically over those mentioned in the Third Schedule, namely:—

(i) Wages, including the period and mode of payment;

(ii) Compensatory and other allowances;

(iii) Hours of work and rest intervals;

(iv) Leave with wages and holidays;

(v) Bonus, profit-sharing, provident fund and gratuity;

(vi) Shift-working otherwise than in accordance with Standing Orders;

(vii) Classification by grades;

(viii) Rules of discipline;

(ix) Rationalisation;

(x) Retrenchment of workmen and closure of establishment; and

(xi) Any other matter that may be prescribed.

POWERS OF THE LABOUR COURT/INDUSTRIAL TRIBUNAL TO MODIFY THE PUNISHMENT OF DISMISSAL OR DISCHARGE

Section 11A of the Act gives wide powers to the Labour Court and the Industrial Tribunal, etc., not only to reappraise the evidence to find out whether the finding of guilt of a workman recorded in the domestic enquiry is correct or not, but also to see whether the punishment inflicted is in proportion to the gravity of the proved misconduct or it is so severe that it has to be altered. It can interfere with the orders of discharge or dismissal of a workman and can impose lesser punishment or even set aside.

NOTICE OF CHANGE IN CONDITIONS OF SERVICE

Section 9A of the Act prohibits a unilateral action on the part of the employer to change the conditions of service to the prejudice of the workmen. This affords an opportunity to the workmen to consider the effect of the proposed change and, if necessary, to present their point of view on the proposal and such consultation would further serve to stimulate a feeling of common joint interest of the management and workmen. It is pertinent to refer to section 9A which reads as under:—

"No employer, who proposes to effect any change in the conditions of service applicable to any workman in respect of any matter specified in the Fourth Schedule, shall effect such change—

(a) without giving to the workmen likely to be affected by such change a notice in the prescribed manner of the nature of the change proposed to be effected; or

(b) within twenty-one days of giving such notice:

Provided that no notice shall be required for effecting any such change—

(a) Where the change is effected in pursuance of any "settlement or award"; or

(b) where the workmen likely to be affected by the change are persons to whom the Fundamental and Supplementary Rules, Civil Service (Classification, Control and Appeal) Rules, Civil Services (Temporary Service) Rules, Revised Leave Rules, Civil Service Regulations, Civilians in Defence Service (Classification, Control and Appeal) Rules or the

Indian Railways Establishment Code or any other rules or regulations that may be notified in this behalf by the appropriate Government in the Official Gazette, apply."

POWER OF THE GOVERNMENT TO REFER A DISPUTE FOR ADJUDICATION

Section 10 of the Act provides that where the appropriate Government is of the opinion that any industrial dispute exists or is apprehended, it may, at any time, by order in writing—

(a) refer the dispute to a Board for promoting a settlement thereof; or

(b) refer any matter appearing to be connected with or relevant to the dispute, to a court for enquiry; or

(c) refer the dispute or any matter appearing to be connected with or relevant to the dispute, if it relates to any other matter specified in the Second Schedule or the Third Schedule, to a Tribunal for adjudication.

It may further be noted that —

(i) the Government may refer a dispute relating to any matter in the Second or Third Schedule to a Labour Court, if such dispute is not likely to affect more than one hundred workmen;

(ii) in a dispute relating to public utility service when a notice of a strike or lockout has been given under section 22 of the Industrial Disputes Act, unless the notice has been frivolously or vexatiously given, the appropriate Government shall, if it thinks that it would be expedient to do so, make a reference under sub-section (1) of section 10.

(1) It is the Central Government alone which can refer a dispute involving any question of national importance or affecting industrial establishments situated in more than one State, to a National Tribunal whether or not it is the appropriate Government in relation to that dispute or any matter relating to that dispute irrespective of its nature, *i.e.*, whether it is specified in the Second or the Third Schedule [sub-section (14) of section 10].

(2) The appropriate Government cannot refuse to refer a dispute, whether jointly or separately applied for by the parties in the prescribed manner, to any of the prescribed authorities under the Act, if it is satisfied that the persons applying represent the majority of each party [sub-section (2) of section 19].

(3) The appropriate Government has power to prohibit the continuance of any strike or lock-out in connection with such dispute when it has been referred to any of the prescribed authorities [sub-section (3) of section 10].

(4) The appropriate Government must specify in the order referring an industrial dispute, the points of the dispute for adjudication, and the Labour Court, Tribunal or the National Tribunal, as the case may be, shall have to confine its adjudication to these points and the matters incidental thereto [sub-section (4) of section 10].

(5) If the appropriate Government while referring a dispute, is of the opinion that the dispute is of such a nature that any other establishment, group or class of establishments of similar nature is likely to be interested in, or affected by such dispute, it may, at the time of making the reference, or at any time thereafter but before the submission of the award, include in that reference such establishment, group, etc., whether or not at the time of such inclusion any dispute exists or is apprended in such establishment or group, etc. [sub-section (5) of section 10].

(6) Notwithstanding any provisions in the Act, no Labour Court, or Tribunal shall have jurisdiction to adjudicate upon any matter which is under adjudication before the National Tribunal.

    (a) Accordingly if the matter referred to the National Tribunal is also pending in a proceeding before a Labour Court or Tribunal, it will be deemed to have been quashed as such reference being made to the National Tribunal;

    (b) It will also be unlawful for the Government to refer a matter under adjudication before the National Tribunal, to any Labour Court or Tribunal for adjudication [sub-section (6) of section 10].

(7) When any industrial dispute in relation to which the Central Government is not the appropriate Government, is referred to the National Tribunal, then notwithstanding anything contained in the Act, any reference in section 15, section 17, section 33A, section 33B, and section 36A to the appropriate Government is to be construed as a reference to the Central Government, but save as aforesaid and as otherwise expressly provided in the Act, any reference in other provision of the Act to the appropriate Government in relation to that dispute shall mean a reference to the State Government.

However, the Government is not bound to refer all the demands put forward to it. The Government has discretion to refer some of them and refuse others for reasons stated in writing. The Government is not also bound to refer the whole dispute or the dispute in all aspects as raised by the parties.

REFERENCE OF DISPUTES TO ARBITRATION

There is also a provision for voluntary reference to arbitration. A reference under section 10A(1) is not the act of the appropriate Government but the act of the parties themselves. The parties to an agreement under section 10A proceed on the footing of an existing or apprehended industrial dispute and cannot thereafter raise an objection that there was no industrial dispute between the parties. In order to constitute a valid reference to arbitration the following conditions must be satisfied:—

   (a) there must exist an industrial dispute or there must be an apprehension of such a dispute;

   (b) the employer and the workmen involved in such dispute, or apprehending such dispute must mutually agree to refer the dispute to arbitration;

   (c) such voluntary reference must be made before the dispute has been referred under section 10 of the Industrial Disputes Act to a Labour Court or Tribunal or National Tribunal;

   (d) the agreement to refer the dispute must be in writing and in the form as prescribed for the purpose and must be signed by the parties in such manner as prescribed;

   (e) a copy of the arbitration agreement must be sent to the appropriate Government and the Conciliation Officer;

(f) the appropriate Government must within one month from the date of the receipt of such copy, publish the same in the Official Gazette.

Section 10A cannot be applied to an arbitration agreement which does not comply with sub-sections (2) and (3) thereof which have been analysed in (c), (d) and (e) above.

ILLEGAL STRIKES

A strike or lock-out in contravention of the provisions of section 22 or 23 of the Industrial Disputes Act, 1947 is declared illegal by section 24 of the said Act. A distinction has been made in this respect by the Act between public utility service and any other industrial establishment. Section 24 of the Act describes as to when the strikes or lockouts are illegal. Section 25 provides that no person shall knowingly expend or apply any money in direct furtherance or support of any illegal strike or lock-out. Section 26 lays down the penalty for illegal strikes and lock-out while section 27 prescribes the penalty for instigation of illegal strike or lock-out. Section 28 provides the penalty for giving financial aid to illegal strikes and lock-outs.

PROHIBITION OF STRIKES AND LOCK-OUTS

1. No person employed in a public utility service shall go on strike in breach of contract—

   (a) without giving to the employer notice of strike, as hereinafter provided, within six weeks before striking;

   (b) within fourteen days of giving such notice; or

   (c) before the expiry of the date of strike specified in any such notice as aforesaid; or

   (d) during the pendency of any conciliation proceedings before a Conciliation Officer and seven days after the conclusion of such proceedings.

2. No employer carrying on any public utility service shall lock-out any of his workmen—

   (a) without giving them notice of lock-out as hereinafter provided, within six weeks before locking out; or

   (b) within fourteen days of giving such notice; or

   (c) before the expiry of the date of lock-out specified in any such notice as aforesaid; or

(d) during the pendency of any conciliation proceedings before a Conciliation Officer and seven days after the conclusion of such proceedings.

3. The notice of lock-out or strike under this section shall not be necessary where there is already in existence a strike, or as the case may be, lock-out in the public utility service, but the employer shall send intimation of such lock-out or strike on the day on which it is declared to such authority as may be specified by the appropriate Government either generally or for a particular area or for a particular class of public utility services.

4. The notice of strike referred to in sub-section (1) shall be given by such number of persons to such person or persons and in such manner as may be prescribed.

5. The notice of lock-out referred to in sub-section (2) shall be given in such manner as may be prescribed.

6. If on any day an employer received from any person employed by him any such notices as are referred to in sub-section (1) or gives to any persons employed by him any such notices as are referred to in sub-section (2), he shall within five days thereof report to the appropriate Government or to such authority as that Government may prescribe, the number of such notices received or given on that day (section 22).

GENERAL PROHIBITION OF STRIKES AND LOCK-OUTS

No workman who is employed in an industrial establishment shall go on strike in breach of contract and no employer of any such workman shall declare a lock out—

(a) during the pendency of conciliation proceedings before a Board and seven days after the conclusion of such proceedings;

(b) during the pendency of proceedings before a Labour Court, Tribunal or National Tribunal and two months after conclusion of such proceedings;

(bb) during the pendency of arbitration proceedings before an arbitrator and two months after the conclusion of such proceedings, where a notification has been issued under sub-section (3A) of section 10A; or

(c) during any period in which a settlement or award is in operation, in respect of any of the matters covered by settlement or award (section 23).

ILLEGAL STRIKES AND LOCK-OUTS

1. A strike or a lock-out shall be illegal if—

    (i) It is commenced or declared in contravention of section 22 or section 23; or

    (ii) It is continued in contravention of an order made under sub-section (3) of section 10 or sub-section (4A) of section 10A.

2. Where a strike or lock-out in pursuance of an industrial dispute has already commenced and is in existence at the time of the reference of disputes to a Board, an arbitrator, a Labour Court, Industrial Tribunal or National Tribunal, the continuance of such strike or lock-out was not at its commencement in contravention of the provisions of this Act or the continuance thereof was not prohibited under sub-section (3) of section 10 or sub-section (4A) of section 10A.

3. A lock-out declared in consequence of illegal strike or a strike declared in consequence of an illegal lock-out shall not be deemed to be illegal (section 24).

PENALTY FOR ILLEGAL STRIKES AND LOCK-OUTS

1. Any workman who commences, continues or otherwise acts in furtherance of a strike which is illegal under this Act, shall be punishable with imprisonment for a term which may extend to one month, or with fine which may extend to fifty rupees, or with both.

2. Any employer who commences, continues, or otherwise acts in furtherance of a lock-out which is illegal under this Act, shall be punishable with imprisonment for a term which may extend to one month, or with fine which may extend to one thousand rupees, or with both. (section 26).

PENALTY FOR INSTIGATION ETC.

Any person who instigates or incites others to take part in, or otherwise acts in furtherance of a strike or lock-out which is illegal under this Act, shall be punishable with imprisonment for a term which may extend to six months, or with fine which may extend to one thousand rupees, or with both (section 27).

GOVERNMENT CAN PROHIBIT THE CONTINUATION OF STRIKES AND LOCK-OUTS

Section 10(3) of the Industrial Disputes Act, 1947 empowers the appropriate Government to prohibit the commencement and continuance of strikes and lock-outs in certain circumstances for investigation and adjudication of the industrial disputes in a peaceful atmosphere. In order to exercise the power to prohibit the strike or lock-out it is necessary that an industrial dispute should have been referred to a Board, Labour Court, Industrial Tribunal or National Tribunal under section 10 or the arbitrator under section 10A of the Industrial Disputes Act, 1947 and that on the date of reference for adjudication there would be a strike or lock-out in existence in connection with such dispute.

An order under section 10B for prohibiting a lock-out or strike requires findings on facts and an adjudication thereon before the power under it could be exercised by the appropriate Government. If an order is made without determining these facts, in certain circumstances it may prove incapable of implementation, for instance, if for any valid reasons, it has become impossible to continue the industry, or the employer has disposed of the same, the order under section 10(3) will become incapable of implementation. The Government may not prohibit the continuance of a lock-out because the workmen have indulged in unlawful and criminal activities, and there is scope for apprehension that, if the work is restored, such activities would continue. Non-compliance with such an order is illegal under section 24(1)(ii) and is punishable with imprisonment and/or fine under section 26 of the Industrial Disputes Act, 1947.

The power to prohibit a strike or lock-out springs into existence only when such dispute has been made the subject of reference under section 10(1) of the Industrial Disputes Act, 1947. If Government feels that it would prohibit a strike under section 10(3) it must give scope for the merits of all the disputes or demands for which the strike had been called to be gone into by some adjudicatory body. In regard to such dispute natural justice would depend upon the circumstances of the case, the nature of enquiry and the subject matter that was being dealt with.

LAY-OFF, RIGHT OF AN EMPLOYER AND ITS DURATION

Chapter VA of the Industrial Disputes Act empowers the employer to lay-off. It determines not merely the right of the workmen to receive compensation but also the wider rights and liabilities with regard to lay-off itself.

According to the definition given in the Act the periods of lay-offs are—

(a) Lay-off for a day occurring when work is denied within two hours of his presenting himself for work.

(b) Lay-off for one-half of day occurring when work is denied in the first half of the shift but the workman is called in the second half of the shift.

LAW GOVERNING LAY-OFF

By virtue of section 25J, these provisions have an overriding effect on other laws like the Industrial Employment (Standing Orders) Act, 1946 or other state industrial relations laws so far as rights and liabilities are concerned. The rights of the employees under the following provisions are not affected by the Chapter:—

(a) any right which a workman has under the Minimum Wages Act, 1948 or any order or notification issued thereunder; or

(b) any right under any operative award; or

(c) any right under any contract with the employer;

(d) any provisions concerning any law for the time being in force in any State for the settlement of industrial disputes.

EMPLOYER'S DUTIES IN CONNECTION WITH A LAY-OFF

The following duties are cast on the employer in connection with a lay-off:—

(a) It must be a justified lay-off effected *bona fide* and not *mala fide*.

(b) The employer must maintain a muster-roll of workmen.

(c) The stoppage of work if resorted to during working hours must be notified by notice put up on the notice board and must be in accordance with the standing orders.

(d) The period of detention of workmen if stoppage occurs during working hours should not exceed two hours after the commencement of the stoppage.

(e) If the unemployment caused by lay-off is for short period the unemployment should be treated as compulsory leave either with or without wages.

(f) If the lay-off is for an indefinite long period, the services may be terminated by due notice or payment of notice-pay in lieu of notice.

(g) The employees must be informed of the following things:—

    (i) whether the employees are to remain on place of work or leave it;

    (ii) when work shall be resumed;

    (iii) the time when the workers are to present themselves for work during normal working hours.

The period of lay-off should not be left indefinite. Where the workers did not suffer any loss, because of this irregularity it was held that the employer could not be penalised.

Where it is not possible to specify the period of lay-off, the worker should be given three weeks' time to rejoin duty when work is resumed. Where the workers are called back to work in batches the union should be consulted as otherwise it may be construed by the union as discrimination. Workmen laid off as a consequence of strike by other workmen are not entitled to lay-off compensation.

QUANTUM OF LAY-OFF COMPENSATION

The compensation must be paid at the rate and for period specified in section 25B of the Industrial Disputes Act.

(1) If the lay-off occurs during working hours and results in the detention of the workmen not exceeding one hour the workmen so detailed shall not be paid for the period of detention.

(2) If the period of detention in clause (1) above exceeds one hour, the workmen so detained shall be paid wages for the whole of the time during which they are detained as a result of stoppage.

(3) Where the workman during the period of twelve months is laid-off, he shall be paid by the employer for all days during which he is so laid-off, except for such weekly

holidays as may intervene, compensation at the rate of fifty per cent. of the total of the basic wages and dearness allowance that would have been payable to him had he not been so laid off.

By Industrial Disputes (Amendment) Act, 1965, section 25C has been re-enacted as:

"Whenever a workman (other than a *badli* workman or a casual workman), whose name is borne on the muster-rolls of an industrial establishment and who has completed not less than one year of continuous service under an employer is laid-off, whether continuously or intermittently, he shall be paid by the employer for all days during which he is so laid-off, except for such weekly holidays as may intervene, compensation which shall be equal to fifty per cent. of the total of the basic wages and dearness allowance that would have been payable to him had he not been so laid off:

Provided that if during any period of twelve months, a workman is so laid off for more than forty-five days, no such compensation shall be payable in respect of any period of the lay-off after the expiry of the first forty-five days, if there is an agreement to that effect between the workman and the employer:

Provided further that it shall be lawful for the employer in any case falling within the foregoing proviso to retrench the workman in accordance with the provisions contained in section 25F at any time after the expiry of the first forty-five days of the lay-off and when he does so, any compensation paid to the workman for having been laid-off during the preceding twelve months may be set-off against the compensation payable for retrenchment.

Explanation.—"*Badli* workman" means a workman who is employed in an industrial establishment in the place of another workman whose name is borne on the muster-rolls of the establishment, but shall cease to be regarded as such for the purposes of this section if he has completed one year of continuous service in the establishment."

Prior practice of paying wages and dearness allowance on a sliding scale for the period of lay-off has also been held to be fair.

A *badli* workman has been held to be entitled to lay-off compensation on satisfying other conditions.

RETRENCHMENT·AND COMPENSATION

'Retrenchment' means discharge of surplus labour or staff in a continuing industry. It means the removal of 'the dead weight of uneconomic surplus'. It is not necessary that removal of surplus must only be when the establishment runs in losses. It may operate at any level of profits. The legislature in using the expression "for any reason whatsoever" says in effect: "It does not matter why you are discharging the surplus if the other requirements of the definition are fulfilled, then it is retrenchment." The words "for any reason whatsoever" in section 2(oo) of the Act exclude closure of the business. Though the reason may be any, but it must essentially be "retrenchment" *i.e.,* discharge of surplus labour or staff by the employer. The definition of "retrenchment" in section 2(oo), though an artificial one, is certainly very wide and would include termination of services even in pursuance of a standing order. The heading of section 25F leaves no doubt that the observance of the provisions thereof is a condition precedent to retrenchment of a workman to whom the section applies. It would, therefore, follow that before action can be taken under standing orders the provisions of section 25F have to be complied with. The retrenchment must be just and fair and its justifiability can be questioned in a reference. Reorganisation of business rationalisation, economy, etc., are good grounds for retrenchment.

CONDITIONS PRECEDENT TO RETRENCHMENT

Reading section 25F of the Industrial Disputes Act, 1947 it is clear that the requirements prescribed by it are a condition precedent for retrenchment of the workmen, non-compliance with which would render the impugned retrenchment invalid and inoperative.

    (a) The retrenchment must be by termination of employment;

    (b) The employee must be given one month's notice in writing indicating the reasons for retrenchment and retrenchment must be effected after expiry of period of notice or the employee should be given wages for the notice period in lieu of such notice [section 25F(a)]. The notice must specify a certain date for retrenchment, otherwise a mere writing would not be a notice. Notice is not necessary if notice pay is given.

(c) The employee should be paid at the time of retrenchment, compensation equivalent to fifteen days average pay for every completed year of service or any part thereof in excess of six months.

EMPLOYER'S OBLIGATIONS AND DUTIES IN RETRENCHING EMPLOYEES

The following further obligations lie on the employer in the matter of retrenchment:—

(i) *Maintenance of Muster-roll:* The employer must maintain a muster-roll as required under section 25D of the Industrial Disputes Act, 1947.

(ii) *Seniority-list :* Rule 77 of the Industrial Disputes (Central) Rules, 1957 further requires that the employer should prepare a list of all workmen in the particular category from which retrenchment is contemplated arranged according to seniority of their service in the category. A copy of this list should be affixed on a notice board at a conspicuous place in the premises of the industrial establishment at least seven days before the actual date of retrenchment. Rule 77 is mandatory and its violation renders retrenchment illegal.

(iii) *The retrenchment should be in consonance with the statutory provisions in section 25G:* The normal rule is to retrench first of all the junior most employees in a particular category. If the employer has sufficient reasons to depart from this rule, only then it may be departed from and reasons for such departure must be recorded.

(iv) *Re-employment:* The retrenched employees have a statutory right of re-employment if the employer proposes to take into employment in future any persons and the retrenched staff has a right of preference over other persons. Section 25F gives statutory sanction to this rule. Under rule 78 of the Industrial Disputes (Central) Rules, the employer has to comply with requisitions mentioned therein. This right is given to citizens of India only.

TRANSFER OF AN UNDERTAKING

Where the ownership or management of an undertaking is transferred, whether by agreement or by operation of law, from the employer in relation to that undertaking to a new employer, every workman who has been in continuous service for not less than one year in that undertaking immediately before such transfer shall be entitled to notice and compensation in accordance with the provisions of section 25F, as if the workman had been retrenched:

Provided that nothing in section 25FF shall apply to a workman in any case where there has been a change of employers by reason of the transfer, if—

(a) the service of the workman has not been interrupted by such transfer;

(b) the terms and conditions of service applicable to the workman after such transfer are not in any way less favourable to the workman than those applicable to him immediately before the transfer; and

(c) the new employer is, under the terms of such transfer or otherwise, legally liable to pay to the workman, in the event of his retrenchment, compensation on the basis that his service has been continuous and has not been interrupted by the transfer. In such cases no compensation will be payable.

CLOSURE AND COMPENSATION

CONCEPT OF CLOSURE

The Industrial Disputes Act, 1947, has defined the word 'closure' recently, as permanent closing down of a place of employment or part thereof. The State Acts of Bombay, and M.P. define it as:

"Closure" means the closing of any place or part of a place of employment or the total or partial suspension of work by an employer or the total or partial refusal by an employer to continue to employ persons employed by him whether such closing, suspension or refusal is or is not in consequence of an industrial dispute.

The essence of closure whether whole or partial is closing down of the place of employment.

CLOSURE—A FUNDAMENTAL RIGHT

It is a fundamental right of a citizen to carry on or close down business, industry or work if he so chooses and nobody can be compelled to carry on against his will. Closure must be, when effected, permanent. This does not mean that the employer is barred from re-starting the closed business or because the business is restarted, it was not closed with the intention of closing permanently. It would be a question of fact whether the closure, when effected, was intended to be a permanent or temporary closure. Refusal to employ a single worker may be a closure. The right is subject to liability of payment of compensation to the workmen as provided by section 25 FFF of the Industrial Disputes Act, 1947 and also to obtain prior permission in cases covered by Chapter VB of the Act.

CLOSURE OF PART OF UNDERTAKING

A closure of a section or department or a branch or a part of undertaking is a "closure" and is valid. It is not retrenchment. Closure may also be effected in stages.

UNFAIR LABOUR PRACTICES

Effective from 21-8-1984, unfair labour practices have been introduced under the Industrial Disputes Act.

An "unfair labour practice" has been defined as any of the practices specified in Fifth Schedule.

Sections 25T and 25U of the Act provide as under—

(1) *Prohibition of unfair labour practice:* No employer or workman or a trade union, whether registered under the Trade Unions Act, 1926 (16 of 1926) or not, shall commit any unfair labour practice.

(2) *Penalty for committing unfair labour practices:* Any person who commits any unfair labour practice shall be punishable with imprisonment for a term which may extend to six months or with fine which may extend to one thousand rupees or with both.

For *exemuration* of such practices refer to Fifth Schedule of the Act.

COMPENSATION TO WORKMEN IN CASE OF CLOSING DOWN OF UNDERTAKINGS

1. Where an undertaking is closed down for any reason whatsoever, every workman who has been in continuous service for not less than one year in that undertaking immediately before such closure shall, subject to the provisions of sub-section (2) of section 25FFF be entitled to notice and compensation in accordance with the provisions of section 25F, as if the workman had been retrenched:

Provided that where the undertaking is closed down on account of unavoidable circumstances beyond the control of the employer, the compensation to be paid to the workman under clause (b) of section 25F shall not exceed his average pay for three months.

Explanation.—An undertaking which is closed down by reason merely of—

    (i) financial difficulties (including financial losses); or

    (ii) accumulation of undisposed of stock; or

    (iii) the expiry of the period of lease or licence granted to it; or

    (iv) in a case where the undertaking is engaged in mining operation, exhaustion of the minerals in the area in which such operations are carried on,

shall not be deemed to be closed down on account of unavoidable circumstances beyond the control of the employer within the meaning of the proviso to this sub-section.

1A. Notwithstanding anything contained in sub-section (1) of section 25FFF where an undertaking engaged in mining operations is closed down by reason merely of ex-workman referred to in that sub-section shall be entitled to any notice or compensation in accordance with the provisions of section 25F, if—

    (a) the employer provides the workman with alternative employment with effect from the date of closure at the same remuneration as he was entitled to receive and on the same terms and conditions of service as were applicable to him, immediately before the closure;

    (b) the service of the workman has not been interrupted by such alternative employment; and

(c) the employer is, under the terms of such alternative employment or otherwise legally liable to pay to the workman, in the event of his retrenchment, compensation on the basis that his service has been continuous and has not been interrupted by such alternative employment.

1B. For the purposes of sub-sections (1) and (1A) of section 25FFF, the expressions "minerals" and "mining operations" shall have the meanings respectively assigned to them in clauses (a) and (d) of section 3 of the Mines and Minerals (Regulations and Development) Act, 1957 (67 of 1957).

2. Where any undertaking set up for the construction of buildings, bridges, roads, canals, dams or other construction work is closed down on account of the completion of the work within two years from the date on which the undertaking had been set up, no workman employed therein shall be entitled to any compensation under clause (b) of section 25F, but if the construction work is not so completed within two years, he shall be entitled to notice and compensation under that section for every completed year of continuous service or any part thereof in excess of six months.

SIXTY DAYS' NOTICE TO BE GIVEN OF INTENTION TO CLOSE DOWN CERTAIN UNDERTAKING

1. An employer who intends to close down an undertaking shall serve, at least sixty days before the date on which the intended closure is to become effective, a notice, in the prescribed manner, on the appropriate Government stating clearly the reasons for the intended closure of the undertaking:

Provided that nothing in this section shall apply to—

(a)   an undertaking in which—

(i) less than fifty workmen are employed, or

(ii) less than fifty workmen were employed on an average per working day in the preceding twelve months;

(b) an undertaking set up for the construction of buildings, bridges, roads, canals, dams or for other construction work or project.

2. Notwithstanding anything contained in sub-section (1), the appropriate Government may, if it is satisfied that owing to such exceptional circumstances as accident in the undertaking or death

of the employer or the like it is necessary so to do, by order, direct that provisions of sub-section (1) shall not apply in relation to such undertaking for such period as may be specified in the order (section 25FFA).

CONTROLS ON RETRENCHMENT, CLOSURE AND LAY-OFF

The Industrial Disputes Act, 1947, prior to enactment of Chapter VB did not contain any provisions for preventing lay-off and retrenchment. The employers had an unfettered right to close down an establishment, subject to the provisions of 60 days' notice and often it was utilised to stifle trade union activities.

There had been many cases of large-scale lay-offs, particularly by large companies and undertakings. This action on the part of the management had resulted in an all-round demoralising effect on the workmen. In order to prevent avoidable hardship to the employees and to maintain higher tempo of production and productivity, it became necessary to put some reasonable restrictions on the employer's right to lay-off, retrenchment, and closure.

By the Amendment Act of 1976 prior approval of the approriate Government is necessary in the case of lay-off, retrenchment and closure in any industrial establishment where 300 or more workmen are employed. In the interests of rehabiliation of workmen and for maintenance of supplies and services essential to the life of the community, a provision is also made in the Act for restarting the undertakings which were already closed down otherwise than on account of unavoidable circumstances beyond the control of the employer.

SPECIAL PROVISIONS OF CHAPTER VB RELATING TO LAY-OFF, RETRENCHMENT AND CLOSURE OF CERTAIN ESTABLISHMENTS

(i) *Application to undertakings employing 100 or more workmen:*

(1) The provisions of this Chapter shall apply to an industrial establishment (not being an establishment of a seasonal character or in which work is performed only intermittently) in which not less than one hundred workmen were employed on an average per working day for the preceding twelve months [section 25K (1)].

(2) If a question arises whether an industrial establishment is of a seasonal character or whether work is performed therein only intermittently, the decision of the appropriate Government thereon shall be final [section 25K(2)].

(ii) *Definitions:* For the purposes of this Chapter—

   (a) "industrial establishment" means—

   (i) a factory as defined in clause (m) of section 2 of the Factories Act, 1948 (63 of 1948);

   (ii) a mine as defined in clause (j) of sub-section (1) of section 2 of the Mines Act, 1952 (35 of 1952); or

   (iii) a plantation as defined in clause (f) of section 2 of the Plantations Labour Act, 1951 (69 of 1951);

   (b) notwithstanding anything contained in sub-clause (ii) of clause (a) of section 2 —

   (i) in relation to any company in which not less than fifty-one per cent, of the paid-up share capital is held by the Central Government; or

   (ii) in relation to any corporation (not being a corporation referred to in sub-clause (i) of clause (a) of section 2) established by or under any law made by Parliament,

the Central Government shall be the appropriate Government (section 25L).

(iii) *Prior permission necessary for lay-off:*

   (1) No workman (other than a *badli* workman or a casual workman) whose name is borne on the muster-rolls of an industrial establishment to which this Chapter applies shall be laid-off by his employer except with the previous permission of such authority as may be specified by the appropriate Government by notification in the Official Gazette unless such lay-off is due to shortage of power or to natural calamity, and in case of a mine such lay-off is due also to fire, flood, excess of inflammable gas or explosion.

   (2) Where the workmen (other than *badli* workmen or casual workmen) of an industrial establishment referred to in sub-section (1) have been laid-off before

the commencement of the Industrial Disputes (Amendment) Act, 1976 and such lay-off continues at such commencement, the employer in relation to such establishment shall, within a period of fifteen days from such commencement, apply to the authority specified under sub-section (1) for permission to continue the lay-off (section 25M).

(2A) Where the workmen (other than *badli* workmen or casual workmen) of an industrial establishment being a mine have been laid-off under sub-section (1) for reasons of fire, flood or excess of inflammable gas or explosion, the employer in relation to such establishment shall, within a period of thirty days from the date of commencement of such lay-off apply to the authority specified under sub-section (1) for permission to continue the lay-off.

(iv) *Procedure for seeking permission:*

(1) In the case of every application for permission under sub-section (1) or sub-section (2), the authority to whom the application has been made may, after making such inquiry as he thinks fit, grant or refuse, for reasons to be recorded in writing, the permission applied for.

(2) Where an application for permission has been made under sub- section (1) or sub-section (2) or (2A) and the authority to whom the application is made does not communicate the permission or the refusal to grant the permission to the employer within a period of two months from the date on which the application is made, the permission applied for shall be deemed to have been granted on the expiration of the said period of two months.

(3) Where no application for permission under sub-section (1) is made, or where no application for permission under sub-section (2) or (2A) has been made within the period specified therein, or where the permission for the lay-off or the continuance of the lay-off has been refused, such lay-off shall be deemed to be illegal from the date on which the workmen

have been laid-off and the workmen shall be entitled to all the benefits under any law for the time being in force as if they had not been laid-off.

(4) The provisions of section 25C (other than the second proviso thereto) shall apply to cases of lay-off referred to in this section.

Explanation.—For the purposes of this section, a workman shall not be deemed to be laid-off by an employer if such employer offers any alternative employment (which in the opinion of the employer does not call for any special skill or previous experience and can be done by the workman) in the same establishment from which he has been laid-off or in any other establishment belonging to the same employer, situate in the same town or village, or situate within such distance from the establishment to which he belongs that the transfer will not involve any hardship to the workman having regard to the facts and circumstances of his case, provided that the wages which would normally have been paid to the workman are offered for the alternative appointment also [section 25M(3) to (6)].

(v) *Conditions precedent to retrenchment of workmen:*

(1) No workman employed in any industrial establishment to which this Chapter applies, who has been in continuous service for not less than one year under an employer shall be retrenched by that employer until—

(a) the workman has been given three months' notice in writing indicating the reasons for retrenchment and the period of notice has expired or the workman has been paid in lieu of such notice, wages for the period of the notice:

Provided that no such notice shall be necessary if the retrenchment is under an agreement, which specifies a date for termination of service;

(b) the workman has been paid, at the time of retrenchment, compensation which shall be equivalent to fifteen days' average pay for every completed year of continuous service or any part thereof in excess of six months; and

(c) notice in the prescribed manner is served on the appropriate Government or such authority as may be specified by the appropriate Government by notification in the Official Gazette, and the permission of such Government or authority is obtained under sub-section (2).

(2) On receipt of a notice under clause (c) of sub-section (1) the appropriate Government or authority may after making such inquiry as such Government or authority thinks fit, grant or refuse, for reasons to be recorded in writing the permission for the retrenchment to which the notice relates.

(3) Where the Government or authority does not communicate the permission or the refusal to grant the permission to the employer within three months of the date of service of the notice under clause (c) of sub-section (1) the Government or authority shall be deemed to have granted permission for such retrenchment on the expiration of the said period of three months [section 25N(1) to (3)].

(vi) *Application for permission:*

(1) Where at the commencement of the Industrial Disputes (Amendment) Act, 1976, the period of notice given under clause (a) of section 25F for the retrenchment of any workman has not expired, the employer shall not retrench the workman but shall, within a period of fifteen days from such commencement, apply to the appropriate Government or to the authority specified in sub-section(2) for permission for retrenchment.

(2) Where an application for permission has been made under sub-section (4) and the appropriate Government or the authority, as the case may be, does not communicate the permission or the refusal to grant the permission to the employer within a period of two months from the date on which the application is made, the permission applied for shall be deemed to have been granted on the expiration of the said period of two months.

(3) Where no application for permission under clause (c) of sub-section (1) is made, or where no application for permission under sub-section (4) is made within the period specified therein or where the permission for the retrenchment has been refused, such retrenchment shall be deemed to be illegal from the date on which the notice of retrenchment was given to the workman and the workman shall be entitled to all the benefits under any law for the time being in force as if no notice has been given to him.

(4) Where at the commencement of the Industrial Disputes (Amendment) Act, 1976, a dispute relating, either solely or in addition to other matters, to the retrenchment of any workman or workmen of an industrial establishment to which this Chapter applies is pending before a Conciliation Officer or the Central Government or the State Government, as the case may be, and—

   (a) there is an allegation that such retrenchment is by way of victimisation; or

   (b) the appropriate Government is of the opinion that retrenchment is not in the interests of the maintenance of industrial peace,

the appropriate Government, if satisfied that it is necessary so to do, may, by order withdraw such dispute or, as the case may be, such dispute in so far as it relates to such retrenchment transfer the same to an authority (being an authority specified by the appropriate Government by notification in the Official Gazette) for consideration whether such retrenchment is justified and any order passed by such authority shall be final and binding on the employer and the workman or workmen [section 25N(4) to (7)].

APPLICATION FOR PERMISSION TO GOVERNMENT

(1) Where an application for permission has been made under sub-section (1), the appropriate Government, after making such enquiry as it thinks fit and after giving a reasonable opportunity of being heard to the employer, the workmen and the persons

interested in such closure may, having regard to the genuineness and adequacy of the reasons stated by the employer, the interests of the general public and all other relevant factors by order and for reasons to be recorded in writing, grant or refuse to grant such permission and a copy of such order shall be communicated to the employer and the workmen [section 25-O(2)].

(2) Where an application has been made under sub-section (1) and the appropriate Government does not communicate the order granting or refusing to grant permission to the employer within a period of sixty days from the date on which such application is made, the permission applied for shall be deemed to have been granted on the expiration of the said period of sixty days.

(3) An order of the appropriate Government granting or refusing to grant permission shall, subject to the provisions of sub-section(5), be final and binding on all the parties and shall remain in force for one year from the date of such order.

MISCELLANEOUS MATTERS

CONDITIONS OF SERVICE, ETC., TO REMAIN UNCHANGED UNDER CERTAIN CIRCUMSTANCES DURING PENDENCY OF PROCEEDINGS

(1) During the pendency of any conciliation proceeding before a Conciliation Officer or a Board or of any proceeding before a Labour Court or Tribunal or National Tribunal in respect of an industrial dispute, no employer shall—

    (a) in regard to any matter connected with the dispute, alter, to the prejudice of the workmen concerned in such dispute, the conditions of service applicable to them immediately before the commencement of such proceedings; or

    (b) for any misconduct connected with the dispute, discharge or punish, whether by dismissal or otherwise, any workman concerned in such dispute,

save with the express permission in writing of the authority before which the proceeding is pending.

(2) During the pendency of any such proceeding in respect of an industrial dispute, the employer may, in accordance with the standing orders applicable to a workman concerned in such dispute or where there are no such standing orders, in accordance

with the terms of a contract whether express or implied between him and the workman—

(a) alter, in regard to any matter not connected with the dispute, the conditions of service applicable to that workman immediately before the commencement of such proceeding, or

(b) for any misconduct not connected with the dispute, discharge or punish, whether by dismissal or otherwise, the workman:

Provided that no such workman shall be discharged or dismissed, unless he has been paid wages for one month and an application has been made by the employer to the authority before which the proceeding is pending for approval of the action taken by the employer.

(3) Notwithstanding anything contained in sub-section (2), no employer shall, during the pendency of any such proceeding in respect of an industrial dispute, take any action against any protected workman concerned in such dispute —

(a) by altering, to the prejudice of such protected workman, the conditions of service applicable to him immediately before the commencement of such proceeding; or

(b) by discharging or punishing, whether by dismissal or otherwise, such protected workman,

save with the express permission in writing of the authority before which the proceeding is pending.

For the purposes of this sub-section, a "protected workman", in relation to an establishment, means a workman who, being an officer of a registered trade union connected with the establishment, is recognised as such in accordance with rules made in this behalf.

(4) In every establishment, the number of workmen to be recognised as protected workmen for the purposes of sub-section (3) shall be one per cent of the total number of workmen employed therein subject to minimum number of five protected workmen and a maximum number of one hundred protected workmen and for the aforesaid purpose the appropriate Government may make rules providing for the distribution of such protected workmen among various trade unions, if any, connected with the

establishment and the manner in which the workmen may be chosen and recognised as protected workmen.

(5) Where an employer makes an application to a Conciliation Officer, Board, an arbitrator, a Labour Court, Tribunal or National Tribunal under the proviso to sub-section (2) for approval of the action taken by him, the authority concerned shall, without delay, hear such application and pass, within a period of three months from the date of receipt of such application such order in relation thereto as it deems fit:

Provided that where any such authority considers it necessary or expedient so to do, it may, for reasons to be recorded in writing, extend such period by such further period as it may think fit:

Provided further that no proceedings before any such authority shall lapse merely on the ground that any period specified in this sub-section had expired without such proceedings being completed.

MAINTENANCE OF PEACE DURING PENDENCY OF PROCEEDINGS

The object of section 33 is to protect the workmen concerned in disputes which form the subject matter of pending proceedings against victimisation by the employer on account of their having raised industrial disputes or their continuing the pending proceedings. The further object of the section is to ensure that proceedings in connection with industrial disputes already pending should be brought to a termination in a peaceful atmosphere and that no employer should, during the pendency of those proceedings, take any action of the kind mentioned in the section which may give rise to fresh disputes likely to further exacerbate the already strained relations between the employer and the workmen.

PROCEDURE FOR CHANGING CONDITIONS

Under the section 33(1) if an employer wants to change the conditions of service in regard to a matter connected with a pending dispute, or to take any action against an employee on the ground of an alleged misconduct connected with the pending dispute he cannot do so unless he obtains previous permission in writing of the appropriate authority.

Section 33(2) deals with the alterations in the conditions of service as well as discharge or dismissal of workmen concerned in any pending dispute where such alteration or such discharge or dismissal is in regard to a matter not connected with the pending dispute.

When an employer, however, wants to dismiss or discharge a workman for alleged misconduct not connected with the dispute he can do so in accordance with the standing orders but a ban is imposed on the exercise of his power by the proviso. The proviso requires that no such workman shall be discharged or dismissed unless two conditions are satisfied, the first is that the employee concerned should be paid wages for one month, and the second is that an application should have been made by the employer to the appropriate authority for approval of the action taken by employer.

WORKMEN CONCERNED IN THE DISPUTE

(i) That expression includes all workmen on whose behalf the dispute has been raised as well as those who would be bound by the award which may be made in the said dispute. It is wider than the phrase 'party to the suit'. All workmen irrespective of membership of union are workmen concerned. Any other workman in the establishment who would be bound by the award under section 18 of the Act and who is also a member of the union espousing the cause is a workman concerned in the dispute.

Workmen subsequently employed are workmen concerned.

(ii) *Workmen held not concerned:* Workmen employed in certain quarries would not be "workmen concerned" in a dispute between the workers in a cement factory and the management of that factory, though the proprietor may be the same. The workmen who were not members of the union and to whom no general notice requiring their appearance was issued, were not considered to be "workmen concerned in the dispute" within the meaning of section 33 of the Act.

APPLICATION WITHOUT PREJUDICE TENABLE

Where the employer has preliminary objection that section 33 does not apply he can make an application without prejudice to his objection.

APPLICATION WHEN NOT NECESSARY

Where services have been suspended pending inquiry or terminated as a contractual measure or on account of real closure, or retrenchment, no application under this provision is necessary.

SCOPE OF INQUIRY WHEN PERMISSION APPLICATION IS MADE TO THE TRIBUNAL

Where an application is made by the employer for the requisite permission under section 33, the jurisdiction of the Tribunal in dealing with such an application is limited to consider whether a *prima facie* case has been made out by the employer for the dismissal of the employee in question, and either grant the permission or refuse it accordingly as it holds whether a *prima facie* case is or is not made out by the employer.

A *prima facie* case does not mean a case proved up to the hilt but a case which can be said to be established if the evidence which is led in support of the same were believed. While determining whether a *prima facie* case had been made out, the relevant consideration is whether on the evidence led it was possible to arrive at the conclusion in question and not whether that was the only conclusion which could be arrived at on that evidence.

Judgment of a criminal court must be considered to be relevant and admissible. It certainly could furnish good material to the Industrial Tribunal to form a *prima facie* opinion about the merits of the case before it. The acquittal of an accused in a criminal case could not stand in the way of the Industrial Tribunal granting the permission if it finds that the employer has made out a *prima facie* case on the evidence on record for the permission asked for.

In these proceedings it is not open to the Tribunal to consider whether the action taken by the employer is proper or adequate or whether it errs on the side of excessive severity; nor can the Tribunal grant permission, subject to certain conditions, which it may deem to be fair.

The Industrial Tribunal has no power to substitute another punishment for the one which was sought to be meted out by the employer to the employee nor to impose any condition on the employer before the requisite permission could be granted.

PERMISSION DOES NOT BAR RAISING OF INDUSTRIAL DISPUTE REGARDING ACTION

The nature and scope of proceedings under section 33 shows that removing or refusing to remove the ban on punishment or dismissal of workmen does not bar the raising of an industrial dispute when as a result of the permission granted by the Tribunal the employer dismisses or punishes the workmen.

EFFECT OF PERMISSION

If the permission is granted, the ban would be lifted and the employer would be at liberty, if he so chooses thereafter, to deal with the punishment to the workmen. The permission granted under section 33 does not have the effect of validating the order of dismissal.

REFUSAL OF PERMISSION

The settled position in law is that permission should be refused if the Tribunal is satisfied that the management's action is not *bona fide* or that the principles of natural justice have been violated or that the materials on the basis of which the management came to a certain conclusion could not justify any reasonable person in coming to such a conclusion.

EFFECT OF REFUSAL

The workman continues in employment and claim for wages will be maintainable.

PROTECTED WORKMAN

He cannot be proceeded against without obtaining permission for dismissal, discharge or punishment from the Tribunal. The law relating to protected workman is contained in section 33(3) of the Industrial Disputes Act read with rule 61 of the Industrial Disputes (Central) Rules.

For the purpose of this sub-section a 'protected workman', in relation to an establishment, means a workman who, being an officer of a registered trade union connected with the establishment, is recognised as such in accordance with rules made in this behalf.

In every establishment, the number of workmen to be recognised as protected workmen for the purposes of sub-section (3) shall be one per cent of the total number of workmen employed therein subject to a minimum number of five protected workmen and a maximum number of one hundred protected workmen and for the aforesaid purpose, the appropriate Government may make rules providing for the distribution of such protected workmen among various trade unions, if any, connected with the establishment and the manner in which the workmen may be chosen and recognised as protected workmen.

No permission is necessary after the main reference is decided.

PRIOR APPROVAL OF ACTION NOT CONTEMPLATED

An application for approval of the action taken, presupposes that there is the order of actual discharge or dismissal made by the employer and it is for the approval of this order that the application is made. This is borne out from Form 'K' under rule 60 of the Rules framed under the Act which corresponds to Form XV under rule 31 of the U.P. Rules.

Sub-section (2)(b) read together with the proviso contemplates that the employer may pass an order of dismissal or discharge before obtaining the approval of the authority concerned and at the same time make an application of the action taken by him.

It is now settled law that if the application for approval is rejected by the appropriate authority including the adjudicator, the concerned workman will be automatically reinstated.

PROVISIONS DO NOT APPLY TO DISCHARGE SIMPLICITER

A discharge which is by way of punishment would fall under the second category, *viz.*, that of punishment, and a discharge which is otherwise than by way of punishment would fall under the first category, *viz.*, discharge simpliciter. Discharge of workman simpliciter whether it is justified or not would not amount to alteration of the conditions of service of the concerned workman within the meaning of section 33(2)(a) of the Act and would not therefore attract it. Similarly the provisions do not apply to retrenchment.

ACTION MUST BE TAKEN IN ACCORDANCE WITH THE STANDING ORDERS

The limitation is imposed by this section that the standing orders will have to be complied with. It cannot however be contended that section 33(2) has no application to a case where there are no standing orders. The existence of standing orders is a prerequisite of the exercise of the powers by the management, and the absence of standing orders will not place it in a better position so as to claim exemption from the operation of the said provision. Model Standing Orders will also apply.

If, therefore, standing orders are applied by him to his workers he cannot escape the operation of sub-section (2) on the ground that the standing orders are not certified. He is required to apply for approval of the action taken by him. Standing Orders regarding considerations for imposing punishment must also be complied with.

PAYiNG OF ONE MONTH'S WAGES IS A MANDATORY CONDITION: AN OFFER OF PAYMENT IS SUFFICIENT COMPLIANCE WITH THE PROVISIONS

Though section 33 speaks of payment of one month's wages, it can only mean that the employer has tendered' the wages and that would amount to payment, for otherwise a workman could always make the section unworkable by refusing to take the wages.

STAGE OF APPLICATION

The Calcutta High Court had held that payment of wages and the making of the application should be simultaneous with the order of discharge or dismissal. The Bombay and Gujarat High Courts have taken contrary views in the matter.

The Supreme Court in a recent case has observed: "Though an express permission in writing is not required in case falling under the proviso to section 33(2)(b) it is desirable that there should not be any time-lag between the action taken by the employer and the order passed by the appropriate authority in an enquiry under the said proviso."

MANNER OF FULFILLING THE CONDITIONS SIMULTANEOUSLY

It is pointed out that the word "simultaneously" must of course be taken reasonably and a notion of split-second timing should not be imported. It should be "done at once and without delay", and it will depend upon the fact of each case whether the application had been made at once without delay. A delay of one month without any reason whatsoever would be inexcusable, but, where the employer was going through a period of very great stress and strain, the undertaking was in a state of collapse there might exist very cogent reason for delay. The offer made the next day is sufficient compliance.

PROCEEDINGS ARE INDEPENDENT OF REFERENCE

The proceedings under this section are totally independent proceedings. They will not die with the death of the reference or its culmination into an award.

The argument that the proceedings if continued beyond the date of the final decision of the main industrial dispute would become futile and meaningless cannot be accepted. The Tribunal does not become *functus officio*.

SUPERANNUATION DOES NOT ATTRACT SECTION 33(2)

Such retirement on superannuation would not amount to 'discharge' within the meaning of section 33(2)(b) of the Act. Further no approval in such a case would be required under the proviso to section 33(2)(b) of the Act.

WITHDRAWAL OF APPLICATION

Where the Industrial Tribunal permitted the concerned workmen to withdraw their complaints under section 33A of the Industrial Disputes Act without prejudice to their objections to the application for approval, they were not barred from objecting to the grant of approval on the ground that order on section 33A applications got the force of an award.

SCOPE OF INQUIRY UNDER SECTION 33(2) IN APPROVAL PROCEEDINGS

The jurisdiction of the appropriate industrial authority in holding an inquiry under section 33(2)(b) is not wider and is more limited than that permitted under section 33(1), and in exercising its powers under section 33(2) of the Act, the appropriate authority must bear in mind the departure deliberately made in separating the two classes of causes falling under the two sub-sections, and in providing for express permission in one case and approval in the other. No interference in punishment can be done.

The employer cannot effect a dismissal by merely suitably amending the original order. The management should ask for opportunity to adduce evidence. If the Tribunal does not approve of the action taken by the employer, the result would be that action taken by him would fall and thereupon the workman would be deemed never to have been dismissed or discharged and would remain in the service of the employer. In such a case no specific provision as to reinstatement is necessary.

COMPLAINTS REGARDING CONTRAVENTION OF SECTION 33

Section 33A provides a summary remedy for adjudication of disputes arising out of contravention of statutory safeguards and protection given under section 33 of the Act to employees during the pendency of conciliation or adjudication proceedings.

By section 33A an employee aggrieved by a wrongful order of dismissal passed against him in contravention of section 33 is given a right to move the Tribunal in redress of his grievance without having to take recourse to section 10 of the Act.

WHO CAN MAKE COMPLAINT ?

An aggrieved workman against whom action is taken can make a complaint under section 33 of the Act. A complaint filed by a union or its Secretary duly authorised by the aggrieved workman must be held to have been properly presented. In the absence of any proof to show that the office bearer of the union was authorised to prefer the complaint, it cannot be considered to be a valid complaint. No complaint can be preferred if no industrial dispute exists. It is not necessary, that when the complaint is made, the main dispute should be pending.

INQUIRY IS CO-EXTENSIVE WITH INQUIRY UNDER SECTION 10 OF THE ACT

The scheme of the section clearly indicates that the authority to whom the complaint is made is to decide both the issues, *viz.* (i) the effect of contravention, and (ii) the merits of the act or order of the employer.

Since the scope of section 33A is co-extensive, the employee would not succeed in obtaining an order of reinstatement merely by proving contravention of section 33 by the employer. After such contravention is proved it would still be open to the employer to justify the impugned dismissal on the merits. The Tribunal has power to order reinstatement in such proceedings.

TRIBUNAL HAS POWER TO GRANT INTERIM RELIEF

In the dispute between the management of Hotel Imperial and their workmen, the Supreme Court held that in view of the language of section 10(4) of the Act interim relief, where it is admissible, can be granted as a matter incidental to the main question referred to the Tribunal without being itself referred to in express terms.

SPECIAL PROVISION FOR ADJUDICATION AS TO WHETHER CONDITIONS OF SERVICE, ETC., CHANGED DURING PENDENCY OF PROCEEDINGS

Where an employer contravenes the provisions of section 33 during the pendency of proceedings before a Conciliation Officer, Board, an arbitrator, Labour Court, Tribunal or National Tribunal, any employee aggrieved by such contravention, may make a complaint in writing, in the prescribed manner—

(a) to such Conciliation Officer or Board, and the Conciliation Officer or Board shall take such complaint into account in mediating in, and promoting the settlement of, such industrial dispute; and

(b) to such arbitrator, Labour Court, Tribunal or National Tribunal and on receipt of such complaint, the arbitrator, Labour Court, Tribunal or National Tribunal, as the case may be, shall adjudicate upon the complaint as if it were a dispute referred to or pending before it, in accordance with the provisions of this Act and shall submit his or its award to the appropriate Government and the provisions of this Act shall apply accordingly.

POWER TO TRANSFER CERTAIN PROCEEDINGS

(1) The appropriate Government may by order in writing and for reasons to be stated therein, withdraw any proceeding under this Act pending before a Labour Court. Tribunal or National Tribunal and transfer the same to another Labour Court, Tribunal or National Tribunal, as the case may be, for the disposal of the proceeding and the Labour Court, Tribunal or National Tribunal to which the proceeding is so transferred may, subject to special directions in the order of transfer, proceed either *de novo* or from the stage at which it was so transferred:

Provided that where a proceeding under section 33 or section 33A is pending before a Tribunal or National Tribunal, the proceeding may also be transferred to a Labour Court.

(2) Without prejudice to the provisions of sub-section (1), any Tribunal or National Tribunal, if so authorised by the appropriate Government, may transfer any proceeding under section 33 or section 33A pending before it to any one of the Labour Courts specified for the disposal of such proceeding by the appropriate Government by notification in the Official Gazette and the Labour Court to which the proceeding is so transferred shall dispose of the same. A general order of transfer or proceedings is valid. It must be a speaking order through Government.

The language of section 33B does not suggest that the transfer permitted by the said provision is only from a Labour Court to Labour Court, from a Tribunal to another Tribunal and from a National Tribunal to another National Tribunal. The section provides that the Government can withdraw a proceeding under this provision pending before a Labour Court or Tribunal or National Tribunal, as the case may be. The expression "as the case may be" clearly indicates as the facts of the particular case demand. Therefore, if in a given case, the State Government is informed that a reference which is already made by it to a Labour Court, is likely to involve more than 100 workmen and, therefore, ultimately does not result in the settlement of the dispute referred to for adjudication in order to achieve the purpose and object of the Act which is investigation and settlement of industrial disputes, the Government is given the power to transfer the reference to an Industrial Tribunal, recording the reasons for doing so, for, in such a case transfer from one Labour Court to another Labour Court would be purposeless and futile. The words "as the case may be" cannot be understood to be permitted only from a Labour Court to another Labour Court or from a Tribunal to another Tribunal and from a National Tribunal to another National Tribunal, the Legislature would have used that expression but the Legislature has designedly used the words "as the case may be" in order to make the provision flexible and give the power to the Government to transfer from one forum to another, as the circumstances and facts of the case demand.

RECOVERY OF MONEY DUE FROM AN EMPLOYER

(1) Where any money is due to a workman from an employer under a settlement or an award or under the provisions of Chapter VA, the workman himself or any other person authorised by him in writing in this behalf, or, in the case of the death of the workman, his assignee or heirs may, without prejudice to any other mode of recovery, make an application to the appropriate Government for the recovery of money due to him, and if the appropriate Government is satisfied that any money is so due, it shall issue a certificate for that amount to the Collector who shall proceed to recover the same in the same manner as an arrear of land revenue:

Provided that every such application shall be made within one year from the date on which the money became due to the workman from the employer:

Provided further that any such application may be entertained after the expiry of the said period of one year, if the appropriate Government is satisfied that the applicant had sufficient case for not making the application within a period, not exceeding three months:

Provided that where the Presiding Officer of a Labour Court considers it necessary or expedient so to do, he may, for reasons to be recorded in writing, extend such period by such further period as he may think fit [section 33C(2)].

(2) Where any workman is entitled to receive from the employer any money or any benefit which is capable of being computed in terms of money and if any question arises as to the amount of money due or as to the amount at which such benefit should be computed, then the question may, subject to any rules that may be made under this Act, be decided by such Labour Court as may be specified in this behalf by the appropriate Government.

(3) For the purposes of computing the money value of a benefit, the Labour Court may, if it so thinks fit, appoint a Commissioner who shall, after taking such evidence as may be necessary, submit a report to the Labour Court and the Labour Court shall determine the amount after considering the report of the Commissioner and other circumstances of the case.

(4) The decision of the Labour Court shall be forwarded by it to the appropriate Government and any amount found due by the Labour Court may be recovered in the manner provided for in sub-section (1).

(5) Where workmen employed under the same employer are entitled to receive from him any money or any benefit capable of being computed in terms of money, then, subject to such rules as may be made in this behalf, a single application for the recovery of the amount due may be made on behalf of or in respect of any number of such workmen.

PENALTIES

The Penalties can be summarised as follows:—

Section	Action/Omission	PENALTY	
		Imprison-ment upto	Fine
25Q	Laying-off, Retrenching workers without prior permission of appropriate authorities in an industrial establishment in which not less than 100 workers were employed on an average per working day for the preceding 12 months	Six months	Rs. 5,000
25R(1)	Closure of an industrial establishment (supra) without permission	Six months	Rs. 5,000
25R(2)	Contravening an order refusing to grant permission		Rs. 2,000 per day
25U	Committing unfair labour practices as specified.	Six months	Rs. 1,000
26	(a) Illegal strikes (b) Illegal lock-outs	one month one month	Rs. 50 Rs. 1,000
27	Instigation for strikes or lock-outs	6 months	Rs. 1,000
28.	Giving financial aid for illegal strikes or lock-outs	6 months	Rs. 1,000
29	Breach of settlement or award	6 months	Rs. 2,500 per day
30	Disclosing confidential information	6 months	Rs. 1,000
30A	Closure without notice under section 25FFA	6 months	Rs. 500
31	Other offences	6 months	Rs. 1,000
31(2)	Contravention of any provision of the Act or Rules	—	Rs. 100

INDUSTRIAL EMPLOYMENT
(STANDING ORDERS) ACT, 1946
CHECK LIST

Applicability of the Act
- Every industrial establishment wherein 100 or more (in many States it is 50 or more).
- Any industry covered by Bombay Industrial Relations Act, 1946.
- Industrial establishment covered by M.P. Industrial Employment (Standing Orders) Act, 1961. **Sec. 1**

Matters to be provided in Standing Orders
- Classification of workmen, e.g., whether permanent, temporary, apprentices, probationers, or badlis.
- Manner of intimating to workmen periods and hours of work, holidays, pay-days and wage rates.
- Shift working.
- Attendance and late coming.
- Conditions of, procedure in applying for, and the authority which may grant, leave and holidays.
- Requirement to enter premises by certain gates, and liability to search.
- Closing and re-opening of sections of the industrial establishments, and temporary stoppages of work and the right and liabilities of the employer and workmen arising therefrom.
- Termination of employment, and the notice thereof to be given by employer and workmen.
- Suspension or dismissal for misconduct, and acts or omissions which constitute misconduct.
- Means of redressal for workmen against unfair treatment or wrongful exactions by the employer or his agents or servants.

Additional Matters
- Service Record - Matters relating to service card, token tickets, certification of service, change of residential address of workers and record of age • Confirmation • Age of retirement • Transfer • Medical aid in case of Accident • Medical Examination • Secrecy • Exclusive service.

Secs. 2(g), 3(2) and Rule 2A

Conditions for Certification of Standing Orders
- Every matter to be set out as per Schedule and Rule 2A.
- The standing orders to be in conformity with the provisions of the Act.

Procedure for Certification of Standing Orders
Certifying Officer to forward a copy of draft standing orders to the trade union or in the absence of union, to the workmen of the industry. The trade union or the other representatives, as the case may be, are to be heard. **Sec.5**

Date of Operation of Standing Orders
On the date of expiry of 30 days from certification or on the expiry of 7 days from authentication of Standing Orders. **Sec. 7**

Posting of Standing Orders
The text of the standing orders as finally certified shall prominently be posted in English or in the language understood by majority of workmen on special board at or near the entrance for majority of workers. **Sec. 9**

Submissions of Draft Standing Orders
Within six months from the date when the Act becomes applicable to an industrial establishment. Five copies of the draft Standing Orders are to be submitted to the Certifying Officer under the Act. **Sec. 3**

Temporary application of Model Standing Orders
Temporary application of mod standing orders shall be deemed to be adopted till the standing orders as submitted are certified. **Sec. 12-A**

Payment of Subsistence Allowance to the Suspended Workers
- At the rate of fifty per cent, of the wages which the workman was entitled to immediately preceding the date of such suspension, for the first ninety days of suspension.
- At the rate of seventy-five percent of such wages for the remaining period of suspension if the delay in the completion of disciplinary proceedings against such workman is not directly attributable to the conduct of such workman. **Sec. 10-A**

PENALTIES
- Failure of employer to submit draft Standing Orders fine of Rs.5000 and Rs.200 for every day on continuation of offence.
- Fine of Rs.100 on contravention and on continuation of offence Rs.25 for every day.

Sec. 13

11A. Industrial Employment (Standing Orders) Act, 1946

WHAT ARE STANDING ORDERS

The Industrial Employment (Standing Orders) Act, 1946 is the first Central enactment with an object to have uniform Standing Orders providing for matters enumerated in the Schedule to the Act. The employers are required to define, with certainty, conditions of service in their establishments to reduce them in writing and to get them certified with a view to avoid unnecessary industrial disputes. It was not intended that there should be different conditions of service for those who are employed before and those employed after Standing Orders came into force. Once the Standing Orders come into force, they bind all those presently in employment of concerned establishment as well as those who are appointed thereafter. The employer cannot enter into an agreement with a workman which is inconsistent with the Standing Orders of the company. The terms of the Standing Orders would prevail over the corresponding terms in the contract of service. The employer cannot enforce simultaneously the Standing Orders regulating the classification of workmen and a special agreement with an individual workman settling his categorisation.

SUBMISSION FOR CERTIFICATION OF DRAFT STANDING ORDERS

After having prepared the draft Standing Orders, the next step is to get the same certified by the concerned Certifying Officer by submitting the same as per provisions of section 3 of the Industrial Employment (Standing Orders) Act, 1946.

The employer is required to submit to the Certifying Officer, five copies of the draft Standing Orders for certification. The Certifying Officer after having gone through in between lines of the draft Standing Orders, will certify them if the provisions are enumerated therein in respect of each and every aspect incorporated in the schedule applicable to the employer's establishment and secondly the provisions made in the Standing Orders are in conformity with the provisions of the Act, *i.e.*, the provisions of the proposed Standing Orders are, as far as possible, in line with the model Standing Orders. In other words, the minimum benefits or advantages offered to the workmen under the provisions of the Act and Rules framed thereunder, including the model Standing Orders, should be provided for in the draft Standing Orders sought to be certified. It does not mean that something more, than what is provided for in the model Standing Orders, cannot be provided by the employer. Even the Certifying Officer has powers to effect increase in any of the provisions of the draft Standing Orders in the interest of workmen while making adjudication upon the fairness or reasonableness of the provisions of any Standing Order giving reasons thereof, as held by the Allahabad High Court.

PROCEDURE FOR CERTIFICATION OF STANDING ORDERS

(1) On receipt of the draft under section 3, the Certifying Officer shall forward a copy thereof to the trade union, if any, of the workmen, or where there is no such trade union, to the workmen in such manner as may be prescribed, together with a

notice in the prescribed from requiring objections, if any, which the workmen may desire to give for the draft Standing Orders to be submitted to him within fifteen days from the receipt of the notice.

(2) After giving the employer and the trade union or such other representatives of the workmen, as may be prescribed, an opportunity of being heard, the Certifying Officer shall decide whether or not any modification of or addition to the draft submitted by the employer is necessary to render the draft Standing Orders certifiable under the Act, and shall make an order in writing accordingly.

(3) The Certifying Officer shall, thereupon, certify the draft Standing Orders, after making any modifications therein which his order under sub-section (2) may require and shall, within seven days thereafter, send copies of the certified Standing Orders authenticated in the prescribed manner and of his order under sub-section (2) to the employer and to the trade union or other prescribed representatives of the workmen.

DATE OF OPERATION OF STANDING ORDERS

Standing Order shall, unless an appeal is preferred under section 6, come into operation on the expiry of thirty days from the date on which authenticated copies thereof are sent under sub-section (3) of section 5, or where an appeal as aforesaid is preferred, on the expiry of seven days from the date on which copies of the order of the Appellate Authority are sent under sub-section (2) of section 6.

REGISTER OF STANDING ORDERS

A copy of all Standing Orders, as finally certified under the Act, shall be filed by the Certifying Officer in a register in the prescribed form maintained for the purpose and the Certifying Officer shall furnish a copy thereof to any person applying therefor on payment of the prescribed fee.

POSTING OF STANDING ORDERS

The text of the Standing Orders, as finally certified under the Act, shall be prominently posted by the employer in English and in the language understood by the majority of his workmen on special boards to be maintained for the purpose at or near the entrance through which the majority of the workmen enter the industrial establishment and in all departments thereof where the workmen are employed.

DURATION AND MODIFICATION OF STANDING ORDERS

(1)   Standing Orders finally certified under the Act shall not, except or agreement between the employer and the workmen or a trade union or other representative body of the workmen, be liable to modification until the expiry of six months from the date on which the Standing Orders or the last modification thereof came into operation.

(2)   Subject to the provisions of sub-section (1), an employer or workman or a trade union or other representative body of the workmen may apply to the Certifying Officer to have the Standing Orders modified and such application shall be accompanied by five copies of the modifications proposed to be made and where such modifications are proposed to be made by agreement between the employer and the workmen, a certified copy of that agreement shall be filed alongwith the application.

(3)   The foregoing provisions of the Act shall apply in respect of an application under sub-section (2) as they apply to the certification of the first Standing Orders.

(4)   Nothing, contained in sub-section (2), shall apply to an industrial establishment in respect of which the appropriate Government is the Government of the State of Gujarat or the Government of the State of Maharashtra.

TEMPORARY APPLICATION OF MODEL STANDING ORDERS

(1) Notwithstanding anything contained in sections 3 to 12 for the period commencing on the date on which the Act becomes applicable to an industrial establishment and ending with the date on which the Standing Orders as finally certified under this Act come into operation under section 7 in that establishment, the prescribed model Standing Orders shall be deemed to be adopted in that establishment and the provisions of section 9, sub-section (2) of section 13 and section 13A shall apply to such model Standing Orders as they apply to the Standing Orders so certified.

(2) Nothing, contained in sub-section (1), shall apply to an industrial establishment in respect of which the appropriate Government is the Government of the State of Gujarat or the Government of the State of Maharashtra.

CERTIFIED STANDING ORDERS BECOME STATUTORY CONDITIONS OF SERVICE

The Supreme Court has held that if any provision of such rules read with Standing Orders confer absolute and unfettered discretion on the employer to allow or disallow rightful claim of employees, that would be unfair and unreasonable as also arbitrary and subject to test of Article 14. It was further observed as follows:—

"The Standing Order Act endeavoured to impose a statutory contract of service between two parties unequal to negotiate, on the footing of equality. The Standing Orders certified under the Act become part of the statutory terms and conditions of service between the employer and his employee and they govern the relationship between the parties. A facet of collective bargaining is that any settlement arrived at between the parties would be treated as incorporated in the contract of service of each employee governed by the settlement. A presumption of more or less systematic translation of the results of collective bargaining into individual contracts is created where these results are in practice operative and effective in controlling the terms on which employment takes place. As soon certified Standing Orders which statutorily prescribe the conditions of service shall be deemed to be incorporated in the contract of employment of each employee with his employer.[1]

---

1. *Sudhir Chandra Sarkar* v. *Tata Iron and Steel Co. Ltd.*, 1984 (3) SCC 369.

INCONSISTENCE BETWEEN CONTRACT OF EMPLOYMENT AND CERTIFIED STANDING ORDERS – LATTER WILL PREVAIL

On the question as to whether the provision contained in the certified Standing Orders will prevail in case of its conflict with the terms and conditions contained in the contract of employment, *i.e.*, appointment letter, it is necessary to bear in mind that certified Standing Orders are framed under the Industrial Employment (Standing Orders) Act, 1946 and once the Standing Orders are framed by the employer and certified, they have the force of law. As against them conditions of service contained in the letter of appointment or contract of employment do not have statutory force. When there is a conflict between a provision of law or an instrument having the force of law and the contract entered into between the parties, the former will prevail.[1] The Rajasthan High Court has followed the judgment of the Supreme Court[2] where exactly an identical question has arisen for decision.

PENALTIES AND PROCEDURE – SECTION 13

(1) An employer, who fails to submit draft Standing Orders as required by section 3 or who modifies his Standing Orders otherwise than in accordance with section 10, shall be punishable with fine which may extend to five thousand rupees, and in the case of a continuing offence with a further fine which may extend to two hundred rupees for every day after the first during which the offence continues.

(2) An employer, who does any act in contravention of the Standing Orders finally certified under Act for his industrial establishment, shall be punishable with fine which may extend to one hundred rupees and in the case of a continuing offence with a further fine which may extend to twenty-five rupees for every day after the first during which the offence continues.

(3) No prosecution for an offence punishable under this section shall be instituted except with the previous sanction of the appropriate Government.

(4) No court, inferior to that of a Metropolitan Magistrate or Judicial Magistrate of the second class, shall try any offence under this section.

---

1. *Eicher Good Earth Ltd.* v. *Rajendra Kumar Soni*, 1993 LLR 524 (Raj HC).

2. *Western India Match Co. Ltd.* v. *Workmen*, AIR 1973 SC 2650: (27) FLR 228.

MATERNITY BENEFIT ACT, 1961

CHECKLIST

Object of the Act
To protect the dignity of motherhood and the dignity of a new person's birth by providing for the full and healthy maintenance of the woman and her child at this important time when she is not working.

Coverage of the Act
Upon all women employees either employed directly or through contractor except domestic women employees employed in mines, factories, plantations and also in other establishments if the State Government so decides. Therefore, if the State Government decides to apply this Act to women employees in shops and commercial establishments, they also will get the benefit of this Act. Bihar, Punjab Haryana, West engal, U.P., Orissa and Andhra have done so.
Sec.3

Conditions for eligibility of benefits
Women indulging temporary or unmarried are eligible for maternity benefit when she is expecting a child and has worked for her employer for at least 80 days in the 12 months immediately preceding the date of her expected delivery.
Sec.5

Cash Benefits
- Leave with average pay for six weeks before the delivery.
- Leave with average pay for six weeks after the delivery.
- A medical bonus of Rs.25 if the employer does not provide free medical care to the woman.
- An additional leave with pay up to one month if the woman shows proof of illness due to the pregnancy, delivery, miscarriage, or premature birth.
- In case of miscarriage, six weeks leave with average pay from the date of miscarriage.

Non Cash Benefits/Privileges
- Light work for ten weeks (six weeks plus one month) before the date of her expected delivery, if she asks for it.
- Two nursing breaks in the course of her daily work until the child is 15 months old.
- No discharge or dismissal while she is on maternity leave.
- No change to her disadvantage in any of the conditions of her employment while on maternity leave.
- Pregnant woman discharged or dismissed may still claim maternity benefit from the employer.

Exception : Women dismissed for gross misconduct lose their right under the Act for Maternity Benefit.
Sec. 7 & 8

Condition for Claiming Benefits
- Ten weeks before the date of her expected delivery, she may ask the employer to give her light work for a month. At that time she should produce a certificate that she is pregnant.
- She should give written notice to the employer about seven weeks before the date of her delivery that she will be absent for six weeks before and after her delivery. She should also name the person to whom payment will be made in case she cannot take it herself.
- She should take the payment for the first six weeks before she goes on leave.
- She will get payment for the six weeks after child-birth within 48 hours of giving proof that she has had a child.
- She will be entitled to two nursing breaks of fifteen minutes each in the course of her daily work till her child is fifteen months old.
- Her employer cannot discharge her or change her conditions of service while she is on maternity leave.
Sec.5

Leave for Miscarriage and Tubectomy Operation
- Leave with wages at the rate of maternity benefit, for a period of six weeks immediately following the day of her miscarriage or her medical termination of pregnancy.
- Entitled to leave with wages at the rate of maternity benefit for a period of two weeks immediately following the day of her tubectomy operation.
Secs. 9 & 13

Leave for illness arising out of pregnancy etc.
A woman suffering from illness arising out of pregnancy, delivery, premature birth of child (miscarriage, medical termination of pregnancy or tubectomy operation) be entitled, in addition to the period of absence allowed to her leave with wages at the rate of maternity benefit for a maximum period of one month.
Sec.10

Prohibition of dismissal during absence of pregnancy
- Discharge or dismissal during or on account of such absence or to give notice of discharge or dismissal on such a day that the notice will expire during such absence, or to vary to her disadvantage any of the conditions of her service.
- At the time during her pregnancy, if the woman but for such discharge or dismissal would have been entitled to maternity benefit or medical bonus, etc.
- Not barred in case of dismissal for gross misconduct.
Sec.12

Failure to Display Extract of Act
Imprisonment may extend to one year or fine.
Sec. 19

Forfeiture of maternity benefit
- If permitted by her employer to absent herself under the provisions of section 6 for any period during such authorized absence, she shall forfeit her claim to the maternity benefit for such period.
- For discharging or dismissing such a woman during or on account of her absence from work, the employer shall be punishable with imprisonment which shall not be less than 3 months, but it will extend to one year and with fine, not exceeding Rs.5,000.
Sec. 18

12. The Maternity Benefit Act, 1961

THE OBJECT

The object of maternity leave and benefit is to protect the dignity of motherhood by providing for the full and healthy maintenance of woman and her child when she is not working. As the number of women employees is growing, maternity leave and other maternity benefits are becoming increasingly common.

In 1961, the Maternity Benefit Act was passed aiming at a uniform maternity benefit all over the country. By an amendment No. 29 of 1995 effective from 1-2-1996 a female employee will be eligible for leave with wages for 6 weeks in case of miscarriage or medical termination of pregnancy or production of such proof.

APPLICABILITY OF THE ACT

The Maternity Benefit Act applies in the first instance, to every establishment being a factory, mine or plantation including any such establishment belonging to Government and to every establishment wherein persons are employed for the exhibition of equestrian acrobatic and other performances, to every shop or establishment within the meaning of any law for the time being in force in relation to shops and establishments in a State, in which ten or more persons are employed, or were employed on any day of the preceding twelve months.

However, the State Government, may, with the approval of the Central Government, after giving not less than two months' notice of its intention of so doing, by notification in the Official Gazette declare that all or any of the provisions of the Act shall apply also to any other establishment or class of establishment, industrial, commercial, agricultural or otherwise. Save as otherwise provided in sections 5A and 5B pertaining to continuance of or payment of maternity benefit in certain cases nothing contained in this Act shall apply to any factory or other establishment to which the provisions of the Employees' State Insurance Act, 1948 apply for the time being.

IMPORTANT TERMS AND EXPRESSIONS

I. "child" includes a still born child;

II. "delivery" means the birth of a child;

III. "prescribed" means prescribed by rules made under this Act;

IV. "State Government", in relation to a Union Territory, means the Administrator thereof;

V. "Wages" means all remuneration paid or payable in cash to a woman, if the terms of the contract of employment, express or implied, were fulfilled and includes—

> such cash allowances (including dearness allowance and house rent allowance) as a woman is for the time being entitled to; incentive bonus; and the money value of the concessional supply of foodgrains and other articles,

but does not include—

(a) any bonus other than incentive bonus;

(b) overtime earnings and any deduction or payment made on account of fines;

(c) any contribution paid or payable by the employer to any pension fund or provident fund or for the benefit of the woman under any law for the time being in force; and

(d) any gratuity payable on the termination of service;

VI. "woman" means a woman employed, whether directly or through any agency, for wages in any establishment;

VII. "employer" means —

    (a) in relation to an establishment which is under the control of the Government, a person or authority appointed by the Government for the supervision and control of employees or where no person or authority is so appointed the head of the department;

    (b) in relation to an establishment under any local authority, the person appointed by such authority for the supervision and control of employees or where no person is so appointed the chief executive officer of the local authority;

    (c) in any other case, the person who, or the authority which has the ultimate control over the affairs of the establishment and where the said affairs are entrusted to any other person whether called a manager, managing director, managing agent, or by any other name, such person;

VIII. "small establishment" means —

    (a) a factory;

    (b) a mine;

    (c) a plantation;

    (d) an establishment wherein persons are employed for the exhibition of equestrian, acrobatic and other performances; or

    (e) a shop or establishment; or

    (f) an establishment to which the provisions of this Act have been declared under sub-section (1) of section 2 to be applicable;

IX. "factory" means a factory as defined in clause (m) of section 2 of the Factories Act, 1948 (63 of 1948);

X. "Maternity Benefit" means the payment referred to in sub-section (1) of section 5;

XI. "Mine" means a mine as defined in clause (j) of section 2 of the Mines Act, 1952 (35 of 1952);

XII. "Miscarriage" means expulsion of the contents of a pregnant uterus at any period prior to or during the twenty-sixth week of pregnancy but does not include any miscarriage, the causing of which is punishable under the Indian Penal Code (45 of 1860);

XIII. "Plantation" means a plantation as defined in clause (f) of section 2 of the Plantation Labour Act, 1951 (69 of 1951).

PROHIBITION OF WORK OR EMPLOYMENT BY WOMEN DURING CERTAIN PERIOD

(i) No employer shall knowingly employ a woman in an establishment during the six weeks immediately following the day of her delivery or her miscarriage.

(ii) No woman shall work in any establishment during the six weeks immediately following the day of her delivery or her miscarriage.

(iii) Without prejudice to the provisions of section 6, no pregnant woman shall, on a request being made by her in this behalf, be required by her employer to do during the period specified in sub-section (iv) (herein below) and work which is of an arduous nature or which involves long hours of standing or which in any way is likely to interfere with her pregnancy or the normal development of the foetus or is likely to cause her miscarriage or otherwise to adversely affect her health.

(iv) The period referred to in clause (iii) shall be—

    (a) the period of one month immediately preceding the period of six weeks, before the date of her expected delivery;

    (b) any period during the said period of six weeks for which the pregnant woman does not avail of leave of absence under section 7.

ENTITLEMENT TO PAYMENT OF MATERNITY BENEFIT

(i) Subject to the provisions of this Act, every woman shall be entitled to, and her employer shall be liable for, the payment of maternity benefit at the rate of the average daily wage for the period of her actual absence, this is to say, the period immediately preceding the day of her delivery, the actual day of her delivery and the period immediately following that day.

Explanation.—For the purpose of this sub-section, the average daily wage means the average of the woman's wages payable to her for the days on which she has worked during the period of three calendar months, immediately preceding the date from which she absents herself on account of maternity, the minimum rate of wage fixed or received under the Minimum Wages Act, 1948 (11 of 1948).

(ii) No woman shall be entitled to maternity benefit unless she has actually worked in an establishment of the employer from whom she claims maternity benefit, for a period of not less than eighty days in the twelve months immediately preceding the date of her expected delivery:

Provided that the qualifying period of eighty days aforesaid shall not apply to a woman who has immigrated into the State of Assam and was pregnant at the time of the immigration.

Explanation.—For the purpose of calculating under this sub-section the days on which a woman has actually worked in the establishment, the days for which she has been laid off or was on holidays declared under any law for the time being in force to be holidays with wages during the period of twelve months immediately preceding the date of her expected delivery shall be taken into account.

(iii) The maximum period for which any woman shall be entitled to maternity benefit shall be twelve weeks of which not more than six weeks shall precede the date of her expected delivery:

Provided that where a woman dies during this period, the maternity benefit shall be payable only for the days upto and including the day of her death:

Provided further that where a woman having been delivered of a child, dies during her delivery or during the period immediately following the date of her delivery for which she is entitled for the maternity benefit, leaving behind in either case the child, the employer shall be liable for the maternity benefit for that entire period but if the child also dies during the said period, then for the days upto and including the date of the death of the child.

CONTINUANCE OF PAYMENT OF MATERNITY BENEFIT IN CERTAIN CASES

Every woman entitled to the payment of maternity benefit under this Act shall, notwithstanding the application of the Employees' State Insurance Act, 1948 (34 of 1948), to the factory or other establishment in which she is employed, continue to be so entitled until she becomes qualified to claim maternity benefit under section 50 of the Act.

PAYMENT OF MATERNITY BENEFIT IN CERTAIN CASES

Any woman

(a) who is employed in a factory or other establishment to which the provisions of the Employees' State Insurance Act, 1948 (34 of 1948) apply;

(b) whose wages (excluding remuneration for overtime work) for a month exceed the amount specified in sub-clause (b) of clause (9) of section 2 of the Act; and

(c) who fulfils the conditions specified in sub-section (2) of section 5,

shall be entitled to the payment of maternity benefit under this Act.

NOTICE OF CLAIM FOR MATERNITY BENEFIT AND PAYMENT THEREOF

(1) Any woman employed in an establishment and entitled to maternity benefit under the provisions of this Act may give notice in writing in such form as may be prescribed, to her employer, stating that her maternity benefit and any other amount to which she may be entitled under this Act may be paid to her or such person as she may nominate in the notice and that she will not work in any establishment during the period for which she receives maternity benefit.

(2) In the case of a woman who is pregnant, such notice shall state the date from which she will be absent from work, not being a date earlier than six weeks from the date of her expected delivery.

(3) Any woman who has not given the notice when she was pregnant may give such notice as soon as possible after the delivery.

(4) On receipt of the notice, the employer shall permit such woman to absent herself from the establishment during the period for which she receives the maternity benefit.

(5) The amount of maternity benefit for the period preceding the date of her expected delivery shall be paid in advance by the employer to the woman on production of such proof as may be prescribed that the woman is pregnant, and the amount due for the subsequent period shall be paid by the employer to the woman within forty-eight hours of production of such proof as may be prescribed that the woman has been delivered of a child.

(6) The failure to give notice under this section shall not disentitle a woman to maternity benefit or any other amount under this Act if she is otherwise entitled to such benefit or amount and in any such case an Inspector may either of his own motion or on an application made to him by the woman, order the payment of such benefit or amount within such period as may be specified in the order.

PAYMENT OF MATERNITY BENEFIT IN CASE OF DEATH OF A WOMAN

If a woman entitled to maternity benefit or any other amount under this Act, dies before receiving such maternity benefit or amount, or where the employer is liable for maternity benefit under second proviso to sub-section (3) of section 5, the employer shall pay such benefit or amount to the person nominated by the woman in the notice given under section 6 and in case there is no such nominee, to her legal representative.

PAYMENT OF MEDICAL BONUS

Every woman entitled to maternity benefit under this Act shall also be entitled to receive from her employer a medical bonus of two hundred and fifty rupees, if no pre-natal confinement and post-natal care is provided for by the employee free of charge.

LEAVE FOR MISCARRIAGE, MEDICAL TERMINATION OF PREGNANCY AND TUBECTOMY OPERATION

In case of miscarriage, a woman shall on production of such proof as may be prescribed, be entitled to leave with wages at the rate of maternity benefit, for a period of six weeks immediately following the day of her miscarriage.

In case of miscarriage or medical termination of pregnancy, a woman shall, on production of such proof as may be prescribed, be entitled to leave with wages at the rate of maternity benefit, for a period of six weeks immediately following the day of her miscarriage or, as the case may be, her medical termination of pregnancy.

In case of tubectomy operation, a woman shall, on production of such proof as may be prescribed, be entitled to leave with wages at the rate of maternity benefit for a period of two weeks immediately following the day of her tubectomy operation.

LEAVE FOR ILLNESS ARISING OUT OF PREGNANCY, DELIVERY, PREMATURE BIRTH OF CHILD, OR MISCARRIAGE

A woman suffering from illness arising out of pregnancy, delivery, premature birth of child or miscarriage shall, on production of such proof as may be prescribed, be entitled, in addition to the period of absence allowed to her under section 6, or as the case may be, under section 9 to leave with wages at the rate of maternity benefit for a maximum period of one month.

NURSING BREAKS

Every woman delivered of a child who returns to duty after such delivery shall, in addition to the interval for rest allowed to her, be allowed in the course of her daily work two breaks of the prescribed duration for nursing the child until the child attains the age of fifteen months.

PROHIBITION FOR DISMISSAL DURING ABSENCE DUE TO PREGNANCY

. (i) When a woman absents herself from work in accordance with the provisions of the Maternity Benefit Act, it shall be unlawful for her employer to discharge or dismiss her during or on account of such absence or to give notice of discharge or dismissal on such a day that the notice will expire during such absence, or to vary to her disadvantage any of the conditions of her service.

(ii) The discharge or dismissal of a workman, at any time during her pregnancy, if the woman but for such discharge or dismissal would have been entitled to maternity benefit or medical bonus referred to in section 8 of the Act, shall not have the effect of depriving her of the maternity benefit or medical bonus:

Provided that where the dismissal is for any prescribed gross misconduct, the employer may, by order in writing communicated to the woman, deprive her of the maternity benefit or medical bonus or both. However, any woman deprived of maternity benefit or medical bonus or both, or discharged or dismissed during or on account of her absence from work in accordance with the provisions of this Act, may, within sixty days from the day on which the order of such deprivation or discharge or dismissal is communicated to her, appeal to such authority as may be prescribed, and the decision of that authority on such appeal, whether the woman should or should not be deprived of maternity benefit or medical bonus or both or discharged or dismissed shall be final.

WAGES NOT TO BE DEDUCTED

No deduction from the normal and usual daily wages of a woman entitled to maternity benefit under the provisions of this Act shall be made by reason only of—

(a) the nature of work assigned to her by virtue of the provisions contained in sub-section (3) of section 4, or

(b) breaks for nursing the child allowed to her under the provisions of section 11 of the Maternity Benefit Act, 1961.

FORFEITURE OF MATERNITY BENEFIT

If a woman works in any establishment after she has been permitted by her employer to absent herself under the provisions of section 6 for any period during such authorised absence, she shall forfeit her claim to the maternity benefit for such period.

EXHIBITION OF ABSTRACTS OF THE ACT

An abstract of the provisions of this Act and the rules made thereunder in the language of the locality shall be exhibited in a conspicuous place by the employer in every part of the establishment in which women are employed.

MAINTENANCE OF MUSTER-ROLLS BY ESTABLISHMENT OF MINES AND CIRCUS

(a) The employer of every mine or circus in which women are employed shall prepare and maintain a muster-roll in Form 'A' and shall enter therein particulars of all women workers in the mine or circus.

(b) All entries in the muster-roll shall be made in ink and maintained upto-date and it shall always be available for inspection by the Inspector during working hours.

(c) The employer may enter in the muster-roll such other particulars as may be required for any other purpose of the Act.

SUBMISSION OF RETURNS BY MINES AND CIRCUS

(a) The employer of every mine or circus shall on or before the 21st day of January in each year submit to the Competent Authority a return in each of the Forms 'L', 'M', 'N' and 'O' giving information as to the particulars specified in respect of the preceding year.

(b) If the employer of a mine or circus to which the Act applies sells, abandons, or discontinues the working of the mine or circus he shall, within one month of the date of sale or abandonment or four months of the date of discontinuance, as the case may be, submit to the Competent Authority a further return in each of the said forms in respect of the period between the end of the preceding year and the date of sale, abandonment or discontinuance.

PENALTY FOR CONTRAVENTION OF ACT BY EMPLOYER

(1) If any employer fails to pay any amount of maternity benefit to a woman entitled under this Act or discharges or dismisses such woman during or on account of her absence from work in accordance with the provisions of this Act, he shall be punishable with imprisonment which shall not be less than three months but which may extend to one year and with fine which shall not be less than two thousand rupees but which may extend to five thousand rupees :

Provided that the court may, for sufficient reasons to be recorded in writing, impose a sentence of imprisonment for a lesser term or fine only in lieu of imprisonment.

(2) If any employer contravenes the provisions of this Act or the rules made thereunder, he shall, if no other penalty is elsewhere provided by or under this Act for such contravention, be punishable with imprisonment which may extend to one year, or with fine which may extend to five thousand rupees, or with both:

Provided that where the contravention is of any provision regarding maternity benefit or regarding payment of any other amount and such maternity benefit or amount has not already been recovered, the court shall, in addition recover such maternity benefit or amount as if it were a fine and pay the same to the person entitled thereto.

PENALTY FOR OBSTRUCTING INSPECTOR

Whoever fails to produce on demand by the Inspector any register or document in his custody kept in pursuance of this Act or the rules made thereunder or conceals or prevents any person from appearing before or being examined by an Inspector shall be punishable with imprisonment which may extend to one year or with fine which may extend to five thousand rupees or with both.

MINES ACT, 1952

CHECKLIST

Applicability of the Act
Throughout India but not to apply in certain cases.
Sec. 3

Notice to be given on minor operation
By owner, agent or manager before the commencement of any minor operation to the Chief Inspector.
Sec. 16

Compensatory day of rest
Within a month of the day work.
Sec. 29

Provisions as to health and safety
Drinking water, Conservancy, Medical appliances etc.
Secs. 19, 20 & 21

Duties and responsibility of the Owners, Agent, and Managers
• Making financial & other provisions of taking such steps as may be necessary.
• To comply with the instructions of the Authorities.
Sec. 18

Notice of accident
Whenever there occurs in or about a mine -
• an accident causing loss of life or serious bodily injury, or
• an explosion, ignition, spontaneous heating, outbreak of fire or irruption or inrush of water or other liquid matter, or
• an influx of inflammable or noxious gases, or
• a breakage of ropes, chains or other gear by which persons or materials, are lowered or raised in a shaft or an incline, or
• an over winding of cages or other means of conveyance in any shaft while persons or materials are being lowered or raised, or
• a premature collapse of any part of the workings, or
• any other accident which may be prescribed.
Sec. 23

Notice of certain diseases
Sec. 25

Extra wages for overtime
Twice of ordinary rate of wages
Sec. 33

Hours of work above ground
Not more than 5 hours continuously and the spread over will be 12 hours to be extended to 14 hours under special circumstances.
Sec. 30

Weekly day of rest
On more than 6 days working in a week.
Sec. 28

Night shift
Sec. 32

Prohibition of employment of certain persons
When working in other mine within prescribed 12 hours.
Sec. 34

Limitation of daily hours and work within overtime
Not more than 10 hours in any day inclusive of overtime.

Hours of work below ground
Below ground not more than 48 hours in any week.

Notice of hours of work
Sec. 36

Exemption of persons
• Below 18 years of age.
• Apprentices and other trainees not below 16 years of age.
Sec. 38

Employment of women
Prohibited in any part of mine which is below ground, in any mine above ground except between 6 a.m. to 7 p.m.
Sec. 46

Annual leave with wages
15 days per annum when below ground or one day for every 20 days of work.
Sec. 52

Payment in advance in certain cases
When leave allowed for not less than 4 days payment to be made.
Sec. 54

PENALTIES

Sec.	Offence	Punishment
Sec.64	Falsification of records etc.	Imprisonment upto 3 months or with fine upto Rs.1000.
Sec. 65	Use of false certificate of fitness	Imprisonment upto one month or with fine upto Rs.200.
Sec. 66	Omission to furnish return	Fine upto Rs.1000.
Sec. 67	Provisions of Sec.38 pertaining to exemption from provision regarding employment	Imprisonment upto 3 months or fine upto Rs.1000
Sec. 68	Providing employment of persons below 18 years of age	Fine upto Rs.500.
Sec. 70	Failure to give notice of accident	Imprisonment upto 3 months. Fine upto Rs.500.
Sec. 72-C	• Contravention of law with dangerous results, when contravention results in loss of life. • When contravention results in serious injuries. • When contravention to persons employed in the mine or other persons in or about the mine.	• Imprisonment upto two years or fine upto Rs.5000. • Imprisonment upto one year or fine upto Rs.3000. • Imprisonment upto 3 months or with fine upto Rs.3000
Sec. 73	General Provisions of disobeyance of orders	Imprisonment upto 3 months or with fine upto Rs.1000
Sec. 74	Enhancement penalty for previous conviction	Imprisonment double than the punishment prescribed.

13. The Mines Act, 1952

■

THE OBJECT

The Mines Act, 1952 seeks to regulate the working conditions in mines by providing for measures to be taken for the safety of workers employed therein and certain amenities for them.

MEANING OF A MINE

"Mine" means any excavation where any operation for the purpose of searching for or obtaining minerals has been or is being carried on and includes—

    (i) all borings, bore holes, oil wells and necessary crude conditioning plants, including the pipe conveying mineral oil within the oilfields;

    (ii) all shafts, in or adjacent to and belonging to a mine, whether in the course of being sunk or not;

    (iii) all levels and inclined planes in the course of being driven;

    (iv) all open cast working;

    (v) all conveyors or aerial ropeways provided for the bringing into or removal from mine of minerals or other articles or for the removal of refuse therefrom;

    (vi) all adits, levels, planes, machinery, work railways, tramways and sidings in or adjacent to and belonging to a mine;

    (vii) all protective works being carried out in or adjacent to a mine;

(viii) all workshops and stores situated within the precincts of a mine and under the same management and used primarily for the purposes connected with that mine or a number of mines under the same management;

(ix) all power stations, transformer sub-stations, convertor stations, rectifier stations and accumulator storage stations for supplying electricity solely or mainly for the purpose of working the mine or number of mines under the same management;

(x) any premises for the time being used for depositing sand or other material for use in a mine or for depositing refuse from a mine or in which any operations in connection with such sand, refuse or other material is being carried on, being premises exclusively occupied by the owner of the mine;

(xi) any premises in or adjacent to and belonging to a mine on which any process ancillary to the getting, dressing or preparation for sale of minerals or of coke is being carried on.

HOURS OF WORK, REST INTERVAL, WEEKLY OFF AND OVERTIME, ETC.

The Act limits hours of work of adult workers to 9 per day and 48 per week if employed above ground and 8 per day and 48 per week, if employed below ground. The maximum daily spread-over in the case of surface workers has been fixed at 12 hours and in the case of underground workers at 8 hours. Slightly longer hours of work have been prescribed for certain categories of underground workers, *viz.*, pump-minders, on-setters or attendants of continuously operated machines. In their case, a maximum of 54 hours week has been prescribed and their daily hours of work and spread-over have been fixed at 9. Under the Act, no adult worker employed above ground is allowed to work continuously for more than five hours unless he is given a rest interval of at least half an hour. No person employed in the mine is allowed to work for more than six days in a week. If the worker is deprived of one or more weekly days of rest as a result of exception provided in the Act, he has to be given an equal number of compensatory days of rest within two months.

Regarding overtime work, the Act provides that except in the case of an emergency involving serious risk to the safety of a mine or persons employed therein, no person shall be allowed to work for more than 10 hours in a day inclusive of overtime. Persons employed above and below ground are entitled to payment at a uniform rate of twice the ordinary rate of wages for overtime work. The period of overtime work is to be calculated on daily or weekly basis whichever is more favourable to the worker. For this purpose the ordinary rate of wages includes any dearness allowance and compensation in cash including such compensation, if any, accruing through the free issue of food grains.

LEAVE WITH WAGES

A person employed in a mine shall be entitled, in addition to weekly rest or festival holidays, to leave with wages after a calendar year's service, at the rate of one day for every 16 days of work performed by him, if employed below ground, and one day for every 20 days of work in the case of other categories of workers. A calendar year's service will, in the case of person engaged in underground work, means not less than 190 attendances at the mine and in the case of others 240 attendances. A person, whose service commences otherwise than on the first day of January, shall be entitled to leave with wages if he has put in, during the remaining calendar year, attendance for not less than half of the total number of days if employed below ground and for not less than two-thirds of the total number of days in any other case. Wages for leave period shall be paid at a rate equal to the daily average of his total full time earnings for the days on which he was employed during the months immediately preceding his leave, exclusive of any overtime wages and bonus but inclusive of any dearness allowance and compensation in cash accruing through free issue of food grains and other articles. Days of lay-off by agreement or contract or as permissible under the Standing Orders; maternity leave not exceeding 12 weeks; and the leave earned in the year prior to that in which the leave is enjoyed shall be deemed to be the days on which the employee has worked in a mine for the purpose of computing his attendances.

Any person employed in a mine who has been allowed leave for not less than 4 days, shall, before his leave begins, be paid the wages due for the period of leave allowed. Any leave not taken by a person in one calendar year shall be added to the leave to be allowed during the succeeding calendar year provided that the total number of days of leave which may be accumulated by any person shall not at any one time exceed 30 days.

In case, where Central Government is satisfied that the leave rules applicable to persons employed in a mine are not less favourable than those provided in the Act, it may exempt the mine from all or any of the provisions of the Act as far as they relate to leave with wages.

DUTIES AND RESPONSIBILITIES OF OWNERS, AGENTS AND MANAGERS

(1) The owner and agent of every mine shall each be responsible for making financial and other provisions and for taking such other steps as may be necessary for compliance with the provisions of this Act and the regulations, rules, bye-laws and orders made thereunder.

(2) The responsibility in respect of matters provided for in the rules made under clauses (d), (e) and (p) of section 58 shall be exclusively carried out by the owner and agent of the mine and by such person (other than the manager) whom the owner or agent may appoint for securing compliance with the aforesaid provisions.

(3) If the carrying out of any instructions given under sub-section (2) or given otherwise than through the manager under sub-section (3) of section 17, results in the contravention of the provisions of this Act or of the regulations, rules, bye-laws or orders made thereunder, every person giving such instructions shall also be liable for the contravention of the provisions concerned.

In spite of the fact that section 17 provides that there shall be a manager for every mine it does not lessen the responsibility of all those persons who are directly concerned with the functioning of the mines.

(4) Subject to the provisions of sub-sections (1), (2) and (3), the owner, agent and manager of every mine shall each be responsible to see that all operations carried on in connection with the mine, are conducted in accordance with the provisions of this Act and of the regulations, rules, bye-laws and orders made thereunder.

(5) On the event of any contravention by any person whosoever, of any of the provisions of this Act or of the regulations, rules, bye-laws or orders made thereunder except those which specifically require any person to do any act or thing or prohibit any person from doing an act or thing, besides the person who contravenes, each of the following persons shall also be deemed to be guilty of such contravention unless he proves that he had used due diligence to secure compliance with the provisions and had taken reasonable measures to prevent such contravention :

   (i) the official or officials appointed to perform duties of supervision in respect of the provisions contravened;

   (ii) the manager of the mine;

   (iii) the owner and agent of the mine;

   (iv) the person appointed, if any, to carry out the responsibility under sub-section (2):

Provided that any of the person aforesaid may not be proceeded against if it appears on inquiry and investigation, that he is not *prima facie* liable.

(6) It shall not be a defence in any proceedings brought against the owner or agent of a mine under this section that the manager and other officials have been appointed in accordance with the provisions of this Act or that a person to carry out the responsibility under sub-section (2) has been appointed.

HEALTH AND SAFETY OF WORKERS

(a) Drinking water

(1) In every mine effective arrangements shall be made to provide and maintain at suitable points conveniently situated a sufficient supply of cool and wholesome drinking water for all persons employed therein:

Provided that in the case of persons employed below ground the Chief Inspector may in lieu of drinking water being provided and maintained at suitable points, permit any other effective arrangement to be made for such supply.

(2) All such points shall be legibly marked "Drinking Water" in a language understood by a majority of the persons employed in the mine and no such point shall be situated within six metres of any washing place and urinal or latrine, unless a shorter distance is approved in writing by the Chief Inspector.

(3) In respect of all mines or any class or description of mines, the Central Government may make rules for securing compliance with the provisions of sub-sections (1) and (2) and for the examination by prescribed authorities of the supply and distribution of drinking water.

(b) Conservancy

(1) There shall be provided, separately for males and females in every mine, a sufficient number of latrines and urinals of prescribed type so situated as to be convenient and accessible to persons employed in the mine at all times.

(2) All latrines and urinals provided under sub-section (1) shall be adequately lighted, ventilated and at all times maintained in a clean and sanitary condition.

(3) The Central Government may specify the number of latrines and urinals to be provided in any mine, in proportion to the number of the males and females employed in the mine and provide for such other matters in respect of sanitation in mines (including the obligation in this regard of persons employed in the mine), as it may consider necessary in the interests of the health of the persons so employed.

(c) Medical Appliances

(1) In every mine there shall be provided and maintained so as to be readily accessible during all working hours such number of first-aid boxes or cupboards equipped with such contents as may be prescribed.

(2) Nothing except the prescribed contents shall be kept in a first-aid box or cupboard or room.

(3) Every first-aid box or cupboard shall be kept in the charge of a responsible person who is trained in such first-aid treatment as may be prescribed and who shall always be readily available during the working hours of the mine.

(4) In every mine there shall be made so as to be readily available such arrangements as may be prescribed for the conveyance to hospitals or dispensaries of persons who, while employed in the mine, suffer bodily injury or become ill.

(5) In every mine wherein more than one hundred and fifty persons are employed, there shall be provided and maintained a first-aid room of such size with equipment and in the charge of such medical and nursing staff as may be prescribed.

NOTICE OF ACCIDENTS

(1) Whenever there occurs in or about a mine—

(a) an accident causing loss of life or serious bodily injury; or

(b) an explosion, ignition, spontaneous heating, outbreak of fire or irruption or inrush of water or other liquid matter; or

(c) an influx of inflammable or noxious gases; or

(d) a breakage of ropes, chains or other gear by which persons or materials are lowered or raised in a shaft or an incline; or

(e) an over winding of cages or other means of conveyance in any shaft while persons or materials are being lowered or raised; or

(f) a premature collapse of any part of the workings; or

(g) any other accident which may be prescribed,

the owner, agent or manager of the mine shall give notice of the occurrence to such authority and in such form and within such time as may be prescribed, and he shall simultaneously post one copy of the notice on a special notice board in the prescribed manner at a place where it may be inspected by trade union officials and shall ensure that the notice is kept on the board for not less than fourteen days from the date of such posting.

(1A) Whenever there occurs in or about a mine an accident causing reportable injury to any person, the owner, agent or manager of the mine shall enter in a register such occurrence in the prescribed form and copies of such entries shall be furnished to the Chief Inspector once in a quarter.

(2) Where a notice given under sub-section (1) relates to an accident causing loss of life, the authority shall make an inquiry into the occurrence within two months of the receipt of the notice and, if the authority is not the Inspector he shall cause the Inspector to make an inquiry within the said period.

(3) The Central Government may, by notification in the Official Gazette, direct that accidents other than those specified in sub-sections (1) and (1A) which cause bodily injury resulting in the enforced absence from work of the person injured for a period exceeding twenty-four hours shall be entered in a register in the prescribed form or shall be subject to the provisions of sub-section (1) or sub-section (1A), as the case may be.

(4) A copy of the entries in the register referred to in sub-section (3) shall be sent by the owner, agent or manager of the mine, on or before the 20th day of January in the year following that to which the entries relate, to the Chief Inspector.

(5) Whenever there occurs in or about a mine an accident causing loss of life or serious bodily injury to any person, the place of accident shall not be disturbed or altered before the arrival or without the consent of the Chief Inspector or the Inspector to whom notice of accident is required to be given under sub-section (1) of section 23, unless such disturbance or alteration is necessary to prevent any further accident, to remove bodies of the deceased, or to rescue any person from danger, or unless discountinuance of work at the place of accident would seriously impede the working of the mine:

Provided that where the Chief Inspector or the Inspector fails to inspect the place of accident within seventy-two hours of the time of the accident, work may be resumed at the place of the accident.

PROHIBITION OF EMPLOYMENT OF PERSONS BELOW EIGHTEEN YEARS OF AGE, ETC.

(1) After the commencement of the Mines (Amendment) Act, 1983, no person below eighteen years of age shall be allowed to work in any mine or part thereof.

(2) Notwithstanding anything contained in sub-section (1) apprentices and other trainees, not below sixteen years of age, may be allowed to work, under proper supervision, in a mine or part thereof by the manager:

Provided that in the case of trainees, other than apprentices, prior approval of the Chief Inspector or an Inspector shall be obtained before they are allowed to work.

Explanation.—In this section and in section 43, "apprentice" means an apprentice as defined in clause (a) of section 2 of the Apprentices Act, 1961(52 of 1961).

CONDITIONS FOR EMPLOYMENT OF WOMEN

(1) No woman shall, notwithstanding anything contained in any law, be employed—

(a) in any part of a mine which is below ground;

(b) in any part of mine above ground except between the hours of 6 a.m. and 7 p.m.

(2) Every woman employed in a mine above ground shall be allowed an interval of not less than eleven hours between the termination of employment on any one day and the commencement of the next period of employment.

(3) Notwithstanding anything contained in sub-section (1), the Central Government may by notification in the Official Gazette, vary the hours of employment above ground of women in respect of any mine or class or description of mines, so, however, that no employment of any woman between the hours of 10 p.m. and 5 a.m. is permitted thereby.

REGISTERS OF PERSONS EMPLOYED

(1) For every mine there shall be kept in the prescribed form and place a register of all persons employed in the mine showing in respect of each such persons—

(a) the name of the employee with the name of his father or, of her husband, as the case may be, and such particulars as may be necessary for purpose of identification;

(b) the age and sex of the employee;

(c) the nature of employment (whether above ground or below ground and if above ground, whether in open cast workings or otherwise) and the date of commencement thereof;

(d) such other particulars as may be prescribed;

and the relevant entries shall be authenticated by the signature or the thumb impression of the person concerned.

(2) The entries in the register prescribed by sub-section (1) shall be such that workers working in accordance therewith would not be working in contravention of any of the provisions of Chapter VI.

(3) No person shall be employed in a mine until the particulars of such person is furnished and no person shall be employed except during the periods of work shown in respect of him in the register.

(4) For every mine other than a mine which, for any special reason to be recorded, is exempted by the Central Government by general or special order, there shall be kept in the prescribed form and place separate registers showing in respect of each person employed in the mine:

(a) below ground;

(b) below ground in open cast workings; and

(c) above ground in other cases:—

    (i) the name of the employee;

    (ii) the class or kind of his employment;

    (iii) where work is carried on by a system of relays, the shift to which he belongs and the hours of the shift.

(5) The register of persons employed below ground referred to in sub-section (4) shall show at any moment the name of every person who is then present below ground in the mine.

Note: No person shall enter any open cast working or any working below ground unless he has been permitted by the manager or is authorised under this Act or any other law to do so.

TO PASTE ABSTRACTS FROM THE ACT, REGULATIONS, ETC.

These shall be kept pasted at or near every mine in English and in such other language or languages as may be prescribed, the prescribed abstracts of the Act and of the regulations and rules.

PENALTIES

(a) Obstruction:

(1) Whoever obstructs the Chief Inspector, Inspector or any person authorised under section 8 in the discharge of his duties, under this Act, or refuses or wilfully neglects to afford the Chief Inspector, Inspector or such person any reasonable facility for making any entry, inspection, examination or inquiry authorised by or under this Act in relation to any mine, shall be punishable with imprisonment for a term which may extend to three months, or with fine which may extend to five hundred rupees, or with both.

(2) Whoever refuses to produce on the demand of the Chief Inspector or Inspector any registers or other documents kept in pursuance of this Act, or prevents or attempts to prevent or does anything which he has reason to believe to be likely to prevent any person from appearing before or being examined by an inspecting officer acting in pursuance of his duties under this Act, shall be punishable with fine which may extend to three hundred rupees.

(b) Falsification of records:

Whoever—

(a) counterfeits, or knowingly makes a false statement in any certificate, or any official copy of a certificate, granted under this Act; or

(b) knowingly uses as true any such counterfeit or false certificate; or

(c) makes or produces or uses any false declaration, statement or evidence knowing the same to be false, for the purpose of obtaining for himself or of any other person a certificate or the renewal of a certificate, under this Act, or any employment in a mine; or

(d) falsifies any plan, section, register or record, the maintenance of which is required by or under this Act or produces before any authority such false plan, action, register or record, knowing the same to be false; or

(e) makes, gives or delivers any plan, return, notice, record or report containing a statement, entry or detail which is not to the best of his knowledge or belief true,

shall be punishable with imprisonment for a term which may extend to three months, or with fine which may extend to one thousand rupees or with both.

(c) Omission to furnish plans:

Any person who, without reasonable excuse the burden of proving which shall lie upon him, omits to make or furnish in the prescribed form or manner or at or within the prescribed time any plan, section, return, notice, register, record or report required by or under this Act to be made or furnished shall be punishable with fine which may extend to one thousand rupees.

(d) Contravention of provisions regarding employment of labour:

Whoever, save as permitted by section 38, contravenes any provision of this Act or of any regulation, rules or bye-law or of any order made thereunder prohibiting, restricting or regulating the employment or presence of person in or about a mine shall be punishable with imprisonment for a term which may extend to three months, or with fine which may extend to one thousand rupees, or with both.

(e) Penalty for employment of persons below eighteen years of age:

If a person below eighteen years of age is employed in a mine in contravention of section 40, the owner, agent or manager of such mine shall be punishable with fine which may extend to five hundred rupees.

(f) Failure to appoint manager:

Whoever, in contravention of the provisions of section 17, fails to appoint a manager shall be punishable with imprisonment for a term which may extend to three months or with fine which may extend to two thousand and five hundred rupees, or with both.

Non-appointment of a qualified manager is violation of section 17, and hence punishable.

(g) Special provision for contravention of certain regulations:

Whoever contravenes any provision of any regulation or of any bye-law or of any order made thereunder, relating to matter specified in clauses (d), (i), (m), (n), (o), (p), (r), (s) and (u) of section 57 shall be punishable with imprisonment for a term which may extend to six months, or with fine which may extend to two thousand rupees, or with both.

(h) Special provision for contravention of orders under section 22:

Whoever continues to work in a mine in contravention of any order issued under sub-section (1A), sub-section (2) or sub-section (3) of section 22 or under sub-section (2) of section 22A shall be punishable with imprisonment for a term which may extend to two years, and shall also be liable to fine which may extend to five thousand rupees:

Provided that in the absence of special and adequate reasons to the contrary to be recorded in writing in the judgment of the court such fine shall not be less than two thousand rupees.

(i) Special provision for contravention of law with dangerous results:

(1) Whoever contravenes any provision of this Act or of any regulation, rule or bye-law or of any order made thereunder other than an order made under sub-section (1A) or sub-section (2) or sub-section (3) of section 22 or under sub-section (2) of section 22A shall be punishable—

(a) if such contravention results in loss of life, with imprisonment which may extend to two years, or with fine which may extend to five thousand rupees, or with both; or

(b) if such contravention results in serious bodily injury, with imprisonment which may extend to one year or with fine which may extend to three thousand rupees, or with both; or

(c) if such contravention otherwise causes injury or danger to persons employed in the mine or other persons in or about the mine, with imprisonment which may extend to three months or with fine which may extend to one thousand rupees, or with both:

Provided that in the absence of special and adequate reasons to the contrary to be recorded in writing in the judgment of the court, such fine, in the case of a contravention referred to in clause (a), shall not be less than three thousand rupees.

(2) Where a person having been convicted under this section is again convicted thereunder, he shall be punishable with double the punishment provided by sub-section (1).

(3) Any court imposing or confirming in appeal, revision or otherwise a sentence of fine passed under this section may, when passing judgment, order the whole or any part of the fine recovered to be paid as compensation to the person injured, or in the case of his death, to his legal representative:

Provided that if the fine is imposed in a case which is subject to appeal, no such payment shall be made before the period allowed for presenting the appeal has elapsed, or, if an appeal has been presented, before the decision of the appeal.

(j) General provision for disobedience of orders:

Whoever contravenes any provision of this Act or of any regulation, rule or bye-law or of any order made thereunder for the contravention of which no penalty is hereinbefore provided, shall be punishable with imprisonment for a term which may extend to three months, or with fine which may extend to one thousand rupees, or with both.

If there is a breach in the maintenance of the creche it is not the owner alone but his agent and manager shall also be liable for the breach.

(k) Enhanced penalty after previous conviction:

If any person who has been convicted for an offence punishable under any of the foregoing provisions (other than sections 72B and 72C) is again convicted for an offence committed within two years of the previous conviction and involving a contravention of the same provision, he shall be punishable for each subsequent conviction with double the punishment to which he would have been liable for the first contravention of such provision.

MINIMUM WAGES ACT, 1948

CHECKLIST

Object of the Act
To provide for fixing minimum rates of wages in certain employments.

Fixation of Minimum Rates of Wages
- The appropriate government to fix minimum rates of wages. The employees employed under part-I or part-II of Schedule.
- To make review at such intervals not exceeding five years the minimum rates or so fixed and revised the minimum rates.

Government can also fix Minimum Wages for
- Time Work • Piece work at piece rate • Piece work for the purpose of securing to such employees on a time work basis • Overtime work done by employees for piece work or time rate workers.

Sec. 3

Minimum Rates of Wages
Such as
- Basic rates of wages etc.
- Variable DA and
- Value of other concessions etc.

Sec. 4

Procedure for fixing and revising Minimum Rates of Wages
- Appointing Committee
- Issue of Notification etc.

Sec. 5

Composition of Committee
Representation of employer and employee in scheduled employment in equal number and independent persons not exceeding 1/3rd or its total number one such person to be appointed by the Chairman.

Sec. 9

Payment of Minimum Rates of Wages
Employer to pay to every employee engaged in scheduled employment at a rate not less than minimum rates of wages as fixed by Notification by not making deduction other than prescribed.

Sec. 12

Fixing Hours for Normal Working
- Shall constitute a normal working day, inclusive of one or more specified intervals.
- To provide for a day of rest in every period of seven days with remuneration.
- To provide for payment for work on a day of rest at a rate not less than the overtime rate.

Sec. 13

Overtime
- To be fixed by the hour, by the day or by such a longer wage-period works on any day in excess of the number of hours constituting a normal working day.
- Payment for every hour or for part of an hour so worked in excess at the overtime rate double of the ordinary rate (1½ times for agriculture labour)

Sec. 14

Wages of workers who work for less than normal working days
Save as otherwise hereinafter provided, be entitled to receive wages in respect of work done by him on that day as if he had worked for a full normal working day.

Sec. 15

Wages for two classes of work
Where an employee does two or more classes of work to each of which a different minimum rate of wages is applicable, wages at not less than the minimum rate in respect of each such class.

Sec. 16

Maintenance of registers and records
- Register of **Fines** - Form I Rule 21(4)
- Annual **Returns** - Form III Rule 21 (4-A)
- Register for **Overtime** - Form IV Rule 25
- Register of **Wages** - Form X, **Wage slip** - Form XI, **Muster Roll** - Form V Rule 26
- Representation of register - for three years Rule 26-A.

Sec. 18

Minimum time rate wages for piece work
Not less than minimum rates wages as fixed.

Sec. 17

Claims by employees
- To be filed before authority constituted under the Act within **6** months.
- Compensation upto **10** rupees

Sec. 20

PENALTIES	Offence	Punishment
Sec. 22	For paying less than minimum rates of wages	Imprisonment upto 6 months or with fine upto Rs.500/- or both
	For contravention of any provisions pertaining to fixing hours for normal working day etc.	Fine upto Rs.500/-.

14. The Minimum Wages Act, 1948

'Wages' are remuneration which the workers are entitled for the work performed by them. The employers always think of how to decrease the production costs while the workers see wages in terms of their pre-occupations, better housing, children's education, medical requirements, minimum recreations, provision for old age, marriage, etc. Our Constitution also enjoins on the Government to endeavour to secure conditions of work ensuring a decent standard of life and full enjoyment of leisure, social and cultural opportunities. The Minimum Wages Act is a landmark legislation for regulating of wages in the country.

THE OBJECT

The object with which the Minimum Wages Act was passed has been more concisely and precisely stated in the preamble of the Act. In other words this Act has been passed to provide for fixing minimum rates of wages in certain employments and the provisions of the Act are intended to achieve the object of doing social justice to the workers employed in the scheduled employments by prescribing minimum rates of wages for them. In brief the Act purports to achieve to prevent exploitation of labour and for that purpose the authorities under the Act have been empowered to take steps to prescribe minimum rates of wages in the scheduled industries.

MINIMUM RATES OF WAGES

The minimum rates of wages may be fixed for different scheduled employments, different classes of work in the same scheduled employment, adults, adolescents, children and apprentices and for different localities.

The Act is being implemented by the Central and State Governments, and as such both are empowered to frame rules. In the text references only to rules of Central Government are made. Employers may have to refer to rules of a State Government if industry comes within the jurisdiction of that Government.

Minimum rate of the wages fixed or revised consists of the following:—

   (i) a basic rate of wages and a special allowance, *viz.,* cost of living allowance;

   (ii) a basic rate of wages with or without cost of living allowance and cash value of concessions for supplies of essential commodities;

   (iii) an all inclusive rate, *i.e.,* basic rate, cost of living allowance and cash value of concessions.

In the case of the *Workmen represented by Secretary* v. *Management of Reptekose Brett & Co. Ltd.* reported in 1992 LLR, the Supreme Court has recommended additional components such as children's education, medical requirements, minimum recreation and provision for old age, marriage, etc.

The Government may fix the minimum rates of wages either by the hour, by the day, by the month or by such large wage-period as may be prescribed which may be revised at intervals and reviewed, if felt necessary.

The employer must pay every employee wages so fixed as notified by the Government.

WAGES MUST BE PAID IN CASH

However, if there is a custom to pay a part or the whole of wages in kind, the Government may authorise payment either wholly or partly in kind. It can also authorise the supply of essential commodities at concessional rates. The Government may prescribe the manner of determining the cash value of wages in kind and of concessions in supplies of essential commodities at concessional rates. However, the matter of estimating the cash value of wages in kind and of concessions is to get the prices from the nearest market and compute accordingly. The cash value of concession in supplies of essential commodities at concessional rates is to be worked out according to the difference between the retail price of commodities at the nearest market and the price charged by the employer.

MANNER AND PROCEDURE OF FIXING AND REVISING MINIMUM RATES OF WAGES

For the fixation of minimum wages, the employment must have been in Schedule originally or added to the Schedule by a notification under section 27 of the Act. The Government may fix or revise minimum wages either by committee procedure or by notification procedure.

Where notification method is adopted for fixation of revisions, the proposals are notified in the Official Gazette for the information of persons likely to be affected, specifying a date not less than two months from the date of notification, after which the proposals will be taken into consideration. In the case of revision by the notification method, the appropriate Government should consult the Advisory Board also. The employers may send their representations against the proposals so published.

While resorting to committee procedure, the Government has to appoint committee consisting of equal number of representatives of employers and employees in the scheduled employment and independent persons not exceeding one-third of total number nominated by the Government. The committee holds inquiries and advises the Government regarding fixation and revision of minimum wages. In both the cases, rates recommended by the committee and accepted by Government or the rates determined by Government after consideration of all representations should be published in the Official Gazette and shall come into force on expiry of 3 months from the date of notification unless otherwise provided.

HOURS OF WORK AND HOLIDAYS

Section 13 of the Act authorises the Government to fix the hours of work, a day of rest with remuneration and payment for the work done on a day of rest at the overtime rate. Under rules 20 to

25 of the Minimum Wages (Central) Rules, 1950 applicable to scheduled employment the number of hours of work in a day should not exceed nine hours for an adult and 4-1/2 hours for a child. The working day of an adult worker shall be so arranged that inclusive of the interval of rest it shall not exceed 12 hours on any day. The number of hours of work for adolescent shall be fixed by the competent medical practitioner as approved by the Government which may either be equal to an adult or child. The child should, however, not be allowed to work for more than $4\,^1/_2$ hours on any day.

In respect of other scheduled employments, for which the appropriate Government is State Government, the employers may refer to the rules prescribed by that Government.

EXTRA WAGES FOR OVERTIME

The employer can take actual work on any day upto nine hours in a 12 hours shift, but he must pay double the rates for any hour or part of an hour of actual work in excess of nine hours or for more than 48 hours in any week.

REST DAY

When a rule made under the Act provides for weekly rest day with wages, the workman must be allowed a day of rest in a week which should ordinarily be a Sunday or any other day of the week as rest day fixed by the employer. An employee could however, claim wages at overtime rate for working on a weekly rest day. This is available also to workmen on a piece-rate basis but in that case "average daily wages" would mean only the notified minimum daily wage and would not include extra earnings for output above the fixed minimum rate of wages.

EMPLOYER'S OBLIGATIONS

(1)As and when proposals for revision of the minimum wages are published in the Official Gazette, the employer may, if he feels necessary, send representations to the Government on the proposed revision.

(2) Once the minimum wages are notified and become effective the employer must pay to every employee engaged in a scheduled employment under him wages at a rate not less than the minimum rate of wages fixed by such notification for that class of employees.

(3) The employer may make deductions out of wages as may be authorised.

(4) The employer shall pay overtime at double the ordinary rate of wages for the period of work done beyond nine hours on any day or 48 hours in any week or for rest day.

(5) The employer should not employ a child for more than $4\frac{1}{2}$ hours on any day.

(6) The employer must pay minimum wages in cash unless the Government authorises their payment wholly or partly in kind.

(7) The employer shall fix wage-period for the payment of wages at intervals not exceeding one month or such other larger period as may be prescribed.

(8) The employer shall pay wages on a working day within seven days of the end of wage period or within 10 days if 1000 or more persons are employed in an establishment.

(9) The employer shall pay the wages to a person discharged not later than the second working day after his discharge.

(10) If an employee is employed on any day for a period less than the normal working day, he shall be entitled to receive wages for a full normal working day provided his failure to work is not caused by his unwillingness to work but by the omission of the employer to provide him work for that period.

(11) Where an employee does two or more classes of work to each of which a different minimum rate of wage is applicable, the employer shall pay to such employee in respect of time respectively occupied in each such class of work, wages not less than the minimum rate in force in respect of each such class.

(12) Where an employee is employed on piece work for which minimum time rate and not a minimum piece rate has been fixed, the employer shall pay to such employee wages at not less than the minimum time rate.

(13) The employer shall fix working days of an adult worker which may be for a maximum of nine hours a day but this period shall not exceed 12 hours on any day.

(14) The employer shall allow a rest day with wages to the employees every week which should ordinarily be Sunday or any other day as fixed by the employer. No employee shall be required to work on a day fixed as rest day, unless he is paid wages for that

day at the overtime rate and is also allowed a substituted rest day with wages (Rule 23).

(15) The employer shall not make deductions from wages except those authorised by or under the rules (Annexure 2).

(16) Every employer shall maintain at the work spot a register of wages in the form prescribed specifying the following particulars for each wage period in respect of each employed person:—

    (a) minimum rate of wages payable;

    (b) the number of days in which overtime was worked;

    (c) the gross wages;

    (d) the wages actually paid and the date of payment.

(17) Every employer shall issue wage slips in the form prescribed containing prescribed particulars to every person employed.

(18) Every employer shall get the signature or the thumb impression of every person employed on the wage book and the wage slips.

(19) The employer or his agent should authenticate the entries in the wage books and the wage slips.

(20) The employer, intending to impose a fine on an employed person or to make deduction for damage or loss caused by him, shall inform personally and in writing to him giving an opportunity to offer any explanation in the presence of another person. The amount of the said fine or deduction shall also be intimated to him.

(21) The employer shall ensure that all such fines imposed and deductions made shall be recorded in the registers in Forms I and II respectively. These registers should be kept at the work spot. Where no fines or deductions are imposed, a nil entry shall be made across the body of the relevant register.

(22) The employer shall exhibit at main entrance to the establishment and its offices, a notice in respect of the following in English and local language in a clean and legible form:—

    (a) minimum rates of wages;

    (b) abstracts of the Acts and rules made thereunder;

    (c) name and address of the Inspector.

(23) The employer shall preserve register of wages, muster-roll, register of fines, register of deductions for damage or loss and register of overtime for a period of three years after the date of last entry made therein.

(24) The employer shall produce all such registers and record on demand before the Inspector. Where an establishment has been closed, the employers should produce such register in his office if asked for.

REGISTERS, RECORDS, NOTICES, ABSTRACT AND RETURNS

Every employer liable to pay minimum rate of wages in the scheduled employment, in terms of the relative Minimum Wages Notification is required to maintain—

I. Register of wages containing the following particulars:—

   (i) the minimum rate of wages payable to each employee;

  (ii) number of days for which each employee worked overtime for each wage period;

 (iii) the gross wages of each employee for the wage period;

 (iv) all deductions from wages, showing the kinds of deduction; and

  (v) the wages actually paid to each employee for each period.

    Note: Signature/thumb impression of each employee is required to be obtained on the wage Register, when wages are paid.

    Entries in wage book are required to be authenticated by the employer or his authorised representative.

II. Register of overtime payment in Form IV.

III. Muster-Roll in Form V.

IV. Register of Fines in Form I

V. Register of deduction for damage or loss caused by the neglect or default of the employees.

Every employer is required to—

    Put up a notice in Form XIII containing the minimum rate of wages fixed and keep it in clean and legible condition.

Exhibit an extract of the Act and Rules thereunder with name and address of the Inspector in English and in the language understood by the majority of the employees. This should be kept clean and legible. (The Inspector will direct the place where notices and abstract, etc., are to be exhibited.)

Give annual Return to the Labour Commissioner in Form III, and

Exhibit a notice in Form XII in the public motor vehicles in case of employment in Public Motor Transport.

SCHEDULED EMPLOYMENT

The Minimum Wages Act used the expression Scheduled Employment section 2(g) and not the usual terms like industry, factory, shops, mine, etc. The emphasis is on the fact of employment of persons, irrespective of what it is called, which Act covers the activity or does not cover. If one or more persons are employed it could be covered provided it is included in the Schedule to the Act and the Government has not opted or refrained from fixing the minimum wages under the provisions of section 3(1A) of the Act. Only requirement is that the activity employing one or more persons should have been included in the Schedule.

Section 2 (g) of the Act reads as follows:

"any employment specified in the Schedule; or any process or branch of work forming part of such employment".

Under this definition every single branch/section of the work is covered. For example the entry "employment in handloom industry" covers not just the employees working on a loom but warping, dyeing of yarn, preparation of spindles for use in weaving, folding of cloth, are also covered by the expression. If sales are made in the same premises as continuation of the process of handloom weaving, selling will also be covered by the entry.

PENALTIES & PUNISHMENT FOR OFFENCES

Section 22 covers the offences of employer like paying to his employees less than the minimum wages fixed to his class of work or fails to pay over time wages and for work done on the day of rest, etc. the punishment could be imprisonment upto six months or fine or both.

Section 22B provides that cognizance of offence should be taken only when the Authority under Section 20 of the Act sanctions the application and the appropriate Government gives its sanction to file a complaint.

Section 22C clarifies who could be held guilty in case the employer happens to be an incorporated body, firm, association of persons, etc.

Section 22D deals with the case of payments found due to an employee who is dead or not traceable.

The provisions of the Act are intended to achieve the objective of doing social Justice to workmen employed in the scheduled employments by prescribing the minimum rates of wages for them.

MOTOR TRANSPORT WORKERS ACT, 1961

CHECKLIST

Object of the Act
To provide for the welfare of motor transport workers and to regulate the conditions of their work.

Running time
In relation to a working day means the time from the moment a transport vehicle starts functioning at the start of the working day until the moment when the transport vehicle ceases to function at the end of the working day, excluding any time during which the running of the transport vehicle is interrupted for a period exceeding such duration as may be prescribed during which period the persons who drive, or perform any other work in connection with the transport vehicle are free to dispose of their time as they please or are engaged in subsidiary work. **Sec. 2(1)**

Applicability of the Act
To every motor transport undertaking employing five or more motor transport workers or by a notification issued by the State Government. **Sec. 1**

Spread-over
Not more than 12 hours in a day. **Sec. 16**

Canteens
Where there are 100 or more workers. **Sec. 8**

Rest room(s)
Wherein such workers are to halt at night. **Sec. 9**

Medical facilities
To be readily available at operating centres and halting points. **Sec. 11**

First aid facilities
To be readily accessible during working hours a first aid box equipped with prescribed contents. **Sec. 12**

Registration of motor transport undertaking
On an application for the registration of a Motor Transport Undertaking to the prescribed authority. **Sec. 3**

Hours of work for adolescents
Not more than 6 hours a day including rest for ½ hour.
Not to work between 10 P.M. and 6 A.M. **Sec. 14**

Daily intervals for rest
After 5 hours working for at least ½ hour for an adult worker and to be allowed rest of at least 9 consecutive hours between the termination of duty on any day and the commencement of duty on the following day. **Sec. 15**

Uniforms
For drivers, conductors and checkers. **Sec. 10**

Split duty
Not more than two spells.
Sec. 17

Notice of hours of work
To be displayed and correctly maintained by the employers. **Sec. 18**

Hours of work
Not more than 8 hours in any day and 48 hours in a week.

To be permitted to work upto 10 hours and 54 hours in a week.

In case of break down etc. the limitation can be prescribed. **Sec. 13**

Compensatory day of rest
Within that particular month. **Sec. 20**

Certificate of fitness for the adolescent
By certifying Surgeon. **Sec. 23**

Prohibition of employment of children
Sec. 21

Medical examination
At the instance of the Inspector any worker can be medically examined. **Sec. 24**

Payment of wages
As per the provisions of the Payment of Wages Act, 1948.
Extra wages for overtime twice his ordinary rates of wages. **Sec. 26**

Weekly rest
A day of rest in every period of 7th day. **Sec. 19**

Annual leave with wages
Besides holidays and on working for 240 days -
One day for every 20 days of work performed by an adult worker during previous calendar year.
For adolescent one day for every 15 days' duty performed during the calendar year. **Sec. 27**

Adolescents employed as motor transport workers to carry tokens and certificate of fitness. **Sec. 22**

Sections	Offence	Punishment
Sec. 29	• Obstructing the Inspectors • Refusing to produce any register or other documents to the Inspector.	• Imprisonment upto 3 months or fine upto Rs.500 or both. • Imprisonment upto 3 months or fine upto Rs.500.
Sec. 30	Use of false certificate of fitness.	Imprisonment upto one month or fine upto Rs.50 or both.
Sec. 31	Contravention of provisions regarding employment of motor transport workers	Imprisonment upto 3 months or fine upto Rs.500 or both and on continuing contravention Rs.75 per day for such contravention
Sec. 32	Wilfully disobeying any direction lawfully given by any person or authority under the Act	Imprisonment upto 3 months or fine upto Rs.500 or with both
Sec. 33	Enhanced penalties after previous conviction	Imprisonment upto six months or fine upto Rs.1000 or with both

15. The Motor Transport Workers Act, 1961

■

THE OBJECT

Though there are enactments such as Motor Vehicles Act, 1988 and the Factories Act, 1948 which cover certain sections of motor transport workers and certain aspects of their conditions of employment, there has been no independent legislation applicable to motor transport workers as a whole for regulating the various aspects of their conditions of employment, work and wages. It was thus considered desirable to have a separate statute for motor transport workers which would cover matters like medical facilities, welfare facilities, hours of work, spread-over, rest periods, overtime, annual leave with pay, etc., on the analogy of similar enactments for workers in factories, mines and plantations.

APPLICABILITY OF THE ACT

The Act applies to motor transport undertakings employing five or more motor transport workers.

The State Government may extend the provisions of the Act to any motor transport undertaking employing less than five motor transport workers.

MOTOR TRANSPORT UNDERTAKING—SCOPE OF

A "motor transport undertaking" means a motor transport undertaking engaged in carrying passengers or goods or both by road for hire or reward, and includes a private carrier. A "private carrier" is defined in the Motor Vehicles Act as denoting an owner of a transport vehicle other than a public carrier who uses that vehicle solely for the carriage of goods which are his property or the carriage of which is necessary for the purposes of his business not being a business of providing transport, or who uses the vehicle for any of the purposes specified in sub-section (2) of section 42 of that Act.

MOTOR TRANSPORT WORKER

A "motor transport worker" means a person who is employed in a motor transport undertaking directly or through an agency, whether for wages or not, to work in a professional capacity on a transport vehicle or to attend to duties in connection with the arrival, departure, loading or unloading of such transport vehicle and includes a driver, conductor, cleaner, station staff, line checking staff, booking clerk, cash clerk, depot clerk, timekeeper, watchman or attendant, but does not include any such person employed in a factory as defined in the Factories Act or any such person to whom Shops and Establishments Act apply. These two groups of excluded employees would however be taken into account for the purpose of determining whether an employer is bound to provide canteens.

The Supreme Court has held that a Municipal Council which owned transport vehicles for carrying nights oil and for the distribution of water is a private carrier coming under the purview of the Act. However, the postal department using vehicles for carrying mails would not be a private carrier covered under the definition of a motor transport undertaking. The reasoning is that the postal department is not carrying on a business and therefore it cannot be said to use the vehicles for the carriage of goods necessary for its business.

Exemptions: The Act does not apply to or in relation to any transport vehicle used—

(i) for the transport of sick or injured persons; or

(ii) for any purpose connected with the security of India, or the security of a State, or the maintenance of public order. In this context "public order" means public peace and tranquility. It does not include public safety or public health.

The factory workers and those covered by Shops and Establishments Act do not come under the Act except for a very limited purpose. The Act has also empowered the Government to exempt—

(i) motor transport workers who hold positions of supervision or management in any motor transport undertaking;

(ii) part-time workers; and

(iii) any class of employers,

from the purview of the Act.

The employees to whom the Shops and Commercial Establishments Act apply are outside the purview of the Motor Transport Workers Act. There have been conflicting decisions on the applicability of these two Acts to a motor transport undertaking.

WELFARE FACILITIES

(i) *Canteens:* The State Government may require in every place wherein 100 or more motor workers employed in a motor transport undertaking call on duty every day, to provide and maintain one or more canteens by the employer, and make rules regarding the date of providing the canteens, number of canteens, foodstuff to be served there and its prices and how it should be managed.

(ii) *Rest Rooms:* Rest rooms are to be provided and maintained at every place where workers are required to halt at night, and these rooms should be sufficiently lighted and ventilated, and have such construction, accommodation and equipment as may be prescribed by the Government.

(iii) *Uniforms:* An employer has also to provide uniforms for the drivers, conductors, and line checking staff employed in his undertaking. Raincoats or other like amenities may also be provided for their protection from rain or cold as may be specified in the rules. Where no arrangement is made for washing uniforms, washing allowance is to be paid to them.

MEDICAL AND FIRST-AID FACILITIES

Every employer has to provide and maintain a first-aid box equipped with prescribed contents in every transport vehicle in the charge of the driver or conductor of the transport vehicle who is to be provided facilities for training in the use thereof. The employer has also to provide and maintain such medical facilities for the workers at such operating and halting stations as may be prescribed by the Government.

HOURS OF WORK, REST INTERVALS AND SPREAD-OVER

(i) *Hours of Work:* No adult worker is to be allowed to work for more than eight hours a day or forty-eight hours in any week. In case of running on long routes or on festive or other occasions, the workers may be allowed to work upto ten hours a day or 54 hours a week with the permission of the prescribed authority. The workers may also be required or allowed to work more than the prescribed hours if there is a breakdown or dislocation of a motor transport service, or if there is interruption of service, or an act of God.

In the case of adolescents, daily hours are not to exceed six, and they are also not to be allowed to work between the hours of 10 P.M. and 6 A.M. Their six hours working is also to include rest interval of half an hour.

(ii) *Rest Intervals:* Every adult worker is to have rest of half an hour after working for five hours, if he is required to work for more than six hours on that day. Again, hours of work on each day are to be so fixed that the worker is allowed a period of rest of at least nine consecutive hours between the termination of duty on any one day and the commencement of duty on the next following day, except when there is breakdown or dislocation of a motor transport service or interruption of traffic or an act of God.

(iii) *Spread-over and Split Duty:* The daily hours of work are not to spread-over for more than 12 hours in the case of adult, and nine hours in case of an adolescent, inclusive of interval for rest, except when there is breakdown or dislocation of service, or interruption of traffic. The hours of work should also not be split into more than two spells on any day, except as may be permitted by other provisions of the Act.

WEEKLY REST DAY

Every worker is to be given a day of rest in every period of seven days, unless his total period of employment is less than six days. If one has to work on the day of rest, it has to be seen that he does not work for more than ten days consecutively without a whole day of rest intervening. If an employer is granted exemption from this provision and the worker is deprived of his days of rest, he is to be allowed within the month in which the days of rest are due to him, or within two months immediately following that month, compensatory days of rest of equal number to the days of rest so lost.

NOTICE OF HOURS OF WORK

Every employer has to display a notice of hours of work in such form and manner as may be prescribed, and the workers are to work in accordance with the notice of hours of work so displayed, except as otherwise provided under this Act.

EXTRA WAGES FOR OVERTIME

If an adult motor transport worker works for more than 8 hours in any day, or if he is required to work on any day of rest to prevent any dislocation of service, he has to be paid wages at twice his ordinary rate of wages in respect of the overtime work or for the work done on the day of rest. If the overtime work results from any breakdown or dislocation of motor transport service or interruption of traffic or act of God, the worker will be entitled to wages in respect of overtime work at such rate as may be prescribed. For the purpose of overtime, the term "ordinary rates of wages" means basic wages and dearness allowances.

EMPLOYMENT OF YOUNG PERSONS

No child or person below the age of 15 years is to be employed in any capacity in any motor transport undertaking.

An adolescent or a person between the age of 15 years and 18 years, can be employed only if he is declared fit for employment in a motor transport undertaking by a certifying surgeon. This certificate is to be granted on the application of any adolescent or his guardian or his parent, and this is to be deposited with the employer. The certificate is to be valid for 12 months, and thereafter it is to be renewed. Any fee payable for obtaining certificate is to be paid by the employer, and is not to be recovered from the adolescent. The latter will have to carry with him a token showing the number of certificate while at work. An inspector appointed under this Act can get any motor transport worker examined by a certifying surgeon if he suspects that the worker concerned is an adolescent, and he cannot work till he is certified to be fit for work.

ANNUAL LEAVE WITH WAGES

A motor transport worker who has worked for a period of 240 days or more in a motor transport undertaking during a calendar year is to be allowed during the subsequent calendar year, leave with wages at the rate of one day for every 20 days of work performed by him in the previous calendar year if he is an adult, and at the rate of one day for every fifteen days of work performed if he is an adolescent. If the worker commences his service after the first day of January, he becomes entitled to leave if he has worked for two-thirds of the total number of days worked in the remainder of the calender year. If he is discharged or dismissed from service during the course of the year, he is entitled to the leave at the prescribed rate even if he has not worked for the period which entitled him to the earned leave.

A motor transport worker can accumulate his earned leave upto thirty days if he is an adult, and upto forty days if he is an adolescent.

Explanation.—For the purposes of earned leave such leave does not include weekly holidays or holidays of festival or other similar occasions whether occurring during or at either end of the period of leave.

WAGES FOR THE LEAVE PERIOD

Wages for the earned leave are to be paid at the rate equal to the daily average of his total full time wages for the days on which he worked during the month immediately preceding his leave, exclusive of any overtime earning and bonus, but inclusive of dearness allowance and value of any concession for foodgrains supplied by the employer. The worker can have wages for the leave period in advance if the leave to be availed of is not for less than four days. The worker has to be paid wages in lieu of the leave refused to him. However, if motor transport worker is entitled to more favourable benefit in respect of leave and other matters under any agreement or any award, or any contract of service or otherwise than those provided by this Act, he will continue to be entitled to the more favourable benefits in respect of other matters under this Act.

PENALTIES

The Act stipulates penalties upto three months imprisonment and fine upto Rs. 500 for contraventions of the provisions of the Act and other offences, such as obstruction of inspector in performing his duty, or supplying of false information or documents. However, use of false certificate of fitness is punishable with imprisonment upto one month and fine upto 50 rupees, or with both. If an offence is continued, it is punishable with additional fine of Rs. 75 per day, and for a repeated offence for which conviction has already been obtained, the punishment is doubled.

Under this Act the Court can take cognizance of the offence if a complaint is made by an Inspector or with his approval, and that also if the complaint is filed within three months from the date the offence has come to the knowledge of the Inspector.

OBLIGATIONS OF EMPLOYERS

An employer is liable to—

(a) provide such welfare amenities to motor transport workers as canteens, rest rooms, uniforms, first-aid and medical facilities as required under this Act and the rules framed thereunder;

(b) observe restrictions in regard to working hours for adults and adolescents, and ensure the workers rest intervals, weekly rest and extra payment for overtime;

(c) avoid employment of adolescents without fitness certificates from the certifying surgeon, and not to employ children below the age of 15 years;

(d) ensure payment of wages to workers in accordance with the provisions of the Payment of Wages Act, 1936, and allow workers leave with wages as provided under this Act;

(e) afford all reasonable facilities to the Chief Inspector and Inspectors for making any entry, inspection, examination or inquiry under this Act, and provide all necessary information and material required to see that the provisions of this Act are being observed;

(f) apply and get his undertaking registered with the prescribed authority.

PAYMENT OF BONUS ACT, 1965

CHECKLIST

Applicability of Act

Every factory wherein **10** or more persons are employed with the aid of power **or**

An establishment in which **20** or more persons are employed without the aid of power on any day during an accounting year. **Sec. 1**

Establishment

Establishment includes departments, undertakings and branches, etc.

Separate establishment

If profit and loss accounts are prepared and maintained in respect of any such department or undertaking or branch, then such department or undertaking or branch is treated as a separate establishment. **Sec. 3**

Computation of available surplus

- Income tax and direct taxes as payable.
- Depreciation as per section 32 of Income Tax Act.
- Development rebate, investment or development allowance.
Sec. 5

Components of Bonus

Salary or wages includes **dearness allowance** but no other allowances e.g. over-time, house rent, incentive or commission. **Sec. 2(21)**

Computation of gross profits

For banking company, as per First Schedule.

Others, as per Second Schedule. **Sec. 4**

Disqualification and Deduction of Bonus

On dismissal of an employee for
- fraud; **or**
- riotous or violent behaviour while on the premises of the establishment; **or**
- theft, misappropriation or sabotage of any property of the establishment; **or**
- Misconduct of causing financial loss to the employer to the extent that bonus can be deducted for that year. **Secs. 9 & 18**

Eligible Employees

Employees drawing wages upto Rs. 10,000 per month or less.
For calculation purposes Rs. 3,500 per month maximum will be taken even if an employee is drawing upto Rs. 10,000 per month. **Sec. 12**

Eligibility of Bonus

An employee will be entitled only when he has worked for **30** working days in that year. **Sec. 8**

Payment of Minimum Bonus

8.33% of the salary or Rs.100 (on completion of 5 years after 1st Accounting year even if there is no profit). **Sec. 10**

Time Limit for Payment of Bonus

Within **8** months from the close of accounting year. **Sec. 19**

Set-off and Set-on

As per Schedule IV. **Sec. 15**

Submission of Return

In Form D to the inspector within **30 days** of the expiry of time limit under Section 19. **Rule 5**

Maintenance of Registers and Records etc.

- A register showing the computation of the **allocable surplus** referred to in clause (4) of section 2, in Form A.
- A register showing the **set-on and set-off** of the allocable surplus, under section 15, in Form B.
- A register showing the details of **the amount of bonus due** to each of the employees, the deductions under sections 17 and 18 and the amount actually disbursed, in Form C.

Sec. 26, Rule 4

Act not applicable to certain employees of LIC, General Insurance, Dock Yards, Red Cross, Universities & Educational Institutions, Chambers of Commerce, Social Welfare Institutions, Building Contractors, etc. **Sec.32**

PENALTY

For contravention of any provision of the Act or the Rules	Upto 6 months or with fine upto Rs.1000.	**Sec. 28**

16. The Payment of Bonus Act, 1965

The Payment of Bonus Act applies to the persons employed in every factory and establishment employing not less than 20 persons on any day during an accounting year. The establishments covered under the Act shall continue to pay bonus even if the number of employees falls below 20 subsequently.

ELIGIBILITY FOR BONUS AND DEFINITION OF AN EMPLOYEE

An 'employee' under the Act means any person other than apprentice, engaged for hire/reward whether the terms of employment be express or implied and includes supervisors/ managerial and administrative employees drawing salary/wages not exceeding Rs. 10,000 per month. Every employee not drawing salary/wages beyond Rs. 10,000 per month who has worked for not less than 30 days in an accounting year, shall be eligible for bonus for a minimum of 8.33% of the salary/wages even if there is loss in the establishment whereas a maximum of 20% of the employee's salary/wages is payable as bonus in an accounting year. However, in case of the employees' salary/ wage range of Rs. 3,500 to Rs. 10,000 per month for the purpose of payment of bonus, their salaries/wages would be deemed to be Rs. 3,500 per month.

INFANCY BENEFIT FOR NEW ESTABLISHMENTS

For the first five accounting years, following the accounting year in which the employer sells goods/renders services, bonus is payable only in respect of the accounting year, in which profits are made but the provisions of set on and set off would not apply.

ELIGIBILITY FOR BONUS

Subject to the above, the Payment of Bonus Act indicates that the following categories of persons will be entitled to bonus:—

(a) skilled or unskilled or manual labour;

(b) managerial staff;

(c) supervisory staff;

(d) administrative staff;

(e) technical staff; and

(f) clerical staff.

An employee who has been engaged on hire or reward on terms which are either express or implied, and

(i) his salary does not exceed Rs. 3500 per mensem, but he must have worked at least 30 working days in a year,

(ii) who is not an apprentice,

is entitled to bonus.

Every person who falls within the definition of the term 'employee' in section 2(13) of the Payment of Bonus Act will be entitled to bonus under the Payment of Bonus Act even if he is not a 'workman' under the definition of section 2(s) of Industrial Disputes Act, 1947.

EXTENT AND APPLICATION OF THE ACT

The Payment of Bonus Act extends to the whole of India. Prior to the Central Labour Law (Extension to Jammu and Kashmir) Act, 1970, this Act had no application to the State of Jammu and Kashmir.

The provisions of this Act shall apply to the following factories/establishments:—

(i) The word 'factory' shall have the same meaning as in clause (m) of section 2 of the Factories Act, 1948. Section 2(m) of the Factories Act defines 'factory' as any premises including the precincts thereof (i) whereon ten or more workers are working, or were working on any day of the preceding twelve months and the manufacturing process is being carried on with the aid of power; or (ii) whereon twenty or more workers are working, or were working on any day of the preceding twelve months and the manufacturing process is being carried on without the aid of power. But the term 'factory' does not include a mine subject to the operation of the Mines Act, 1952 or a Railway running shed.

(ii) Every other establishment in which twenty or more persons are employed on any day during an accounting year. An establishment in public sector means an establishment owned, controlled or managed by Government company as defined in section 67 of the Companies Act, 1956. Section 617 of the Companies Act defines a 'Government company' as a company in which not less than fifty-one per cent of the paid up share capital is held by the Central Government or by any State Government or Governments or jointly by the Central and State Governments. An establishment in public sector also means a Corporation in which not less than forty per cent of its capital is held whether singly or taken together by (i) the Government, or (ii) the Reserve Bank of India, or (iii) a Corporation owned by the Government or the Reserve Bank of India. On the other hand, an establishment in private sector means any establishment other than an establishment in public sector.

APPLICABILITY OF ACT TO PUBLIC UNDERTAKINGS

The Act also applies to public sector in certain cases. If in any accounting year an establishment in public sector sells any goods produced or manufactured by it or renders any services, in competition with an establishment in private sector and the income from such sales or services or both is not less than twenty per cent, of the gross income of the establishment in public sector for that year, then the provisions of this Act shall apply to such establishment in public sector. In other words, section 20 of the Act provides for the application of the bonus formula to those public sector establishments which fulfil the twenty per cent compensation test. Once the bonus formula is applied to such establishment, it shall continue to apply even if the 20 per cent compensation test is not satisfied in any subsequent accounting year. It is to be noted in this connection that an establishment engaged in any industry carried on by or under the authority of any department of the Central Government or a State Government or a local authority is not an "establishment in public sector".

EXEMPTED ESTABLISHMENTS

The Act will not apply to the following classes of employees:—

(i) Employees employed by the Life Insurance Corporation of India.

(ii) Seaman as defined in clause (42) of section 3 of the Merchant Shipping Act, 1958.

(iii) Employees registered or listed under any scheme made under the Dock Workers (Regulation of Employment) Act, 1948, and employed by registered or listed employers.

(iv) Employees employed by an establishment engaged in any industry carried on by or under the authority of any department of the Central Government or a State Government or a local authority.

(v) Employees employed by (a) the Indian Red Cross Society or any other institution of a like nature (including its branches); (b) Universities and other educational institution; (c) Institutions (including Hospitals, Chambers of Commerce and Social Institutions) established not for the purpose of profit.

(vi) Employees employed through contractors on building operations.

(vii) Employees of the Reserve Bank of India.

(viii) Employees of (a) the Industrial Finance Corporation of India, (b) any financial corporation established under section 3 or section 3A of the State Financial Corporation Act, 1951, (c) the Deposit Insurance Corporation, (d) the Agriculture Refinance Corporation, (e) the Unit Trust of India, (f) the Industrial Development Bank of India, (g) any other financial institution being an establishment in public sector which the Central Government notifies in the Official Gazette with regard to its capital structure, its objects, its extent of financial assistance and any other relevant factor.

(ix) Employees of inland water transport establishments operating on routes passing through any other country.

An appropriate Government is also empowered to exempt an establishment or class of establishments from the operation of all or any of the provisions of this Act provided appropriate Government is of the opinion that having regard to the financial position and other relevant circumstances, it would not be in the public interest to apply all or any of the provisions of the Act. The appropriate Government on taking decision of exemption will notify in the Official Gazette the period for which exemption is granted and specify therein conditions, if any, to be imposed on the exempted establishment. The exemption of an establishment from the operation of the Act by the appropriate Government depends on the conditions specified in section 36 of the Act. Power of exemption is to be exercised by the appropriate Government in a quasi-judicial manner. This section contemplates a determination and exercise of discretion as guided and limited by the provision itself. The discretion is not absolute and is justifiable. An order rejecting an application for exemption must be a speaking order.

ACCOUNTING YEAR

Section 2(1) of the Act defines accounting year as defined in relation to (i) a corporation, (ii) a Company, and (iii) any other cases. In case of corporation accounting year means the year ending on the day on which the books and accounts of the corporation are closed and balanced. In case of a company it means the period in respect of which any profit and loss account of the company laid before it in annual general meeting is made up, whether that period is a year or not. In any other case it means the year commencing on the 1st day of April, or if the accounts of an establishment maintained by the employer thereof are closed or balanced on any day other than the 31st day of March, then at the option of the employer, the year ending on the day on which the accounts are so closed and balanced.

ALLOCABLE SURPLUS

In case of a company other than a banking company allocable surplus means sixty-seven per cent of the available surplus in an accounting year of the company which has not made the arrangements prescribed under the Income-tax Act for the declaration and payment within India of the dividends payable out of its profits in accordance with the provisions of section 194 of that Act. In all other cases allocable surplus in an accounting year.

AVAILABLE SURPLUS

Available surplus in any accounting year is computed under section 5 of the Act. The available surplus as provided by section 5 of the Act in respect of any accounting year shall be the gross profit for that year after deducting therefrom those sums referred to in section 6 of the Act. Prior to the Payment of Bonus (Amendment) Act, 1969 one of the sums referred to in section 6 was the tax which the employer was liable to pay for the accounting year in respect of his income, profits and gains during the year.

The available surplus in respect of the accounting year commencing on any day in the year 1968 and in respect of every subsequent accounting year shall be the aggregate of (a) the gross profit for that accounting year after deducting those sums as referred to in section 6; and (b) an amount equal to the difference between (i) the direct tax, calculated in accordance with the provisions of section 7 in respect of an amount equal to the gross profits of the employer for the immediately preceding accounting year, and (ii) the direct tax calculated in the same manner but after deducting therefrom the amount of bonus which the employer has paid or is liable to pay to his employees in accordance with the provisions of this Act for that year.

The following sums shall be deducted from the gross profits as prior charges:—

(a) Any amount by way of depreciation admissible in accordance with the provisions of the Income-tax law. In case an employer has been paying bonus to his employees under a settlement or an award or an agreement made before the 29th May, 1965 and subsisting on that date after deducting from the gross profits notional normal depreciation, then the amount of depreciation to be deducted shall continue at the option of such employer to be such notional normal depreciation. But the employer must exercise this option once and within one year from that date. In all other cases amount of income-tax payable for bonus year is to be calculated after deducting statutory depreciation and not notional normal depreciation. A claim for depreciation on account of double or multiple shifts can be allowed even though such amount is not claimed under the Income-tax Act.

(b) Any amount by way of development rebate or investment allowance or development allowance which the employer is entitled to deduct from his income under the Income-tax Act. Amount actually allowable as development rebate under section 33 of the Incom-tax Act, 1961 should be allowed as deduction and not seventy per cent of that amount contemplated by section 34(3) of the Income-tax Act as development rebate reserve. Rehabilitation reserve is also a substantial item which goes to reduce the available surplus. But it is equitable in the larger interest of the industry as well as of the employees that proper rehabilitation reserve should be built up taking into consideration the increase in prices of plant and machinery which has to be replaced at a future date and by the determination of a multiplier and its divisor.

(c) Any direct tax which the employer is liable to pay for the accounting year in respect of his income, profits and gains during that year. This charge shall operate subject to the provisions of section 7 of the Act. The direct taxes are to be worked out on the gross profits worked out under section 4, less the prior charges under section 6, namely depreciation and development rebate but without deducting from such balance the bonus payable by the company in the particular accounting year. The amendment of the Act in 1969 has not altered this position. Further, in calculating the allocable surplus the tax concession by way of rebate that an employer will get under the Income-tax Act on the bonus found to be payable need not be taken into consideration.

(d) Such further sums as are specified in respect of the employer in the Third Schedule. In the Third Schedule to the Act employers have been classified into six categories, namely— (1) Company other than a Banking Company, (2) Banking Company, (3) Corporation, (4) Co-operative Society, (5) Any other employer not falling under any of the aforesaid categories, and (6) Any employer falling under item No. 1 or item No. 3 or item No. 4 or item No. 5 and being a licensee within the meaning of the Electricity Supply Act, 1948. Each class of employer will be entitled to deduct further sums as provided in column 3 of the said Schedule. Where interest is paid by one office of the company to its another office on advances received from that office, it will be disallowed in calculating gross profit of the office even if such expenditure is accepted as a proper expenditure by auditors.

Under clause l(iii) of the Third Schedule if the directors of a company once decide to declare a particular amount as dividend for the previous year and set apart the required amount from the General Reserve, it relates back to the date of the commencement of the accounting year. Hence the amount subsequently declared as dividend is deductible from Reserves though on the date of commencement of the year no dividend us declared. Strict interpretation of the expression "on the date of the commencement of the year" is not possible.

ACCURACY OF BALANCE SHEET AND PROFIT AND LOSS ACCOUNT

Section 226(1) of the Companies Act provides that a company or a corporation need not prove the accuracy of the balance sheet and profit and loss account by affidavit or any other mode. However, the proviso to the said section enables the authority that in case there is any doubt, steps can be taken to find out the accuracy. Sub-section (2) enables a party challenging the correctness of such statement by applying for clarification by the management and the authority before whom the proceedings are pending and the company will be given an opportunity to give clarification. In one case the opposite party had not challenged the accuracy of a particular item but simply attached the statement in general terms pertaining to method of accounting nor did he move the authority for direction, the presumption of accuracy could not be rebutted by the authority. The burden to prove accuracy lies upon the party challenging the correctness. In another case, it has been held that in case of dispute about accuracy of the balance sheet and profit and loss account, the industrial tribunal has the powers and duty to enquire into the accuracy of balance sheet and profit and loss account but it cannot make any fishing enquiry. It has been further held that if the Company fails to produce the material for purpose of calculating available surplus, the tribunal has to make its own calculation.

DEARNESS ALLOWANCE

Dearness Allowance is included in the definition of 'salary' or 'wages' under section 2(21) of the Payment of Bonus Act.

BONUS ON COMMISSION

Section 2(21) of the Payment of Bonus Act defines 'salary' or 'wages'. Its opening provision includes within it all remunerations (other than the remuneration in case of overtime work) capable of being expressed in terms of money, which would, if the terms of employment, express or implied, were fulfilled, be payable to an employee in respect of his employment and includes dearness allowance, yet in express terms, the definition does not include any commission payable to the employee *vide* clause (vii) of section 2(21) of the Act.

FORFEITURE OF BONUS

An employee who is dismissed from service on the grounds of fraud, riotous or violent behaviour at the premises of the establishment or for theft, misappropriation or sabotage of any property of the establishment as contained in section 9 of the Payment of Bonus Act shall not only be disqualified from receiving the bonus for the accounting year in which he was dismissed but also for the past years remained unpaid to him.

WAGES FOR BONUS

Salary or wages for payment of wages other than house rent allowance includes dearness allowance.

Hereinbelow are clarifications with regard to components of wages or salary.

TIME LIMIT FOR PAYMENT OF BONUS

All amounts payable to an employee by way of bonus are to be paid in cash:

(a) Where there is dispute regarding payment of bonus pending before an authority (under the I.D. Act) within one month from the date on which the award becomes enforceable or settlement comes into operation, in respect of such dispute; and

(b) in all other cases within 8 months from the close of the accounting year.

WORKING DAYS AND BONUS

As per the provisions of section 14 of the Payment of Bonus Act, 'working days' include days not worked because of leave (disablement caused by accident arising out of and in the course of employment) and days involved in lay-offs under an agreement or as permitted by standing orders under the relevant laws relating to industrial disputes as applicable to the establishment. The reference to 'working day' appears in section 8 in the context of eligibility for bonus, where it is provided that such eligibility depends upon the employee having worked in the establishment for at least 30 working days (not necessarily continuous) in the year, as well in section 13 which refers to proportionate reduction of the minimum bonus when it is paid on the basis of Rs.100 per adult employee and Rs.60 per non-adult employee respectively, in which case such minimum bonus is proportionately reduced by reference to the number of days worked, as compared to the total number of working days in the year. While section 14 indicates the meaning of 'days worked" as applicable to a particular employee, there is no definition of what constitute the total number of 'working days' in the accounting year. This should, therefore, be calculated under any normally acceptable meaning of this phrase which is appropriate to the facts and circumstances of each case.

HELD TO BE WAGES	HELD NOT TO BE WAGES
Retaining Allowance paid to the workmen of seasonal establishment during off season. *Managing Director, Chalthan Vibhag Sahakari Khand Udyog, Chalthan v. Govt. Labour Officer,* 1981 Lab IC 292.	**Adhoc Allowance, Family Allowance, House Rent Allowance, and Tiffin Allowance** - Cannot be considered as Dearness Allowance. *Scindia Steam Navigation Company Ltd. v. Scindia Employees' Union,* 1983 II LLN 63.
City Compensatory Allowance paid to the employee since it is attached to the post. *S. Krishnamurthy v. Presiding Officer, Central Govt. Labour Court Madras,* 1986 I LLJ 133 (SC).	**Subsistence Allowance** would not amount to remuneration or wages within the meaning of section 2(21) of the Act. *Motor Industries Company Ltd. v. Popat Murlidhar Patil,* 1997 I LLN 749:1997 (2) LLJ 1206 (Bom HC).
Lay Off Compensation paid to the workmen during lay off. 1. *Mohan Kumar v. Dy. Labour Commissioner,* 1991 (62) FLR 903. 2. *P.K. Mohan Kumar v. Deputy Labour Commissioner,* 1996 LLR 765 (Ker HC).	However, in one case, the Gujarat High Court has held that a suspended employee will not be disqualified for bonus. *Project Manager, Oil and Natural Gas Commission v. Sham Kumar Sehgal,* 1995 LLR 618 (Guj HC). **Value of Uniform and Chappals** *T.C. Panuswamy v. Labour Court, Coimbatore,* 1970 (2) LLJ 507. **Commission payable to the Salesmen.** *All India Voltas & Volkart Employees Federation v. Voltas Ltd.,* 1973 Lab IC 645.

PAYMENT OF
GRATUITY
ACT, 1972

CHECK LIST

Sec. 1

Applicability
Every factory, mine, oil field, plantation, port, railways, company, shop, establishment or educational institutions employing 10 or more persons

Sec. 2(s)

Wages for Calculation
@15 days' wages for every completed year as if the month comprises of 26 days at the last drawn wages

Sec. 2(e)

Employee
All employees irrespective of status or salary

Qualifying period
On rendering of 5 years' service, either termination, resignation or retirement

Entitlement
On completion of five years' service except in case of death or disablement

Sec. 4

Calculation Piece-rated employee
@15 days' wages for every completed year on an average of 3 months' wages

Calculation Seasonal employee
@ 7 days' wages for every completed year of service

Rule 4

Display of Notice
On conspicuous place at the main entrance in English language or the language understood by majority of employees of property, etc

Sec.6 Rule 6

Nomination
To be obtained by employer after expiry of one year's service, in Form F

Sec. 4(3)

Total Ceiling
Rs.3,50,000

Rule 9

Mode of Payment
Cash or, if so desired, by Bank Draft or Cheque

Sec. 9

Penalties
- Imprisonment for 6 months or fine upto Rs.10,000 for avoiding to make payment by making false statement or representation
- Imprisonment not less than 3 months and upto one year with fine on default in complying with the provisions of Act or Rules.

Sec.8 Rule 8

Recovery of Gratuity
To apply within 30 days in Form I when not paid within 30 days

Sec. 4(6)

Forfeiture of Gratuity
- On termination of an employee for moral turpitude and riotous or disorderly behaviour
- Wholly or partially for wilfully causing loss, destruction of property, etc

Sec. 13

Protection of Gratuity
Can not be attached in execution of any decree

17. The Payment of Gratuity Act, 1972

The Payment of Gratuity Act as enacted in 1972 applies to every shop or establishment within the meaning of any law for the time being in force in a State in which 10 or more persons are employed or were employed on any day of the preceding 12 months. A shop or establishment to which this Act has become applicable shall continue to be governed by the Act notwithstanding the number of persons employed therein at any time after it has become applicable.

The original Act covered those employees who were getting salary upto Rs. 1,000 and it was increased to Rs. 3,500 per month with effect from 31-12-1992. The total payment of gratuity was restricted to Rs. 50,000. By an amending Act 34 of 1994, effective from 24th May, 1994, the salary limit for eligibility of gratuity to an employee has been removed but total limit of amount of gratuity has been restricted to Rs. 1,00,000. Thereafter by an amendment Act 11 of 1998, effective from 26th September, 1997, the gratuity limit has been raised to Rs. 3,50,000.

Gratuity shall be payable to an employee on termination of his employment after he has rendered continuous service for not less than five years—(a) On his superannuation, or (b) On his retirement, resignation, or (c) On his death or disablement due to accident or disease.

An employer will be liable to pay gratuity to the legal heirs/nominees of the deceased employee even if the employee had not completed five years of service. For every completed year of service or part thereof in excess of six months the employer shall pay gratuity to an employee at the rate of fifteen days' wages based on the rate of wages last drawn by the employee concerned:

Provided that in the case of a piece-rated employee, daily wages shall be computed on the average of the total wages received by him for a period of three months immediately preceding the termination of his employment, and, for this purpose, the wages paid for any overtime work shall not be taken into account:

Provided further that in the case of an employee who is employed in a seasonal establishment and who is not so employed throughout the year, the employer shall pay the gratuity at the rate of seven days' wages for each season.

Explanation.—In the case of a monthly rated employee, the fifteen days' wages shall be calculated by dividing the monthly rate of wages last drawn by him by twenty-six and multiplying the quotient by fifteen.

The amount of gratuity payable to an employee shall not exceed fifty thousand rupees.

For the purpose of computing the gratuity payable to an employee who is employed, after his disablement, on reduced wages, his wages for the period preceding his disablement, shall be taken to be the wages received by him during that period, and his wages for the period subsequent to his disablement shall be taken to be the wages as so reduced.

For payment of gratuity, 'wages' means all emoluments which are earned by an employee while on duty or on leave in accordance with the terms and conditions of his employment and which are paid or are payable to him in cash and includes dearness allowance but does not include any bonus, commission, house rent allowance, overtime wages and any other allowance.

ACTUALLY WORKED – MEANING OF

In Explanation I to section 4 of the Payment of Gratuity Act, the legislature has used the words 'actually employed'. If it was contemplated by Explanation I that it was sufficient that there should be a subsisting contract of employment, then it was not necessary for the legislature to have used the words 'actually employed'. It is not permissible to attribute redundancy to the legislature to defeat the purpose of enacting the explanation. The expression 'actually employed', in Explanation I to section 2(c) must in the context in which it occurs mean 'actually worked'.

ATTACHMENT OF GRATUITY – PAYABLE TO LEGAL HEIRS

If the gratuity is payable to the employee then it is not liable to attachment. But if the employee is dead, obviously the gratuity cannot be deemed to be payable to the employee. If the said gratuity becomes payable to the heirs of the employees the same becomes attachable but the employer is not legally bounded to pay the said gratuity to the legal heirs of the employee.

'AVERAGE MONTHLY WAGES' – CALCULATION

The expression *'average of the monthly basic wages'* can only mean the wage earned by an employee during a month divided by the number of days for which he has worked and multiplied by 26 days in order to arrive at the monthly wages for computation of gratuity payable under a scheme of gratuity framed by the employer. For instance, the calculation of gratuity for an employee having served for 20 years and drawing salary of Rs. 2,600 per month will be as under:

- Rs. 2,600 per month last drawn salary
- Rs. 100 per day x 15 days x 20 years of service.
- Rs. 30,000 gratuity payable.

CONTINUOUS SERVICE – MEANING OF

The term 'continuous service' has been controversial ever since the Payment of Gratuity Act, 1972 has come into force. In one case, the Supreme Court has also interpreted the terms which has led to the amendment of the definition by the Amending Act 25 of 1984 where by a separate section 2A definition of 'continuous service' was added. Again by an Amending Act 22 of 1987 the amendment was made in the definition. In order to determine as to what 'continuous service' means it is imperative to reproduce the section 2A defining 'continuous service' which reads as under:

(1) An employee shall be said to be in continuous service for a period if he has, for that period, been in uninterrupted service, including service which may be interrupted on account of sickness, accident, leave, absence from duty without leave not being absence in respect of which an

order treating the absence as break in service has been passed in accordance with the standing orders, rules or regulations governing the employees of the establishment, lay off, strike or a lock-out or cessation of work not due to any fault of the employee, whether such uninterrupted or interrupted service was rendered before or after the commencement of this Act.

(2) Where an employee not being an employee employed in a seasonal establishment is not in continuous service within the meaning of clause (1) for any period of one year or six months, he shall be deemed to be in continuous service under the employee—

(a) for the said period of one year, if the employer during the period of twelve calendar months preceding the date with reference to which calculation is to be made, has actually worked under the employer for not less than—

   (i) one-hundred and ninety days, in the case of an employee employed below the ground in a mine or an establishment which works for less than six days in a week; and

   (ii) two hundred and forty days, in any other case.

(b) for the said period of six months, if the employee during the period of six calendar months preceding the date with reference to which the calculation is to be made, has actually worked under the employer for not less than—

   (i) ninety-five days, in the case of an employee employed below the ground in a mine or in an establishment which works for less than six days in a week; and

   (ii) one hundred and twenty days, in any other case.

Explanation.—For the purpose of clause (2) the number of days on which an employee has actually worked under an employer shall include the days on which—

   (i) he has been laid off under an agreement or as permitted by standing orders made under the Industrial Employment (Standing Orders) Act, 1946

(20 of 1946) or under the Industrial Disputes Act, 1947 or under any other law applicable to the establishment;

(ii) he has been on leave with full wages, earned in the previous year;

(iii) he has been absent due to temporary disablement caused by accident arising out of and in the course of his employment; and

(iv) in the case of a female, she has been in maternity leave; however, that the total period of such maternity leave does not exceed twelve weeks.

(3) Where an employee employed in a seasonal establishment is not in continuous service within the meaning of clause (1) for any period of one year or six months, he shall be deemed to be in continuous service under the employer for such period if he has actually worked for not less than seventy-five per cent of the number of days on which the establishment was in operation during such period.

DUTY OF AN EMPLOYER TO PAY GRATUITY

Section 4 of the Act casts an obligation on an employer of an establishment to which the Payment of Gratuity Act applies, to consider the case of each individual employee in the matter of payment of gratuity to him. This is a statutory duty or obligation cast on the employer by the Act and the factory, shop or establishment is thereunder bound to consider the case of an employee whether he is entitled to receive gratuity. The employer shall arrange to pay the amount of gratuity within thirty days from the date it becomes payable to the person to whom the gratuity is payable. If the amount of gratuity payable under section 4 is not paid by the employer within the period specified, the employer shall pay, from the date on which the gratuity becomes payable to the date on which it is paid, simple interest at such rate, not exceeding the rate notified by the Central Government from time to time for repayment of long term deposits, as that Government may, by notification specify. The rate of interest for delayed payment of gratuity has been fixed at 10% per annum by amendment by Act 22 of 1987. Be it made clear that the amount of interest payable by the employer shall in no case exceed the amount of gratuity payable under the Act. However, no such interest shall be payable if the delay in the payment is due to the fault of the employee and the employer has obtained permission in writing from the controlling authority for the delayed payment on this ground.

FORFEITURE OF GRATUITY

The gratuity payable to an employee shall be wholly forfeited—

(i) if the service of such employee has been terminated for his riotous or disorderly conduct or any other act of violence on his part; or

(ii) if the services of such employee has been terminated for any act which constitutes an offence involving moral turpitude provided that such offence is committed by him in the course of his employment. In order to forfeit gratuity of an employee, there must be termination order containing the charges as established to the effect that the employee was guilty of any of the aforesaid misconducts. In one case, it has been held that in the absence of termination order containing any of the above allegations, the gratuity of an employee cannot be forfeited.

TIME LIMIT FOR CLAIMING GRATUITY

If an employer fails to pay gratuity to an employee or his legal heirs or the nominee, the Payment of Gratuity Act prescribes time limit of one year for claiming of gratuity and filing an appeal within 60 days from the receipt of the order, to the appellate authority when a person is aggrieved by the order of the controlling authority. Since the Gratuity Act is a beneficial legislation, it does not prohibit the authorities in condoning delay for making claim for gratuity whenever there is sufficient cause in not making the claim or filing of an appeal before the authorities.

MODE FOR PAYMENT OF GRATUITY

The mode for payment of gratuity is prescribed in section 9 of the Payment of Gratuity Act, 1972. The said section contemplates that gratuity payable under the Act should be paid in cash, or if so desired by the payee, by demand draft or bank cheque to the eligible employee, nominee or legal heir, as the case may be. The second proviso to sub-section (1) of section 4 of the Act further lays down that in case of death of the employee, gratuity payable to him should be paid to his nominee, or if no nomination has been made, to his heirs. The use of word, 'eligible' before the expression, 'employee, nominee or legal heir' is also not without significance. In case of death, the gratuity amount payable under the Act has to be paid to the 'eligible' nominee or the guardian of such nominee and where no nomination has been made, to his heirs. A further obligation of the employer is to intimate the details of payment to the controlling authority of the area while making payment of the gratuity amount. Where, however, the eligible employee, his nominee, legal heir or the guardian of the nominee, as the case may be, so desires and the amount of gratuity payable is less than one thousand rupees payment may be made by postal money order after deducting the postal money order commission thereof from the amount payable.

NOTICE OF OPENING, CHANGE OR CLOSURE OF AN ESTABLISHMENT

An employer has to send a notice in Form A to the Controlling Authority of the area within 30 days of the Rules as becoming applicable. In addition to that, Form B is to be submitted within 30 days of any change in the name, address, employer or nature of business whereas an employer has to send Form C intending to close down the business atleast 60 days before intended closure.

NOMINATION

Under rule 6, a nomination shall be in Form F and will be submitted in duplicate within one year from the employment of the employee.

DISPLAY OF NOTICE

There is statutory obligation under rule 4(1) to display a notice conspicuously at or near the main entrance of the establishment in bold letters in English and in language understood by the majority of the employees specifying the name of the officer with designation authorised to receive notices under the Act or the Rules. A fresh notice is required to be displayed as per rule 4(2) of the Rules immediately after the notice referred to in sub-rule (1) becomes illegible or requires a change. The displaying of abstract of the Act and Rules at a conspicuous place at or near the main entrance of the establishment by the employer has also been made obligatory, under rule 20 of the Payment of Gratuity (Central) Rules, 1972. The rule provides that the employer shall display an abstract of the Act and the Rules made thereunder as given in Form 'U' in English and in the language understood by the majority of the employees at a conspicuous place at or near the main entrance of the establishment.

PAYMENT OF WAGES ACT, 1936

CHECKLIST

Applicability of the Act
• Factory • Industrial Establishment • Tramway service or motor transport service engaged in carrying passengers or goods or both by road for hire or reward • Air transport service • Dock, Wharf or Jetty • Inland vessel, mechanically propelled • Mine, quarry or oil-field • Plantation • Workshop or other establishment etc.

Object of the Act
To regulate the payment of wages of certain classes of employed persons.

Time of payment of wages
The wages of every person employed be paid
• When less than 1000 persons are employed, shall be paid before the expiry of the 7th day of the following month.
• When more than 1000 workers, before the expiry of the 10th day of the following month.

Sec. 5

Wages to be paid in current coins or currency notes
• All wages shall be paid in current coins or currency notes or in both.
• After obtaining the authorization, either by cheque or by crediting the wages in employee's bank account.

Sec. 6

Coverage of Employees
Drawing average wage upto Rs. 10,000 per month.

Fines as prescribed by
• Not to be imposed unless the employer is given an opportunity to show cause.
• To record in the register. **Sec. 8**

Deduction made from wages
Deductions such as, fine, deduction for amenities and services supplied by the employer, advances paid, over payment of wages, loan, granted for house-building or other purposes, income tax payable, in pursuance of the order of the Court, PF contributions, cooperative societies, premium for Life Insurance, contribution to any fund constituted by employer or a trade union, recovery of losses, ESI contributions etc.

Sec. 7

Deduction for absence from duties for unauthorised absence
Absence for whole or any part of the day -
• If ten or more persons absent without reasonable cause, deduction of wages upto 8 days.

Sec. 9

Deductions for services rendered
When accommodation amenity or service has been accepted by the employee.

Sec. 11

Deduction for damages or loss
• For default or negligence of an employee resulting into loss.
• Show cause notice has to be given to the employee. **Sec. 10**

PENALTIES (Sec. 20)

On contravention of S. 5 (except sub-sec.4), S.7, S.8 (except sub-sec.8), S.9, S.10 (except sub-sec. 2) and Secs.11 to 13.	Fine not less than Rs.1000 which may extend to Rs.5000. On subsequent conviction fine not less than Rs.5000, may extend to Rs.10,000. On contravention of S.4, S.5(4), S.6, S.8(8), S.10(2) or S.25 fine not less than Rs.1000 - may extend to Rs.5000. On subsequent conviction fine not less than Rs.5000 - may extend to Rs.10,000.
• For failing to maintain registers or records; or • Wilfully refusing or without lawful excuse neglecting to furnish information or return; or • Wilfully furnishing or causing to be furnished any information or return which he knows to be false; or • Refusing to answer or wilfully giving a false answer to any question necessary for obtaining any information required to be furnished under this Act.	• Fine which shall not be less than Rs.1000 but may extend to Rs.5000 - On record conviction fine not less than Rs.5000, may extend to Rs.10,000. • For second or subsequent conviction, fine not less than Rs.5000 but may extend to Rs.10,000.
• Wilfully obstructing an Inspector in the discharge of his duties under this Act; or • Refusing or wilfully neglecting to afford an Inspector any reasonable facility for making any entry, inspection etc. • Wilfully refusing to produce on the demand of an Inspector any register or other document kept in pursuance of this Act; or preventing any person for appearance etc.	Fine not less than Rs.1000 extendable upto Rs.5000 - On subsequent conviction fine not less than Rs.5000 - may extend to Rs.10,000.
• On conviction for any offence and again guilty of contravention of same provision. • Failing or neglecting to pay wages to any employee.	• Imprisonment not less than one month extendable upto six months and fine not less than Rs.2000 extendable upto Rs.15000. • Additional fine upto Rs.100 for each day.

18. The Payment of Wages Act, 1936

For the working class there cannot be any injustice greater than that which deprives a worker of his or her wages due to him from his employer. Also, it causes more hardship and distress than delays in receiving the wages a person needs for day-to-day living. Therefore, the Payment of Wages Act, 1936 has a historical background.

The Government found it necessary to regulate the payment of wage in industry because there were many abuses, payments denied or delayed, arbitrary deductions, heavy fines, and payment in kind instead of cash.

OBJECT OF THE ACT

The Payment of Wages Act regulates the payment of wages to certain classes of persons employed in industry and its importance cannot be under-estimated. The Act guarantees payment of wages on time and without any deductions except those authorised under the Act. The Act provides for the responsibility for payment of wages, fixation of wage period, time and mode of payment of wages, permissible deduction as also casts upon the employer a duty to seek the approval of the Government for the acts and permission for which fines may be imposed by him and also sealing of the fines, and also for a machinery to hear and decide complaints regarding the deduction from wages or in delay in payment of wages, penalty for malicious and vexatious claims. The Act does not apply to persons whose wage is Rs. 10,000 or more per month. The Act also provides to the effect that a worker cannot contract out of any right conferred upon him under the Act.

APPLICABILITY OF THE ACT

The Act applies to Railways, factories, mines and following establishments:—

(a) tramway or motor transport service engaged in carrying passengers or goods or both by road for hire or reward;

(b) dock, wharf or jetty;

(c) inland vessel, mechanically propelled;

(d) mine, quarry or oil-fields;

(e) plantation;

(f) workshop or other establishment in which articles are produced, adapted or manufactured with a view to their use, transport or sale;

(g) establishment in which any work relating to the construction, development or maintenance of building, road, bridges or canals or relating to operations connected with navigations, irrigation or other supply of water, or relating to the generation, transmission and distribution of electricity or any other form of power, is being carried on;

(h) any other establishment covered by Central/State Government through notification in Official Gazette.

WAGES

"Wages" means all remuneration (whether by way of salary, allowances or otherwise) expressed in terms of money and includes —

(a) any remuneration payable under any award or settlement between the parties;

(b) remuneration in respect of overtime, holiday, or any leave period;

(c) additional remuneration payable under terms of employment (whether called a bonus or by any other name);

(d) sum payable under any law by reason of termination of employment but not providing any time limit;

(e) sum under the scheme if any, but does not include —

    (i) any bonus (whether under a scheme of profit sharing or otherwise) which does not form part of the remuneration payable under term of employment or which is not payable under any award or settlement between the parties or orders of a court;

    (ii) value of house accommodation or of the supply of light, water, medical attendance or other amenity or of any service excluded from the computation of wages by a general or special order of the State Government;

(iii) Provident Fund;

(iv) travelling allowance or value of travelling concession;

(v) special expenses on account of the nature of his employment;

(vi) gratuity.

TIMELY PAYMENT OF WAGES

Wages must be paid—

(a) before the expiry of the seventh day after the last day of the wage-period, if less than 1000 workmen are employed and in other case on the 10th day;

(b) in current coin or currency notes and by cheques or by crediting the wages in the employee's bank account after obtaining his written authority;

(c) on a working day;

(d) before the expiry of the second day, to the person whose employment is terminated.

No wage-period should exceed one month.

RESPONSIBILITY FOR PAYMENT OF WAGES

Every employer shall be responsible for the payment of all wages required to be paid under this Act to persons employed by him and in case of persons employed,—

(a) in factories, if a person has been named as the manager of the factory under clause (f) of sub-section (1) of section 7 of the Factories Act, 1948 (63 of 1948);

(b) in industrial or other establishments, if there is a person responsible to the employer for the supervision and control of the industrial or other establishment;

(c) upon railways (other than in factories), if the employer is the railway administration and the railway administration has nominated a person in this behalf for the local area concerned;

(d) in the case of contractor, a person designated by such contractor who is directly under his charge; and

(e) in any other case,

a person designated by the employer as a person responsible for complying with the provisions of the Act, the person so named, the person responsible to the employer, the person so nominated or the person so designated, as the case may be, shall be responsible for such payment.

DEDUCTIONS FROM WAGES

The following are the main deductions as allowed:—

- fines;
- deduction for the actual period of absence;
- deduction for damage or loss of goods expressly entrusted to the employed person for custody, or for loss of money for which he is required to account, where such damage or loss is directly attributed to his negligence or default;
- deduction for house-accommodation;
- deduction for amenities and services supplied by the employer as agreed by to between the employer and the employed person. However, the services do not include the supply of tools and raw materials required for the purposes of employment;
- deduction for recovery of advances and interest, and for adjustment of over-payment of wages;
- deduction for recovery of loans from any fund constituted for the welfare of labour as agreed to between the employer and the employed person;
- deduction for recovery of loans for house building or for other purposes as agreed to between employer and the employed person;
- deduction for income-tax;
- deduction on orders of a court or other authority;
- deduction for subscription and repayment of advance from any Provided Fund;
- deduction for payments to co-operative societies as agreed to between employer and the employed person;
- deduction of premium for LIC policy on written authorisation of the employed person, or for Post Office Savings Scheme;

- deduction on written authorisation by the employee for contribution to any fund constituted by the employer or trade union for welfare of employed persons as agreed to between employer and the employed persons;
- deduction on written authorisation of the employed person for payment of fees for membership of trade union as agreed to between employer and the employed person;
- deduction made on written authorisation of the employed person, for contribution to Prime Minister's National Relief Fund or for such other fund as the Central Government may notify in the Official Gazette.

Total amount of deductions should not exceed 75% of wages of the employed person in any wage-period if whole or part of the deductions are meant for payments to co-operative societies. In other cases it should not exceed 50%.

(For full details *refer* to section 7 of the Act).

LEVY OF FINES
Fines can be imposed only for acts and omissions the list of which has been approved by the appropriate Government. Fines should not exceed 3% of the wages in a month; be recovered within 90 days of the date of the act or omission; be imposed after a proper show cause procedure and cannot be imposed on an employed person of less than 15 years of age.

DEDUCTION FOR DAMAGE AND LOSS
If any employee causes damage or loss to the employer due to his negligence the employer may deduct such damage or loss after giving the employee an opportunity of showing cause.

CLAIM
Claims arising out of deduction from wages or delay in payment of wages and penalty for malicious claims will be heard and decided by the authority appointed by the appropriate Government for any specified area.

Employees of the same unpaid group may file joint application for realisation of the dues and compensation.

EMPLOYER'S OBLIGATIONS
1. To fix the wage-period not exceeding one month (section 5).

2. To pay wages in cash or by cheque after taking written authorisation of the employed person (section 6).

3. To pay wages on any working day.

4. To make deductions permissible only under section 7 from the wages of the employed person.

5. To ensure that deductions do not exceed 75% where payment to a co-operative society is to be made, and in other cases, deductions do not exceed 50%.

6. To seek, before imposing fines, approval of list of acts and omissions from the prescribed authority.

7. Not to impose fines exceeding 3% of the wages on the employee.

8. To give show-cause notice to the employed person before imposing fines.

9. To recover fines within 60 days of the date of offence.

10. To afford facilities to Inspectors for entry, inspection, supervision, examination or inquiry under the Act.

11. To display abstract of the Act and the Rules in English and in a language understood by the majority of workmen.

12. To maintain following registers in the prescribed forms:—

    (i) Register of wages;

    (ii) Register of fines;

    (iii) Register of deduction for damage or loss;

    (iv) Register of advances.

PENALTIES FOR CONTRAVENTION OF
THE PROVISIONS OF THE ACT

CONTRAVENTION/OFFENCE	FINE & PUNISHMENT OR BOTH
On contravention of S. 5 (except sub-sec. 4), S. 7, S. 8 (except sub-sec. 8), S. 9, S. 10 (except sub-sec. 2) and Secs. 11 to 13.	Fine not less than Rs. 1,000 which may extend to Rs. 5,000. On subsequent conviction fine not less than Rs. 5,000, may extend to Rs. 10,000. On contravention S.4, S.5(4), S.6, S.8(8), S.10(2) or S.25 fine not less than Rs. 1,000 - may extend to Rs.5000. On subsequent conviction fine not less than Rs. 5,000 - may extend to Rs. 10,000.
• For failing to maintain registers or records; or • Wilfully refusing or without lawful excuse neglecting to furnish information or return; or • Wilfully furnishing or causing to be furnished any information or return which he knows to be false; or • Refusing to answer or wilfully giving a false answer to any question necessary for obtaining any information required to be furnished under this Act.	• Fine which shall not less than Rs. 1,000 but may extend to Rs. 5,000. On record conviction fine not less than Rs.5,000, may extend to Rs. 10,000. • For second or subsequent conviction, fine not less than Rs. 5,000 but may extend to Rs. 10,000.
• Wilfully obstructimg an Inspector in the discharge of his duties under this Act; or • Refusing or wilfully neglecting to afford an Inspector any reasonable facility for making any entry, inspection etc. • Wilfully refusing to produce on the demand of an Inspector any register or other document kept in pursuance of this Act; or preventing any person for appearance, etc.	• Fine not less than Rs. 1,000 extendable upto Rs. 5,000 - On subsequent conviction fine not less than Rs. 5,000 - may extend to Rs. 10,000.
• On conviction for any offence and again guilty of contravention of same provision. • Failing or neglecting to pay wages to any employee.	• Imprisonment not less than one month extendable upto six months and fine not less than Rs. 2,000 extendable upto Rs. 15,000. • Additional fine upto Rs. 100 for each day.

CHECKLIST

SALES PROMOTION EMPLOYEES (CONDITIONS OF SERVICE) ACT, 1976 & THE RULES

Object of the Act
To regulate certain conditions of service of sales promotion employees in certain establishments.

Applicability of the Act
Whole of India with effect from 6-3-1976.

Applicability of other Acts
- Workmen's Compensation Act, 1923
- Industrial Disputes Act, 1947
- Minimum Wages Act, 1948
- Maternity Benefit Act, 1961
- Payment of Bonus Act, 1965
- Payment of Gratuity Act, 1972

Maintenance of register
- A register of sales promotion employees in Form B.
- Service Books for every employee in Form C.
- A register of service books in Form D.
- Leave account of each employee in Form E.
  Sec. 7 Rule 23

Wages for weekly day of rest
Entitled to wages on weekly days of rest as if he was on duty.
Rule 7

Affixing of holidays to leave
Prefixing or suffixing of any leave not permissible.
Rule 11

Quarantine leave
Upto 30 days on the recommendations of authorised medical attendant or Public Health Officer.
Rule 16

Leave
- Earned leave and cash compensation on earned leave not availed of.
- On full wages for not less than 1/11th of the period spent on duty.
- Leave on medical certificate
- Cn one-half of the wages for not less than 1/18th of the period of service.
- Cashable on voluntary relinquishment or termination other than by way of punishment.
  Sec. 4

Number of holidays in a year
10 in a calendar year.
Rule 4

Compensatory holidays
Within 30 days of the day when he was required to work.
Rule 5

Application for leave
When other than casual leave, not less than one month before commencement of leave except for urgent or unforeseen circumstances.
Rule 9

Holidays intervening during the period of leave
Except casual leave granted or day of weekly rest, other holidays shall be part of leave. **Rule 12**

Extraordinary leave
At the discretion of the employer.
Rule 17

Maximum limit upto which earned leave
- Can be accumulated 180 days of which the employee can avail himself 90 days at a time.
- Encashment of leave 120 days.
  Rule 14

Issue of Appointment Letter in Form A
Within three months from the commencement of the Act and in other case on appointment.
Sec. 5 Rule 22

Wages for holidays
To be entitled for wages on all holidays as if he was on duty.
Rule 6

Recording of reason for refusal or postponement of leave
Rule 10

Medical leave
On production of medical certificate.
Rule 15

Casual leave
15 days in a calendar year.
Rule 20

PENALTY
On contravention of provisions relating to 'Leave', Issue of Appointment Letter or Maintenance of Registers fine upto Rs.1000.

19. The Sales Promotion Employees (Conditions of Service) Act, 1976

THE OBJECT

As a result of the Supreme Court judgment in the case of *May and Baker (India) Limited* v. *Their Workmen,* 1961 (2) LLJ 94, the persons engaged in sales promotion did not come within the purview of the definition of "workman" under the Industrial Disputes Act, 1947 and as such they did not have any protection regarding security of employment and other benefits under that Act. These persons, particularly the medical representatives in the pharmaceutical industry have been demanding from time to time that they should be covered by Industrial Disputes Act. On a petition made by the Federation of Medical Representatives Associations of India, the Committee on Petitions (Rajya Sabha) in its thirteenth report submitted on March 14, 1972, came to the conclusion that "the ends of social justice to this class of people will not be met only by suitably amending the definition of the term "workman" in the Industrial Disputes Act, 1947, in a manner that the medical representatives are also covered by the definition of 'workman' in the said Act". It was, therefore considered, more appropriate to have a separate legislation for governing the conditions of service of sales promotion employees instead of amending Industrial Disputes Act to bring such employees within its purview. The Act has been amended by Act No. 48 of 1986 as published in Gazette of India, Extraordinary, Part II, Section 1, dated 24-11-1986.

The Act extends to whole of India and applies at the first instance to every establishment engaged in pharmaceutical industry. The Central Government may by notification in the Official Gazette apply the provisions of the Sales Promotion Employees (Conditions of Service) Act, 1976, with effect from such date as may be specified in the notification to any other establishment engaged in any notified industry.

IMPORTANT WORDS AND PHRASES UNDER THE ACT

(a) "Sales promotion employees" mean any person by whatever name called (including an apprentice) employed or engaged in any establishment for hire or reward to do any work relating to promotion of sales or business or both, but does not include any such person—

(i) who, being employed or engaged in a supervisory capacity, draws wages exceeding sixteen hundred rupees per mensem; or

(ii) who is employed or engaged mainly in a managerial or administrative capacity.

Explanation.—For the purpose of this clause, the wages per mensem of a person shall be deemed to be the amount equal to thirty times his total wages (whether or not including, or comprising only of commission) in respect of the continuous period of his service falling within the period of twelve months immediately preceding the date with reference to which the calculation is to be made, divided by the number of days comprising that period of service;

(b) all words and expressions used but not defined in this Act, and defined in the Industrial Disputes Act, 1947 (14 of 1947), shall have the meanings respectively assigned to them in that Act.

ISSUE OF APPOINTMENT LETTER

Every employer in relation to a sales promotion employee shall furnish to such employee letter of appointment, in such form as may be prescribed—

(a) in a case where he holds appointment as such at the commencement of this Act, within three months of such commencement; and

(b) in any other case, on his appointment as such.

MAINTENANCE OF REGISTER

Every employer in relation to an establishment shall keep and maintain such registers and other documents and in such manner as may be prescribed. Rule 23 of the Sales Promotion Employees (Conditions of Service) Act provides that an establishment shall prepare and maintain following registers and records:—

(a) A register of Sales Promotion Employees in Form B;

(b) Service book for every employee in Form C;

(c) A register of service book in Form D;

(d) Leave account of each employee in Form E.

PENALTY

If any employer contravenes the provisions of section 4 (pertaining to grant of leave) or section 5 (pertaining to issue of appointment letters) or section 7 (pertaining to maintenance of registers) or any rules made under the said Act, he shall be punishable to fine which may extend to one thousand rupees.

OFFENCES BY COMPANIES

(1) Where an offence under this Act has been committed by a company, every person who, at the time the offence was committed, was in charge of, and was responsible to, the company for the conduct of the business of the company, as well as the company, shall be deemed to be guilty of the offence and shall be liable to be proceeded against and punished accordingly:

Provided that nothing contained in this sub-section shall render any such person liable to any punishment provided in this section, if he proves that the offence was committed without his knowledge or that he exercised all due diligence to prevent the commission of such offence.

(2) Notwithstanding anything contained in sub-section (1), where an offence under this Act has been committed by a company and it proved that the offence has been committed with the consent or connivance of, or is attributable to, any neglect on

the part of any director, manager, secretary or other officer of the company, such director, management, secretary or other officer shall also be deemed to be guilty of such offence and shall be liable to be proceeded against and punished accordingly.

(3) For the purposes of this section—

    (a) "company" means any body corporate and includes a firm or other association of individuals; and

    (b) "director", in relation to a firm, means a partner in the firm.

TRADE UNIONS ACT, 1926

Object of the Act

To provide for the registration of Trade Union and in certain respects to define the law relating to registered Trade Unions.

Registration of trade union

- Any **7** or more members of a trade union may, by subscribing their names to the rules of the trade union and its compliance.

- There should be at least **10%**, or **100** of the workmen, whichever is less, engaged or employed in the establishment or industry with which it is connected.

- It has on the date of making application not less than **7** persons as its members, who are workmen engaged or employed in the establishment or industry with which it is connected.

Sec. 4

Application for registration

Prescribed form with following details:

- Names, occupations and addresses of the members' place of work;

- Address of its head office; and

- Names, ages, addresses and occupations of its office bearers.

Sec. 5

Minimum requirements for membership of trade union

Not less than **10%**, or **100** of the workmen, whichever is less, subject to a minimum of **7**, engaged or employed in an establishment etc.

Sec. 9A

Cancellation of registration

- If the certificate has been obtained by fraud or mistake or it has ceased to exist or has willfully contravened any provision of this Act

- If it ceases to have the requisite number of members.

Sec. 10

Criminal conspiracy in trade disputes

No office-bearer or member of a registered trade union shall be liable to punishment under sub-section (2) of conspiracy u/s 120B of IPC in respect of any agreement made between the members for the purpose of furthering any such object of the Trade Union.

Sec. 17

Disqualification of office-bearers of Trade Union

- If one has not attained the age of **18** years.

- Conviction for an offence involving moral turpitude.

- Not applicable when **5** years have elapsed.

Sec.21-A

Returns

Annually to the Registrar, on or before such date as may be prescribed, a general statement, audited in the prescribed manner, of all receipts and expenditure of every registered Trade Union during the year ending on the **31st December**.

Sec. 28

Penalties	Offence	Punishment
Sec. 31	▪ For making false entry in or any omission in general statement required for sending returns.	▪ Fine upto Rs.500. On continuing default, additional fault, Rs.5 for each week (not exceeding Rs.50).
	▪ For making false entry in the form.	• Fine upto Rs.500.
Sec. 32	▪ Supplying false information regarding Trade Union.	• Fine upto Rs.200.

20. The Trade Unions Act, 1926

The trade unions in India came into existence long before independence in 1926 when Trade Unions Act was passed. It provides that any seven persons can form a trade union and get it registered. The Act has granted immunity from criminal prosecution for any agreement furthering trade union objectives, and from civil suit for action which would induce workers to break contract of employment or otherwise interfere with trade, business or employment.

Since trade unions had no legal protection before 1926, the purpose of the Trade Unions Act was to give the trade unions a legal status. Thus a registered trade union becomes a legal person and it can act or dispose of property and exist as a legal body distinct from the members of which the union is composed.

The Constitution of free India also recognises the right of a citizen to form a union since the right to form and continue a trade union is a fundamental right guaranteed under Article 19(l)(c) of the Constitution of our country which can only be subjected to reasonable restriction in the public interest as provided by Article 19(1)(6) of the Constitution. Provision is also made in the Indian Trade Unions Act, 1926, for providing them immunities from criminal prosecution in certain circumstances which further ensure the safe conduct of the trade unions. Under the various laws, the trade unions are required to get themselves registered for certain purposes. Every trade union is required to register itself under the Trade Unions Act in order to operate as a trade union.

"Trade Union" means any combination, whether temporary or permanent, formed primarily for the purpose of regulating the relations between workmen and employers or between workmen and workmen, or between employers and employers, or for imposing restrictive conditions on the conduct of any trade or business, and includes any federation of two or more trade unions.

IMPORTANT DEFINITIONS

'Appropriate Government' means, in relation to Trade Unions whose objects are not confined to one State, the Central Government, and in relation to other Trade Unions, the State Government, and unless there is anything repugnant in the subject or context.

'office bearer' means in the case of a Trade Union, which is registered under this Act as the Head Office thereof.

'Registered Office' means that office of a Trade Union, which is registered under this Act as the Head Office thereof.

'registered trade union' means a Trade Union registered under this Act.

'registrar' means (i) a Registrar of Trade Unions appointed by the appropriate Government under section 3 and includes any Additional or Deputy Registrar of Trade Unions, and (ii) in relation to any Trade Union, the Registrar appointed for the State in which the head or registered office, as the case may be, of Trade Union is situated.

'trade dispute' means any dispute between employers and workmen or between workmen and workmen, or between employers and employers, which is connected with the employment or non-employment, or the terms of employment, or the conditions of labour, of any person.

'workmen' means all persons employed in trade or industry whether or not in the employment of the employer with whom the trade dispute arises.

REGISTRATION OF A TRADE UNION

(1) Any seven or more members of a Trade Union may, by subscribing their names to the rules of the Trade Union and by otherwise complying with the provisions of this

Act with respect to registration, apply for registration of the Trade Union under this Act.

(2) Where an application has been made under sub-section (1) for the registration of a Trade Union, such application shall not be deemed to have become invalid merely by reason of the fact that, at any time after the date of the application, but before the registration of the Trade Union, some of the applicants, but not exceeding half of the total number of persons who made the application, have ceased to be members of the Trade Union or have given notice in writing to the Registrar dis-associating themselves from the application.

Be it made clear that even after its registration there is no provision of recognition of trade union. Thus recognition of a trade union is, by and large, a matter of agreement between the employer and the trade union except in the State of Madhya Pradesh and Maharashtra where there is a separate legislation in this context. However, in public undertakings, recognition to trade unions is accorded under the 'Code of Discipline in Industries' but that too is by mutual agreement since the Code of Discipline in Industries has no legal force.

APPLICATION FOR REGISTRATION

(1) Every application for registration of a Trade Union shall be made to the Registrar, and shall be accompanied by a copy of the rules of the Trade Union and a statement of the following particulars, namely:—

    (a) the names, occupations and addresses of members making the application;

    (b) the name of the Trade Union and the address of its head office; and

    (c) the titles, names, ages, addresses and occupations of the office bearers of the Trade Union.

(2) Where a Trade Union has been in existence for more than one year before the making of an application for its registration, there shall be delivered to the Registrar, together with the application, a general statement of the assets and liabilities of the Trade Union prepared in such form and containing such particulars as may be prescribed.

PROVISIONS TO BE CONTAINED IN THE RULES OF A TRADE UNION

A Trade Union shall not be entitled to registration under this Act, unless the executive thereof is constituted in accordance with the provisions of the Trade Unions Act, the rules thereof provide for the following matters, namely :—

(a) the name of the Trade Union;

(b) the whole of the objects for which the Trade Union has been established;

(c) the whole of the purposes for which the general funds of the Trade Union shall be applicable, all of which purposes shall be purposes to which such funds are lawfully applicable under this Act;

(d) the maintenance of a list of the members of the Trade Union and adequate facilities for the inspection thereof by the office bearers and members of the Trade Union;

(e) the admissions of ordinary members who shall be persons actually engaged or employed in an industry with which the Trade Union is connected and also the admission of the number of honorary or temporary members as office bearers required under section 22 to form the executive of the Trade Union;

(ee) the payment of a subscription by members of the Trade Union which shall not be less than twenty-five paise per month per member;

(f) the conditions under which any member shall be entitled to any benefit assured by the rules and under which any fine or forfeiture may be imposed on the members;

(g) the manner in which the rules shall be amended, varied or rescinded;

(h) the manner in which the members of the executive and the other office bearers of the Trade Union shall be appointed and removed;

(i) the safe custody of the funds of the Trade Union, and annual audit in such a manner as may be prescribed, of the accounts thereof, and adequate facilities for the inspection of the account books by the office bearers and members of the Trade Union; and

(j) the manner in which the Trade Union may be dissolved.

REGISTRATION AND ITS CERTIFICATE

The Registrar, on being satisfied that the Trade Union has complied with all the requirements of the Act, in regard to registration shall register the Trade Union by entering in a register to be maintained in such form as may be prescribed, the particulars relating to the Trade Union contained in the statement accompanying the application for registration. The Registrar, on registering a Trade Union under section 8, shall issue a certificate of registration in the prescribed form which shall be conclusive evidence that the Trade Union has been duly registered under this Act.

CANCELLATION OF REGISTRATION

A certificate of registration of a Trade Union may be withdrawn or cancelled by the Registrar —

(a) on the application of the Trade Union to be verified in such manner as may be prescribed, or

(b) if the Registrar is satisfied that the certificate has been obtained by fraud or mistake, or that the Trade Union has ceased to exist or has wilfully and after notice from the Registrar contravened any provision of this Act or allowed any rule to continue in force which is inconsistent with any such provision; or has rescinded any rule providing for any matter, provision for which is required by section 6:

Provided that not less than two months' previous notice in writing specifying the ground on which it is proposed to withdraw or cancel the certificate shall be given by the Registrar to the Trade Union before the certificate is withdrawn or cancelled otherwise than on the application of the Trade Union.

REGISTERED OFFICE

All communications and notices to a registered Trade Union may be addressed to its registered office. Notice of any change in the address of the head office shall be given within fourteen days of such change to the Registrar in writing, and the changed address shall be recorded in the register referred to in section 8.

CRIMINAL CONSPIRACY IN TRADE DISPUTES

No office bearer or member of a registered Trade Union shall be liable to punishment under sub-section (2) of section 20B of the Indian Penal Code (45 of 1860), in respect of any agreement made between the members for the purpose of furthering any such object of the Trade Union as is specified in section 15 of the Trade Unions Act unless the agreement is an agreement to commit an offence.

IMMUNITY FROM CIVIL SUIT IN CERTAIN CASES

No suit or other legal proceeding shall be maintainable in any Civil Court against any registered Trade Union or any office bearer or any member thereof in respect of any act done in contemplation or furtherance of a trade dispute to which any member of the Trade Union is a party on the ground only that such act induces some other person to break a contract of employment, or that it is in interference with the trade, business or employment of some other person or with the right of some other person to dispose of his capital or of his labour as he wills.

RETURNS

(1) There shall be sent annually to the Registrar on or before such date as may be prescribed, a general statement audited in the prescribed manner, of all receipts and expenditures of every registered Trade Union during the year ending on the 31st day of December next preceding such prescribed date and of the assets and liabilities of the Trade Union existing on such 31st day of December. The statement shall be prepared in such form and shall comprise such particulars as may be prescribed.

(2) Together with the general statement there shall be sent to the Registrar a statement showing all changes of office bearers made by the Trade Union during the year to which the general statement refers, together with a copy of the rules of the Trade Union corrected up to the date of the despatch thereof.

(3) A copy of every alteration made in the rules of a registered Trade Union shall be sent to the Registrar within fifteen days of the making of the alteration.

(4) For the purpose of examining the documents referred to in sub-sections (1), (2) and (3), the Registrar or any officer authorised by him, by general or special order, may at all reasonable times inspect the certificate of registration, account books, registers, and other documents, relating to a Trade Union at its registered office or may require their production at such place as he may specify in this behalf, but no such place shall be at a distance of more than ten miles from the registered office of a Trade Union.

FAILURE TO SUBMIT RETURNS

(1) If default is made on the part of any registered Trade Union in giving any notice or sending any statement or other document as required by or under any provision of this Act, every office bearer or other person bound by the rules of the Trade Union to give or send the same, or, if there is no such office bearer or person, every member of the executive of the Trade Union, shall be punishable with fine which may extend to five rupees and, in the case of a continuing default, with an additional fine which may extend to five rupees for each week after the first during which the default continues:

Provided that the aggregate fine shall not exceed fifty rupees.

(2) Any person who wilfully makes, or causes to be made, any false entry in, or any omission from, the general statement required by section 28 pertaining to 'Returns' or in or from any copy of rules or of alterations of rules sent to the Registrar under that section, shall be punishable with fine which may extend to five hundred rupees.

SUPPLYING FALSE INFORMATION REGARDING TRADE UNIONS

Any person who with intent to deceive, gives to any member of a registered Trade Union or to any person intending or applying to become a member of such Trade Union any document purporting to be a copy of the rules of the Trade Union or of any alterations to the same which he knows, or has reason to believe is not a correct copy of such rules or alterations as are for the time being in force or any person who, with like intent gives a copy of any rules of an unregistered Trade Union to any person on the pretence that such rules are the rules of a registered Trade Union, shall be punishable with fine which may extend to two hundred rupees.

COGNIZANCE OF OFFENCES

(1) No court inferior to that of a Presidency Magistrate or a Magistrate of the first class shall try an offence under this Act.

(2) No court shall take cognizance of any offence under this Act, unless complaint thereof has been made by, or with the previous sanction of, the Registrar or, in the case of an offence under section 32, pertaining to supplying false information regarding Trade Unions, by the person to whom the copy was given, within six months of the date on which the offence is alleged to have been committed.

PRESCRIBED FORM A FOR APPLICATION FOR REGISTRATION OF TRADE UNION

Dated the...............................day of.......................20.....

1. We hereby apply for the registration of a Trade Union under the name of

2. The address of the head office of the Union is ....

3. The Union came into existence on the........ day of..... 20...

4. The Union is a Union of employees (workers engaged in the industry or profession).

5. The particulars required by section 5(1)(c) of the Indian Trade Unions Act, 1926.

6. The particulars given in Schedule II show the provision made in the rules for the matters detailed in section 6 of the Indian Trade Unions Act, 1926.

7. (To be struck out in the case of Unions which have not been in existence for one year before the date of application) The particulars required by section 5(2) of the Indian Trade Unions Act, 1926, are given in Schedule III.

8. We have been duly authorised to make the application.

	Signature	Occupation	Address
1			
2			
3			
4			
5			
6			
7			

To the Registrar of Central Trade Unions.

SCHEDULE I

LIST OF OFFICERS

Title	Name	Age	Address	Occupation

Note: Enter in this Schedule the names of all members of the executive of the Union showing in Column I the names of any posts held by them (*e.g.*, President, Secretary, Treasurer, etc.) in addition to their offices as members of the executive.

WORKMEN'S COMPENSATION ACT, 1923

CHECKLIST

Applicability

All over India
Sec.1

Coverage of Workmen

All workers irrespective of their status or salaries either directly or through contractor or a person recruited to work abroad.
Sec.1(3)

Employer's liability to pay compensation to a workman

On death or personal injury resulting into total or partial disablement or occupational disease caused to a workman arising out of and during the course of employment.
Sec.3

Amount of compensation

- Where death of a workman results from the injury
  - an amount equal to fifty per cent of the monthly wages of the deceased workman multiplied by the relevant factor or an amount of eighty thousand rupees, whichever is more.
- Where permanent total disablement results from the injury.
  - an amount equal to sixty per cent of the monthly wages of the injured workman multiplied by the relevant factor or an amount of ninety thousand rupees, whichever is more.

Procedure for calculation
Higher the age - Lower the compensation

- Relevant factor specified in second column of Schedule IV giving slabs depending upon the age of the concerned workman.
- Example : In case of death
  - Wages Rs.3000 PM • Age 23 years
  - Factor as schedule IV Rs.219.95
  - Amount of compensation Rs.329935
  - In case of total disablement Rs.395910

Sec.4

When an employee is not liable for compensation

- In respect of any injury which does result in the total or partial disablement of the workman for a period exceeding three days.
- In respect of any injury, not resulting in death or permanent total disablement caused by an accident which is directly attributable to—
  - The workman having been at the time thereof under the influence of drink or drugs, or
- Wilful disobedience of the workman to an order expressly given, or to a rule expressly framed, for the purpose of securing the safety of workmen, or
- Wilful removal or disregard by the workman of any safety guard or other device which he knew to have been provided for the purpose of securing the safety of workman.

Sec. 3(a) & (b)

Wages

When the monthly wages are more than Rs.4000 per month it will be deemed Rs.4000.
Sec.4 Exh.b

Notice of accident

As soon as practicable
Sec.10

Report of accident
Rule 11 Form EE

Report of fatal accident and serious injury within 7 days to the Commissioner (not applicable when ESI Act applies).
Sec.10B

Bar upon contracting out

Any workman relinquishing his right for personal injury not permissible.
Sec.14

PENALTY

- In case of default by employer
- Deposit of Compensation

- 50% of the compensation amount + interest to be paid to the workman or his dependents as the case may be.
- Within one month with the Compensation Commissioner.

Sec.4A

21. The Workmen's Compensation Act, 1923

■

THE OBJECT

This Act provides compensation to certain classes of workmen by their employers for injury which may be suffered by the workmen as a result of an accident during the course of employment. The general principle is that a workman who suffers injury in course of his employment should be entitled to compensation and in case of a fatal injury his dependents should be compensated. The Act provides security to the workmen who receive partial incapacity resulting in a loss in the earning capacity. The compensation becomes payable under the Act not because of a tort or wrong doing by the employer. The liability under the Act has no connection with any wrong doing on the part of the employer. A workman means any person who is employed otherwise than for the purpose of employer's trade or business and is employed in any such capacity as is specified in Schedule II. Also a person recruited for work abroad by a company will also be covered by this Act. The rate of compensation is provided in the Schedule IV appended to the Act.

IMPORTANT DEFINITIONS AND CLARIFICATIONS

"Compensation" means compensation as provided by this Act.

"Dependent" means any of the following relatives of a deceased workman, namely:—

(i) a widow, a minor legitimate or adopted son, an unmarried legitimate or adopted daughter or a widowed mother; and

(ii) if wholly dependent on the earnings of the workman at the time of his death, a son or a daughter who has attained the age of 18 years and who is infirm;

(iii) if wholly or in part dependent on the earnings of the workman at the time of his death;

    (a) a widower;

    (b) a parent other than a widowed mother;

    (c) a minor illegitimate son, an unmarried illegitimate daughter or a daughter legitimate or illegitimate or adopted if married and a minor or if widowed and a minor;

    (d) a minor brother or an unmarried sister or a widowed sister if a minor;

    (e) a widowed daughter-in-law;

    (f) a minor child of a pre-deceased son;

    (g) a minor child of a pre-deceased daughter where no parent of the child is alive; or

    (h) a paternal grandparent if no parent of the workman is alive.

Explanation.—"For the purposes of sub-clause (ii) and items (f) and (g) of sub-clause (iii), references to a son, daughter or child include an adopted son, daughter or child respectively.

"Employer" includes a body of persons whether incorporated or not and any managing agent of an employer and the legal representative of a deceased employer, and when the services of a workman are temporarily lent on hire to another person by the person with whom the workman has entered into a contract of service of apprenticeship, means such other person while the workman is working for him.

"Managing Agent" means any person appointed or acting as the representative of another person for the purpose of carrying on such other person's trade or business, but does not include an individual manager subordinate to an employer.

"Partial disablement" means where the disablement is of a temporary nature, such disablement as reduces the earning capacity of a workman in any employment in which he was engaged at the time of the accident resulting in the disablement, and, where the disablement is of a permanent nature, such disablement as reduces his earning capacity in every employment which he was capable of undertaking at that time :

Provided that every injury specified in Part II of Schedule I shall be deemed to result in permanent partial disablement.

"Qualified Medical Practitioner" means any person registered under any Central Act, or an Act of the Legislature of a State providing for the maintenance of a register of a medical practitioner, or, any area where no such last mentioned Act is in force, any person declared by the State Government, by notification in the Official Gazette, to be a Qualified Medical Practitioner for the purposes of this Act.

"Seaman" means any person forming any part of the crew of any ship, but does not include the master of the ship.

"Total Disablement" means such disablement, whether of a temporary or permanent nature, as incapacitates a workman for all work which he was capable of performing at the time of the accident resulting in such disablement:

Provided that permanent total disablement shall be deemed to result from every injury specified in Part I of Schedule I or from any combination of injuries specified in Part II thereof where the aggregate percentage of the loss of earning capacity, as specified in the said Part II against those injuries amount to one hundred per cent, or more.

"Wages" includes any privilege or benefit which is capable of being estimated in money, other than a travelling allowance or the value of any travelling concession or a contribution paid by the employer to a workman towards any pension or provident fund or a sum paid to a workman to cover any special expenses entailed on him by the nature of his employment.

"Workman" means any person who is—

    (i) a railway servant as defined in clause (34) of section 2 of the Railways Act, 1989, not permanently employed in any administrative, district or sub-divisional office of a

Railway and not employed in any such capacity as specified in Schedule II, or

(iA) (a) a master, seaman or other member of the crew of a ship,

    (b) a captain or other member of the crew of an aircraft,

    (c) a person recruited as driver, helper, mechanic, cleaner or in any other capacity in connection with a motor vehicle,

    (d) a person recruited for work abroad by a company,

and who is employed outside India in any such capacity as is specified in Schedule II and the ship, aircraft or motor vehicle, or company, as the case may be is registered in India, or;

(ii) employed in any such capacity as is specified in Schedule II, whether the contract of employment was made before or after the passing of this Act and whether such contract is expressed or implied, oral or in writing; but does not include any person working in the capacity of a member of the Armed Forces of the Union,

and any reference to a workman who has been injured shall, where the workman is dead, include a reference to his dependents or any of them.

LIABILITY OF AN EMPLOYER FOR COMPENSATION

(1) If personal injury is caused to a workman by accident arising out of and in the course of his employment, his employer shall be liable to pay compensation in accordance with the provisions of Chapter II of the Act:

Provided that the employer shall not be so liable—

    (a) in respect of any injury which does not result in the total or partial disablement of the workman for a period exceeding a period of three days;

    (b) in respect of any injury, not resulting in death or permanent total disablement caused by an accident which is directly attributable to—

        (i) the workman having been at the time thereof under the influence of drink or drugs; or

    (ii) the wilful disobedience of the workman to an order expressly given, or to a rule expressly framed, for the purpose of securing the safety of workmen; or

   (iii) the wilful removal or disregard by the workman of any safety guard or other device which he knew to have been provided for the purpose of securing the safety of workmen.

(2) If a workman employed in any employment specified in Part A of Schedule III contracts any disease specified therein as an occupational disease peculiar to that employment, or if a workman, whilst in the service of an employer in whose service he has been employed for a continuous period of not less than six months (which period shall not include a period of service under any other employer in the same kind of employment) in any employment specified in Part B of Schedule III, contracts any disease specified therein as an occupational disease peculiar to that employment, or if a workman whilst in the service of one or more employers in any employment specified in Part C of Schedule III for such continuous period as the Central Government may specify in respect of each such employment, contracts any disease specified therein as an occupational disease peculiar to that employment, the contracting of the disease shall be deemed to be an injury by accident within the meaning of this section, and unless the contrary is proved the accident shall be deemed to have arisen out of and in the course of the employment:

Provided that if it is proved—

   (a) that a workman whilst in the service of one or more employers in any employment specified in Part C of Schedule III has contracted a disease specified therein as an occupational disease peculiar to that employment during a continuous period which is less than the period specified under this sub-section for that employment, and

   (b) that the disease has arisen out of and in the course of the employment,

the contracting of such disease shall be deemed to be an injury by accident within the meaning of this section:

Provided further that if it is proved that a workman who having served under any employer in any employment specified in Part B of Schedule III or who having served under one or more employers in any employment specified in Part C of that Schedule, for a continuous period specified under this sub-section for that employment and he has after cessation of such service contracted any disease specified in the said Part B or the said Part C, as the case may be, as an occupational disease peculiar to the employment and that such disease arose out of the employment the contracting of the disease shall be deemed to be an injury by accident within the meaning of this section.

(2A) If a workman employed in any employment specified in Part C of Schedule III contracts any occupational disease peculiar to that employment, the contracting whereof is deemed to be an injury by accident within the meaning of this section, and such employment was under more than one employer, such employers, shall be liable for the payment of the compensation in such proportion as the Commissioner may, in the circumstances, deem just.

(3) The Central Government or the State Government, after giving, by notification in the Official Gazette, not less than three months' notice of its intention so to do may, by a like notification, and any description of employment to the employments specified in Schedule III, and shall specify in the case of employments so added the diseases which shall be deemed for the purposes of this section to be occupational disease peculiar to those employments respectively and thereupon the provisions of sub-section (2) shall apply in the case of a notification by the Central Government, within the territories to which this Act extends, or in case of a notification by the State Government, within the State as if such diseases had been declared by this Act to be occupational diseases peculiar to those employments.

(4) Save as provided by sub-sections (2), (2A) and (3), no compensation shall be payable to workman in respect of any disease unless the disease is directly attributed to a specific injury by accident arising out of and in the course of this employment.

(5) Nothing herein contained shall be deemed to confer any right to compensation on a workman in respect of any injury if he has instituted in a Civil Court a suit for damages in respect of the injury against the employer or any other person; and no suit for damages shall be maintainable by a workman in any court of law in respect of any injury—

(a) if he has instituted a claim to compensation in respect of
the injury before a Commissioner; or

(b) if an agreement has been made between the workman and
his employer providing for the payment of compensation
in respect of the injury in accordance with the provisions
of this Act.

AMOUNT OF COMPENSATION AND METHOD OF CALCULATION

(1) Subject to the provisions of this Act, the amount of
compensation shall be as follows, namely:—

(a) Where death results from the injury	an amount equal to fifty per cent of the monthly wages of the deceased workman multiplied by the relevant factor; or an amount of eighty thousand rupees, whichever is more;
(b) Where permanent total disablement results from the injury	an amount equal to sixty per cent of the monthly wages of the injured workman multiplied by the relevant factor; or an amount of ninety thousand rupees, whichever is more.

Explanation I.—For the purposes of clause (a) and clause (b),
"relevant factor" in relation to a workman means the factor
specified in the second column of Schedule IV against the entry in
the first column of that Schedule specifying the number of years
which are the same as the completed years of the age of the
workman on his last birthday immediately preceding the date on
which the compensation fell due.

Explanation II.—Where the monthly wages of a workman
exceed four thousand rupees, his monthly wages for the purposes
of clause (a) and clause (b) shall be deemed to be four thousand
rupees only;

(c) Where permanent partial disablement results from the injury	(i) in the case of an injury specified in Part II of Schedule I, such percentage of the compensation which would have been payable in the case of permanent total

> disablement as is specified therein as being the percentage of the loss of earning capacity caused by that injury, and
>
> (ii) in the case of an injury not specified in Schedule I, such percentage of the compensation payable in the case of permanant total disablement as is proportionate to the loss of earning capacity (as assessed by the qualified medical practitioner) permanently caused by the injury.

Explanation I.—Where more injuries than one are caused by the same accident, the amount of compensation payable under this head shall be aggregated but not so in any case as to exceed the amount which would have been payable if permanent total disablement had resulted from the injuries.

Explanation II.—In assessing the loss of earning capacity for the purposes of sub-clause (ii), the qualified medical practitioner shall have due regard to the percentages of loss of earning capacity in relation to different injuries specified in Schedule I;

(d) Where temporary disablement, whether total or partial results from the injury — a half-monthly payment of the sum equivalent to twenty-five per cent of monthly wages of the workman, to be paid in accordance with the provisions of sub-section (2).

(1A) Notwithstanding anything contained in sub-section (1), while fixing the amount of compensation payable to a workman in respect of an accident occurred outside India, the Commissioner shall take into account the amount of compensation, if any, awarded to such workman in accordance with the law of the country in which the accident occurred and shall reduce the amount fixed by him by the amount of compensation awarded to the workman in accordance with the law of that country.

(2) The half-monthly payment referred to in clause (d) of sub-section (1) shall be payable on the sixteenth day—

(i) from the date of disablement where such disablement lasts for a period of twenty-eight days or more; or

(ii) after the expiry of a waiting period of three days from the date of disablement where such disablement lasts for a period of less than twenty-eight days; and thereafter half-monthly during the disablement or during a period of five years, whichever period is shorter :

Provided that—

(a) there shall be deducted from any lump sum or half-monthly payments to which the workman is entitled the amount of any payment or allowance which the workman has received from the employer by way of compensation during the period of disablement prior to the receipt of such lump sum or of the first half-monthly payment, as the case may be; and

(b) no half-monthly payment shall in any case exceed the amount, if any, by which half the amount of the monthly wages of the workman before the accident exceeds half the amount of such wages which he is earning after the accident.

Explanation I.—Any payment or allowance which the workman has received from the employer towards his medical treatment shall not be deemed to be a payment or allowance received by him by way of compensation within the meaning of clause (a) of the proviso.

(3) On the ceasing of the disablement before the date on which any half-monthly payment falls due there shall be payable in respect of that half-month a sum proportionate to the duration of the disablement in that half-month.

(4) If the injury of the workman results in his death, the employer shall, in addition to the compensation under sub-section (1) deposit with the Commissioner a sum of two thousand five hundred rupees for payment of the same to the eldest surviving defendant of the workman towards the expenditure of the funeral of such workman or where the workman did not have a dependent or was not living with his dependant at the time of his death to the person who actually incurred such expenditure.

Calculation of Wages for Compensation: Section 4 of the Act provides that where the monthly wages of a workman exceed four thousand rupees, his monthly wages for the purpose of clause (a) and clause (b) shall be deemed to be four thousand rupees only. Now, therefore, all workmen except managerial and clerical staff without any wage limit are covered under the Act, the total lump sum compensation is determined by first determining the monthly wages, then finding out the relevant multiplying factor given in Schedule IV pertaining to the age of workman at the time of accident and then dividing it by the percentage payable *vide* section 4(a) for death and 4(b) for permanent total disablement.

Illustrations

(1) Amount of compensation in case of death:

If a workman meets with an accident and dies in the course of employment at the age of 35 and at that time he drew monthly wages of Rs. 3,900 per month as per Schedule IV of the Act the relevant factor applicable to his case would be Rs. 197.06. According to section 4(a) of the Act compensation payable would be an amount equal to fifty per cent of the monthly wages of deceased multiplied by the relevant factor, *i.e.*, Rs. 197.06 and as such the amount of compensation payable to his dependants will be Rs. 3,84,267.00. The determination of the compensation will be arrived in the following manner:—

$$50\% \text{ of Rs. } 3,900 = 1950 \times 197.06$$
$$= \text{Rs. } 3,84,267.00$$

The minimum compensation in the case of death in no circumstances will be less than Rs. 80,000.

(2) Amount of compensation in case of total disablement:

If instead of death a workman suffers permanent total disablement as per section 4(b) of the Act the compensation payable will be an amount equal to 60% of the monthly wages of the injured workman multiplied by the relevant factor. However, the minimum amount of compensation will be Rs. 90,000 when it is less than that amount. Hence the amount of compensation would be 60 per cent of Rs. 3,900, *i.e.*, equal to Rs. 2,340 *vide* section 4(b) multiplied by relevant factor in Schedule IV, *i.e.*, Rs. 197.06 and as such the amount of compensation payable will be Rs. 4,61,120.40.

(3) Determination of compensation in case of injury (loss of thumb):

If such a workman loses his thumb of one hand the calculation of compensation will be 30% of Rs. 4,61,120.40, *i.e.*, Rs. 1,38,336.12 (*vide* Schedule I Part II Serial No. 5)

(4) Determination of compensation either in case of death, total disablement or injury:

Assuming that a workman of 35 years of age has been getting Rs. 4,000 per month as his wages and meets with an accident then for the purpose of determining the amount of compensation, *Explanation* II of section 4 of the Act should be referred. While applying the aforesaid principle, the employee or his/her dependants as the case may be, will be entitled to the compensation, which shall be determined as follows:—

   (i) In case of death - Rs. 3,94,120.00

  (ii) In case of total disablement - Rs. 4,72,944.00

 (iii) In case of loss of thumb - Rs. 2,36,472.00

COMPENSATION TO BE PAID WHEN DUE AND PENALTY FOR DEFAULT

(1) Compensation under section 4 pertaining to amount of compensation shall be paid as soon as it falls due.

(2) In cases where the employer does not accept the liability for compensation to the extent claimed he shall be bound to make provisional payment based on the extent of liability which he accepts, and such payment shall be deposited with the Commissioner or made to the workman, as the case may be, without prejudice to the right of the workman to make any further claim.

(3) Where any employer is in default in paying the compensation due under this Act within one month from the date it fell due, the Commissioner shall—

    (a) direct that the employer shall, in addition to the amount of the arrears, pay simple interest thereon at the rate of twelve per cent per annum or at such higher rate not exceeding the maximum of the lending rates of any scheduled bank as may be specified by the Central Government, by notification in the Official Gazette, on the amount due; and

(b) If, in his opinion, there is no justification for the delay, direct that the employer shall, in addition to the amount of the arrears, and interest thereon pay a further sum not exceeding fifty per cent, of such amount by way of penalty:

Provided that an order for the payment of penalty shall not be passed under clause (b) without giving a reasonable opportunity to the employer to show cause why it should not be passed.

Explanation.—For the purposes of this sub-section, "scheduled bank" means a bank for the time being included in the Second Schedule to the Reserve Bank of India Act, 1934.

The interest payable under sub-section (3) shall be paid to the workman or his dependant as the case may be.

METHOD OF CALCULATING WAGES

Under the Workmen's Compensation Act and for the purposes thereof the expression "monthly wages" means the amount of wages deemed to be payable for a month's service whether the wages are payable by the month or by whatever other period or at piece rates and calculated as follows, namely :—

(a) where the workman has, during a continuous period of not less than twelve months immediately preceding the accident, been in the service of the employer who is liable to pay compensation, the monthly wages of workman shall be one-twelfth of the total wages which have fallen due for payment to him by the employer in last twelve months of that period;

(b) where the whole of the continuous period of service immediately preceding the accident during which the workman was in the service of the employer who is liable to pay the compensation was less than one month, the monthly wages of the workman shall be the average monthly amount which, during the twelve months immediately preceding the accident, was being earned by a workman employed by the same employer or, if there was no workman so employed, by a workman employed on similar work in the same locality;

(c) in other cases including cases in which it is not possible for want of necessary information to calculate the monthly wages under clause (b), the monthly wages shall be thirty times the total wages earned in respect of last continuous period of service immediately preceding the accident from the employer who is liable to pay compensation, divided by the number of days comprising such period.

Explanation.—A period of service shall, for the purposes of this section, be deemed to be continuous which has not been interrupted by a period of absence from work exceeding fourteen days.

DISTRIBUTION OF COMPENSATION

(1) No payment of compensation in respect of workman whose injury has resulted in death, and no payment of a lump sum as compensation to a workman or a person under legal disability, shall be made otherwise than by deposit with the Commissioner, and no such payment made directly by an employer shall be deemed to be a payment of compensation:

Provided that, in the case of a deceased workman, an employer may make to any dependent advances on account of compensation of an amount equal to three months' wages of such workman and so much of such amount as does not exceed the compensation payable to that dependant shall be deducted by the Commissioner from such compensation and repaid to the employer.

(2) Any other sum amounting to not less than ten rupees which is payable as compensation may be deposited with the Commissioner on behalf of the person entitled thereto.

(3) The receipt of the Commissioner shall be a sufficient discharge in respect of any compensation deposited with him.

(4) On the deposit of any money under sub-section (1), as compensation in respect of a deceased workman the Commissioner shall, if he thinks necessary, cause notice to be published or to be served on each dependant in such manner as he thinks fit, calling upon the dependants to appear before him on such date as he may fix for determining the distribution of the compensation. If the Commissioner is satisfied after any inquiry which he may deem necessary, that no dependant exists, he shall repay the balance of the money to the employer by whom it was

paid. The Commissioner shall, on application by the employer, furnish a statement showing in detail all disbursements made.

(5) Compensation deposited in respect of a deceased workman shall, subject to any deduction made under sub-section (4) be apportioned among the dependants of the deceased workman or any of them in such proportion as the Commissioner thinks fit, or may, in the discretion of the Commissioner, be allotted to any one dependant.

(6) Where any compensation deposited with the Commissioner is payable to any person, the Commissioner shall, if the person to whom the compensation is payable is not a woman or a person under a legal disability, and may, in other cases, pay the money to the person entitled thereto.

(7) Where any lump sum deposited with the Commissioner is payable to a woman or a person under a legal disability, such sum may be invested, applied or otherwise dealt with for the benefit of the woman, or of such person during his disability, in such manner as the Commissioner may direct; and where a half-monthly payment is payable to any person under a legal disability the Commissioner may, on his own motion or on an application made to him in this behalf, order that the payment be made during the disability to any dependant of the workman or to any other person whom the Commissioner thinks best fitted to provide for the welfare of the workman.

(8) Where, on application made to him in this behalf or otherwise, the Commissioner is satisfied that, on account of neglect of children on the part of a parent or on account of the variation of the circumstances of any dependant or for any other sufficient cause, an order of the Commissioner as to the distribution of any sum paid as compensation or as to the manner in which any sum payable to any such dependant is to be invested, applied or otherwise dealt with, ought to be varied, the Commissioner may make such orders for the variation of the former order as he thinks just in the circumstances of the case:

Provided that no such order prejudicial to any person shall be made unless such person has been given an opportunity of showing cause why the order should not be made, or shall be made in any case in which it would involve the repayment by a dependant of any sum already paid to him.

(9) Where the Commissioner varies any order under sub-section (8) by reason of the fact that payment of compensation to any person has been obtained by fraud, impersonation or other improper means any amount so paid to or on behalf of such person may be recovered in the manner hereinafter provided in section 31.

POWER OF COMMISSIONER TO REQUIRE FROM EMPLOYER, STATEMENT REGARDING FATAL ACCIDENT

(1) Where a Commissioner receives information from any source that a workman has died as a result of an accident arising out of and in the course of his employment, he may send by Registered Post a notice to the workman's employer requiring him to submit within thirty days of the service of the notice, a statement, in the prescribed form, giving the circumstances attending the death of the workman, and indicating whether, in the opinion of the employer, he is or is not liable to deposit compensation on account of the death.

(2) If the employer is of opinion that he is liable to deposit compensation he shall make the deposit within thirty days of the service of the notice.

(3) If the employer is of opinion that he is not liable to deposit compensation, he shall in his statement indicate the grounds on which he disclaims liability.

(4) Where, the employer has so disclaimed liability the Commissioner after making such inquiry as he may think fit, may inform any of the dependants of the deceased workman, that it is open to the dependant to prefer a claim for compensation, and may give them such other further information as he may think fit.

REPORT OF FATAL ACCIDENTS AND SERIOUS BODILY INJURIES

(1) Where, by any law for the time being in force, notice is required to be given to any authority, by or on behalf of an employer, of any accident occurring on his premises which results in death or serious bodily injury, the person required to give the notice shall, within seven days of the death or serious bodily injury, send a report to the Commissioner giving the circumstances attending the death or serious bodily injury:

Provided that where the State Government has so prescribed the person required to give the notice may instead of sending such report to the Commissioner send it to the authority to whom he is required to give the notice.

Explanation.--"Serious bodily injury" means an injury which involves, or in all probability will involve, the permanent injury to, any limb or the permanent loss of the use of, or permanent loss of or injury to the sight or hearing, or the fracture of any limb, or the enforced absence of the injured person from work for a period exceeding twenty days.

(2) The State Government may, by a notification in the Official Gazette, extend the provisions of sub-section (1) to any class of premises other than those coming within the scope of that sub-section and may, by such notification, specify the persons who shall send the report to the Commissioner.

(3) Nothing in this section shall apply to the factories to which the Employees' State Insurance Act, 1948, applies.

RETURN AS TO COMPENSATION

The State Government may, by notification in the Official Gazette, direct that every person employing workmen, or that any specified class of such persons, shall send at such time and in such form and to such authority, as may be specified in the notification, a correct return specifying the number of injuries in respect of which compensation has been paid by the employer during the previous years and the amount of such compensation, together with such other particulars as to the compensation as the State Government may direct.

CONTRACTING OUT

Any contract or agreement whether made before or after the commencement of this Act, whereby a workman relinquishes any right of compensation from the employer for personal injury arising out of or in the course of the employment, shall be null and void in so far as it purports to remove or reduce the liability of any person to pay compensation under this Act.

POWER OF COMMISSIONER TO REQUIRE FURTHER DEPOSIT IN CASE OF FATAL ACCIDENT

(1) Where any sum has been deposited by an employer as compensation payable in respect of a workman whose injury has resulted in death, and in the opinion of the Commissioner such

sum is insufficient the Commissioner may, by notice in writing stating his reasons, call upon the employer to show cause why he should not make a further deposit within such time as may be stated in the notice.

(2) If the employer fails to show cause to the satisfaction of the Commissioner, the Commissioner may make an award determining the total amount payable and requiring the employer to deposit the deficiency.

REGISTRATION OF AGREEMENTS

(1) Where the amount of any lump-sum payable as compensation has been settled by an agreement, whether by way of redemption of a half-monthly payment or otherwise, or where any compensation has been so settled as being payable to a woman or a person under a legal disability, a memorandum thereof shall be sent by the employer to the Commissioner, who shall, on being satisfied as to its genuineness, record the memorandum in a register in the prescribed manner :

Provided that—

(i) no such memorandum shall be recorded before seven days after communication by the Commissioner of notice to the parties concerned;

(ii) the Commissioner may at any time rectify the register;

(iii) where it appears to the Commissioner that an agreement as to the payment of lump-sum whether by way of redemption of half-monthly payment or otherwise, or an agreement as to the amount of compensation payable to a woman or a person under a legal disability ought not to be registered by reason of the inadequacy of the sum or amount, or by reason of the agreement having been obtained by fraud or undue influence or other improper means, he may refuse to record the memorandum of the agreement and may make such order, including an order as to any sum already paid under the agreement, as he thinks just in the circumstances.

(2) An agreement for the payment of compensation which has been registered under the above provisions shall be enforceable under this Act, notwithstanding anything contained in the Indian Contract Act, 1872, or in any other law for the time being in force.

EFFECT OF FAILURE TO REGISTER AGREEMENT

Where a memorandum of any agreement the registration of which is required by section 28, is not sent to the Commissioner as required by that section the employer shall be liable to pay the full amount of compensation which he is liable to pay under the provisions of this Act, and notwithstanding anything contained in the proviso to sub-section (1) of section 4, shall not, unless the Commissioner otherwise directs, be entitled to deduct more than half of any amount paid to the workman by way of compensation whether under the agreement or otherwise.

PENALTIES

(1) Whoever—

   (a) fails to maintain notice-book which he is required to maintain under sub-section (3) of section 10 pertaining to notice of claim; or

   (b) fails to send to the Commissioner a statement which he is required to send under sub-section (1) of section 10A pertaining to powers of the Commissioner required from an employer regarding fatal accident;

   (c) fails to send a report which he is required to send under section 10B pertaining to report of fatal accidents and serious bodily injuries;

   (d) fails to make a return which he is required to make under section 16,

shall be punishable with fine which may extend to five thousand rupees.

(2) No prosecution under this section shall be instituted except by or with the previous sanction of a Commissioner, and no court shall take cognizance of any offence under this section, unless complaint thereof is made within six months of the date on which the alleged commission of the offence came to the knowledge of the Commissioner.

––––––––

OTHER RELATED MATTERS

Hours of work-rest, overtime and spread-over

Leave & holidays

Leave admissible to workers under the Factories Act

Transfer of employees

Procedure for disciplinary action

Procedure to conduct a domestic enquiry

Punishment

Resignation of an employee and legal implications

Law relating to retirement of an employee

Retiral benefits to employees in private employment

22. Other Related Matters

Although all the important Labour Acts have been dealt and explained in this book there are many areas of day-to-day importance which are not enacted by the Government but have developed by practices and judicial interpretations. In order to enhance the utility of the book and for the information of the readers, the important subjects are dealt with hereinafter.

HOURS OF WORK

The health and efficiency of workers depend mostly on the number of hours they have to work. In case of long working hours, the operative is bound to be tired and slack in his duties. Such tiresomeness often becomes the cause of his shattered health, which ultimately tells upon the efficiency of a worker. Besides, if the hours of work are long, the workers develop the habit of loitering and loafing away the time under various pretexts.

According to Factories Act, 1948, the hours of work remain the same, *i.e.*, 48 hours per week and 9 hours per day with a 'spread over' of 10½ hours. It removes the distinction between perennial and seasonal factories. For children and adolescents, the hours have been fixed at 4½ per day with a 'spread-over' of 5 hours. After every five hours of work, a rest interval of half an hour is provided for adult workers. Provisions have also been made for weekly holidays and leave with wages. Employment of women and children between 7 p.m. and 6 a.m. is prohibited but is being allowed in some of the States. Overtime is to be paid twice the normal rate of wages. No worker is allowed to work in two factories on the same day. In case of workers in night shifts, it has become necessary to provide them 24 consecutive hours' rest every week. The State Governments have been empowered to grant exemption to certain categories of workers from the provision relating to hours of work but in case of such exemptions the total number of hours of work should not exceed 10 hours a day and 50 hours a week and the 'spread-over' 12 hours a day. When an employee is not working in a factory, then his working hours are fixed under the Shops and Establishments Act of that particular State. Like Factories Act, forty-eight hours working in a week is provided in Shops and Establishments Act. Although, the daily time limit is 9 hours for factory workers it ranges from 8 to 12 hours for shops and establishments employees but total hours for the week must not exceed 48.

HOURS OF WORK—REST, OVERTIME AND SPREAD-OVER UNDER SHOPS & ESTABLISHMENTS ACT OF THE STATES

State	Ordinary		With overtime		Quarterly over-time limit	Period of Rest in hour(s)	Spread-over
	Daily	Weekly	Daily	Weekly			
Andhra Pradesh	8	48	11	54	50	1 after 5	12
Assam							
Shops	8	48	10		50	1 after 4	10½
Commercial Establishment	8	48	10		50	1 after 4	10½
Bihar	9	48	10	60		½ after 5	12
Bombay (Maharashtra Gujarat)							
Shops	9	48		51		1 after 5	11(12)
Commercial Establishment	9	48		51		1 after 5	11
Restaurant	9			51		1 after 5	14
Theatre	9			54		1 after 5	11
Delhi							
Shops	9	48		54	150	½ after 5	12
Commercial Establishment	9	48		54	150	½ after 5	10½

Haryana	9	48		50		½	10
Himachal Pradesh	9	48	10	50		½	10
Karnataka	9	48			50	1 after 5	12
Kerala	8	48			50	1 after 4	10½
Madhya Pradesh							
Shops	9	48		51			12
Commercial Establishment	10	48		51			12
Restaurant	9			54			14
Theatre	9		10				12
Orissa	9	48			50	½ after 5	12
Punjab	9	48	10		50	½ after 5	12
Rajasthan	9	48	10		50	½ after 5	12
Tamil Nadu	8	48	10	54		1 after 4	12
Uttar Pradesh	8	48	10		50	½ after 5	12
West Bengal	8½	48			120	1 after 6	10½

Note.—'Hours of work' means the time during which the persons employed at the disposal of the employer exclusive of any interval allowed for rest and meals and hours worked has corresponding meaning.

'Week' means the period of seven days beginning at mid-night on Saturday.

'Day' means a period of twenty-four hours beginning at mid-night. Provided that in the case of an employee whose hours of work extended beyond mid-night, day means the period of twenty-four hours beginning when such employment commences irrespective of mid-night.

'Rest' means that no period of continuous work shall exceed the prescribed number of hours.

'Spread-over' means the period between the commencement and the termination of the work of an employee on any day.

LEAVE AND HOLIDAYS

Although 'leave' has been dealt under the Chapter on Factories Act this subject being of day-to-day importance it is imperative to explain it separately also.

DISTINCTION BETWEEN LEAVE AND HOLIDAYS

A reference to item 4 of Schedule III appended to the Industrial Disputes Act, 1947 would make it abundantly clear that holidays stand on a different footing altogether from leave with wages, or leave facilities. Holidays are off-days granted by the employer to their workmen either voluntarily or compulsorily under the force of law. On a holiday the entire business is closed and no one works while in case of leave the entire business is running. It would thus be seen that there is a fundamental distinction between leave and holidays.

FESTIVAL AND NATIONAL HOLIDAYS

The holidays declared under the Negotiable Instruments Act are usually applicable to Government departments more particularly to banks and they are not generally adopted by factories and other establishments in the private and public sector. The factory legislations also do not provide for the grant of festival holidays to industrial workers. But inspite of that, some quantum of festivals and national holidays with pay is prevalent in factories and other industrial establishments. Generally, the occupiers of factories fix the number of such holidays in their standing orders or service rules. Apart from this, States are very generous in declaring paid holidays.

LEAVE ADMISSIBLE TO WORKERS UNDER THE FACTORIES ACT

Leave to employees is granted on the basis of statutory provisions, agreements, settlements, customs, usages or practices. Section 79 of the Factories Act, 1948 as amended by Act 94 of 1976 with effect from 26th October, 1976 provides for earned leave with wages to the workers in addition to the weekly offs and compensatory holidays.

(i) **Qualifying service for entitlement of leave.**—Under section 79 of the Act as amended w.e.f. 26th October, 1976, every worker who has worked for a period of 240 days or more in a factory during a calendar year is qualified for annual leave with wages to be availed by him during the subsequent calendar year or during any other calendar year. But a worker whose service commences otherwise than on the first day of January shall be entitled to leave with wages only if he has worked for two-thirds of the total number of days in the remainder of the calendar year.

(ii) **Calculation of leave.**—In regard to an adult employee, the leave with wages is to be calculated at the rate of one day for every twenty days of work performed by him during the previous calendar year while in the case of a child worker, such leave is to be calculated at the rate of one day for every fifteen days of work performed by him during the previous calendar year and for the purpose of computation of the period of 240 days or more, the following should be deemed to be the days on which such workers have worked in a factory:—

(a) any days of lay-off, by agreement or contract or as permissible under the standing orders;

(b) in the case of a female worker, maternity leave for any number of days not exceeding twelve weeks; and

(c) the leave earned in the year prior to that in which the leave is enjoyed.

The leave admissible under the above provisions is exclusive of all holidays whether occurring during or at either end of the period of leave. But it may be noted that an adult worker whose service commences otherwise than on the first day of January is entitled to one day leave with wages for every twenty days of work performed by him while in the case of a child worker, such leave is to be calculated at the rate of one day for every fifteen days of work performed by him provided such workers have worked for two-thirds of the total number of days in the remainder of the calendar year.

(iii) **Leave to discharged or dismissed worker.**—If a worker is discharged or dismissed from service or quits his employment or is superannuated or dies while in service during the course of the calendar year, he or his heir or nominee, as the case may be, is entitled to wages in lieu of the quantum of leave to which he was entitled immediately before his discharge, dismissal, quitting of employment, superannuation or death calculated at the rates specified above even if he had not worked for the entire period of 240 days or for two-thirds of the total number of days in the remainder of the calender year and the payment in lieu of such unavailed leave is to be made before the expiry of the second working day from the date of discharge, dismissal or quitting but where the worker is superannuated or dies while in service the payment in lieu of such unavailed leave is to be made before the expiry of two months from the date of such superannuation or death and in calculating leave under this provision of the Act, fraction of leave of half a day or more is to be treated as one full day's leave but fraction of less than half a day should be omitted. In addition to the above, it may also be borne in mind that if a worker does not in any one calendar year avail the whole of the leave allowed to him during the previous calendar year then any such leave not taken by him should be added to the leave to be allowed to him in the succeeding calendar year provided that the total number of days of leave that may be carried forward to the succeeding year should not exceed thirty in the case of an adult or forty in the case of a child. It has been further provided in the Factories Act that a worker who has applied for leave with wages but has not been given such leave as aforesaid shall be entitled to carry forward leave refused without any limit.

In other words, in a case where the worker applies for leave with wages but is not given such leave, then in that eventuality he is entitled to carry forward the entire unavailed leave without any limit.

(iv) **Leave—How to be availed of ?**—A worker desirous of availing of the leave earned by him during the preceding calender year has to make an application for such leave at least fifteen days before the date on which he wishes to proceed on leave in writing to the manager but in case the worker is employed in a public utility service as defined in clause (n) of section 2 of the Industrial Disputes Act, 1947 then such leave application in writing should be made not less than thirty days before the date on which he wants his leave to begin. Such leave can be availed in minimum three instalments during the year. The leave as aforesaid can also be availed in case of illness and when such leave is to be availed due to illness then even the formalities for applying for leave in advance as stated above are not necessary. In short, the Factories Act contemplates that if a worker wants to avail himself of the leave with wages due to him to cover a period of illness, he shall be granted such leave even if the application for leave is not made within the time specified above and in such a case wages as admissible under section 81 of the said Act shall be paid within fifteen days in non-public utility service and in case of a public utility service within thirty days from the date of the application for leave. An application for leave which is made well in time should not ordinarily be refused.

(v) **Payment in lieu of unavailed leave on termination, etc.**—If the employment of a worker, who is entitled to leave as aforesaid, is terminated by the occupier before he has taken the entire leave to which he is entitled, or if having applied for and having not been granted such leave, the worker quits his employment before he has taken the leave, the occupier of the factory has to pay him the amount payable under section 80 in respect of the leave not taken and such payment is to be made, where the employment of the worker is terminated by the occupier, before the expiry of the second working day after such termination, and where a worker who quits his employment, on or before the next pay day. It may also be borne in mind that the unavailed leave of a worker has not to be taken into consideration in computing the period of any notice required to be given before discharge or dismissal. The intention of the legislature in enacting sub-section (ii) of section 79 seems to enjoin upon the occupier to make payment on a day on which the factory is working, providing punishment for breach if payment is not made on the second working day after termination of the service, without affecting the right of the aggrieved worker to recover the amount in accordance with law.

(vi) **Whether leave can be claimed as of right?**—The dictionary meaning of the word, "leave" being permission and unless such permission is given or leave sought is granted, no person can absent himself from duty in an unauthorised manner. In other words, "leave" means permission obtained by an employee from his employer relieving him from the duty to attend his work. It, therefore, follows that leave should be taken in advance before an employee intends to proceed on leave. In short, no workman can proceed on leave without first applying for and obtaining it.

When leave has accrued to an employee then normally it is his right to get it but from what time leave should be sanctioned has to be adjusted according to the exigencies as and when it accrues or is applied for irrespective of the consideration for the business exigencies and necessities. This shows that even though an employee is entitled to and eligible for a certain period of leave, he cannot as a matter of right demand that the same should be granted to him at a particular time when he applies for the same or whenever he applies for the same. The reason is that at the particular time when he applies for leave the pressure of work or exigencies of service may be such that his services cannot be spared. But at the same time it cannot also be denied that he has got a right to have his leave application considered and disposed of properly, *bona fide* and in accordance with law. In other words, when a discretion is conferred on the employer then the exercise of that discretion has to be exercised in the *bona fide* exercise of the powers and not in a *mala fide* manner.

(vii) **Obligation of an employer to grant leave.**—Unless leave is applied for, the question of its sanction does not arise and in case a worker remains absent from work without leave having been granted or sanctioned to him, he exposes himself to disciplinary action. Normally when leave has accrued to an employee it is his right to get it but from what time leave should be sanctioned has to be adjusted according to the exigencies of business of the employer and that leave cannot be sanctioned as and when it accrues or is applied for, irrespective of the consideration for the business exigencies and necessities. An employer is, however, under an equitable obligation to grant leave to an employee upto the maximum limit at his credit for *bona fide* reasons and so long as the employee does not exceed that limit or does not absent himself without any prior sanction or previous intimation under unforeseen circumstances, he cannot be charged with any irregularity in attendance. The reason is that every man is likely to have social obligations and he may fall ill at times and there may be deaths and illness in his family. It will be idle for the employer to expect that one cannot be taken ill. Though in law the anxiety of employer to carry on his business has preference within certain limits set out by statutory provisions and service rules the fact that sometimes the requirements of an employee may be so urgent and pressing that it may be impossible for him to wait, cannot be lost sight of. It, therefore, follows that the employer cannot refuse leave to a workman due to circumstances beyond his control.

(viii) **Application for leave with reasons if necessary.**—It is now well established that whenever an employee wishes to proceed on leave, it is necessary that he must make an application for leave with reasons therefor. The reasons for taking leave should also not be vague. In fact, remaining absent without any application or intimation is a serious misconduct. Even if the close relation of an employee is stated to be ill, the employee cannot walk out of the establishment without applying and taking anybody's permission and when such an act is repeated then he can be discharged and in that eventuality his discharge would be *bona fide*. The principle that leave should be taken in advance is also applicable in case of extension of leave. A worker is, therefore, under an obligation to send his application for leave sufficiently in advance so that the leave may be sanctioned to him before his original leave expires. The reason is that if a belated application is received then it is entirely at the discretion of the employer whether to sanction it or not. In case the leave is sanctioned then the absence is completely justified because the employer retains the right to sanction leave with retrospective effect. In case, the extension is not granted then the worker would be treated as absent and would be liable to disciplinary action. Sending of an application for extension of leave the same day on which the employee is scheduled to report for duty by ordinary post is a misconduct. The ordinary rule, however, is that extension should be applied for well in time with reasons therefor.

(ix) **Obligation of workers to produce medical certificates in case of sickness.**—The ordinary rule is that in case of grant of leave, application should be sent in advance but this rule is subject to some relaxation in case of sickness. It is now generally recognised that the employer has a right to demand leave application even in case of sickness accompanied by the medical certificate, but when the application for sick leave is accompanied by a medical certificate then the said certificate should generally be believed. It is also generally held that when the application for sick leave accompanied by the medical certificate is received then it should be granted. In such a case when the leave is refused by the employer without any sufficient reason the action of the employer cannot be sustained as being arbitrary and capricious. But it does not mean that the employer cannot demand a medical certificate and cannot refuse sick leave when asked for on account of the failure of the workman to produce the medical certificate. The reason being that it is within the right of the employer to insist upon the production of medical certificate, specially when the leave applied for is for a fairly long period. In such cases, if the workman remains absent without leave he is to blame himself and not the employer.

Note:

The shops and establishments which are not governed by the Factories Act are covered by the Shops and Establishment Acts as enacted by every State. The quantum, qualifying period and accumulation of leave varies in some States but the principles pertaining to leave are by and large the same.

TRANSFER OF EMPLOYEES

Transfers are the part and parcel of employment. Of course, there is no dearth of such instances when many people have spent their whole life at one place. Transferring of an employee is nothing new. It was prevalent even during the rules of Mauryas and Guptas. One reason given for the transfers is that it helps maintain the national integrity because an employee is able to understand more about many regions. Apart from this, it is also seen that people develop vested interests if they are allowed to work at a particular place, for a very long period of time.

Transfers have caused a lot of bad blood, anger, frustration and disgust. There are no two opinions that if transfers are done for improving the functioning they are most welcome, but if done with ill intentions or for punishment then they certainly cause dispute and frustration. As per the rules an employer has the right to transfer the employees from one place to another. Non-compliance of the transfer order by the employee amounts to misconduct. There are, however, certain norms which are to be observed by an employer while transferring any employee.

It is necessary that there is an exigency of work which has prompted the management for the transfer, of the employee. Further, an employer should always have uppermost the interest of an employee in his mind and transfers should not be actuated with even any indirect ulterior motive or any kind of *mala fides*.

The transfers should not be made for the purpose of victimising or harassing any employee.

As a matter of fact, the right of employer to transfer his employees is inherent and implicit in the contract of employment. There is no doubt that any employer is the best judge to know the capacity of his employees. He also knows well where and when the capacities of any employee could best be utilised. But at the same time, employer has no right to transfer his employee to a new concern started by him subsequent to the date of employment of his employee unless it is so stated in the terms of his employment that he would also be liable to be transferred to any of the existing concerns or new ones started by him in future. However, the right of an employer to transfer his employee from one station to another though within the discretion of the employer is always subject to the condition that the terms of contract of employment of an employee are not adversely affected.

The powers of Labour Courts/Industrial Tribunals to interfere with the order of transfer of an employee from one place or station to another are very limited. Ordinarily, it would be proper for them to accept as correct any submission by the employer that the impugned order of transfer was made only because it was found unavoidable in the interest of the business. In such cases, the submission of the employer, that the transfer was unavoidable must be accepted without calling upon him to lead positive evidence. The only exception to this principle is the case where there is reason to believe that the action is *mala fide* or victimisation or unfair labour practice or due to some other ulterior motive not connected with the business interest of the employer. In other words, the powers of transfer from one station to another or from one establishment or branch to another can be exercised only when such transfer is in the interest of the business. The order of transfer is liable to be set aside only if it is shown that it has not been effected *bona fide* or for ordinary and normal reasons of trade or business but has been the result of an unfair labour practice. The orders of transfer are generally challenged on the ground of victimisation, unfair labour practice, or *mala fide* but when they are challenged on such grounds, the employees have to lead positive evidence of their own to show that they were transferred because of their union activities.

The position is the same when an order of transfer is challenged on compassionate grounds. The compassionate ground also has to be considered in the back-ground of administrative interest which is also one of the vital considerations to be taken into account.

PROCEDURE FOR DISCIPLINARY ACTION
Surprisingly there is no procedure prescribed for disciplinary action either in Industrial Disputes Act or in the rules made thereunder, which should be complied with, before inflicting punishment on an industrial worker who has been guilty of a misconduct. The procedure is evolved by various High Courts and Supreme Court in appeal under Article 226 and Article 136 of the

Constitution of India respectively. This procedure is based on principles of natural justice. Broadly speaking the following requirements are *sine qua non* for inflicting punishment upon a workman—(1) charge-sheet, (2) holding a domestic enquiry according to principles of natural justice, (3) report of the enquiry officer, (4) show cause notice, (5) order of punishment. Breach of this procedure also does not give worker a right to re-instatement unless injustice is caused. What has to be seen in these types of cases is not whether this procedure is followed, but whether alleged misconduct is proved.

MISCONDUCT

The first duty of the employee is to obey the orders which the employer is justified in giving under the terms of employment. All orders concerning the work which the employee is required to do and the time, the manner and the place of performing it are presumable and in the absence of any special circumstances, are within the control of the employer.

Though there is no fixed rule of law defining the degree of 'misconduct' which will justify dismissal misconduct inconsistent with the fulfilment of an express or implied condition of service justifies dismissal. Misconduct is made of two words. 'Mis' means bad and 'conduct' means behaviour. In fact, 'misconduct' is a relative term and occurs in various enactments and so it has to be construed with reference to the subject matter and the context in which it occurs, having regard to the scope of the enactment under reference. It literally means, to conduct amiss, to mismanage, wrong or improper conduct, bad behaviour unlawful behaviour or conduct. The synonyms are misbehaviour; misdemeanour; mismanagement; misdeed; delinquency; offence. It implies a wrongful intention and not a mere error of judgment. It does not necessarily imply corruption or criminal intent. An omission to do what is expected of a person to do constitutes misconduct whereas if such failure is directed to intentionally cause mischief or loss, to any person then it is called wilful misconduct. This shows that, "misconduct" is a specific connotation. It is not mere inefficiency or slackness. It is something far more positive and certainly, deliberate disobedience of any order of a superior authority would be a species of misconduct. Where the employer levels the charge of "misconduct", *i.e.*, a charge of some positive act or of conduct which would be quite incompatible with express and implied norms of the relationship of the workman to the employer, there must be material in support of such a serious charge. Such a charge cannot be brought against a workman for not having obeyed the directions of a third party who was not a person in authority over the workman, even though such third person had some interest in the business of the employer. The term, 'misconduct' usually implies an act done wilfully with a wrong intention and as applied to professional acts, even though such acts are not inherently wrongful, it also means dereliction of or deviation from duty. The word, 'misconduct' is a generic term while the insubordination, neglect of work, etc., are species thereof.

Thus 'misconduct' is the doing of something or the omitting to do something which is wrong to do or omit, whereas the person who is guilty of the act or the omission knows that the act which he is doing, or that which he is omitting to do, is wrong thing to do or omit. It, therefore, follows that 'misconduct' may or may not be wilful. In fact, the term 'misconduct' is wide enough to include wrongful commission or omission whether done or omitted to be done intentionally or unintentionally, or to put it in another way a 'misconduct' arises if a person does what he should not have done and does not do what he should have done or any unbusiness like conduct including negligence or want of necessary care.

The conclusion that emerges from the above discussion is that a misconduct need not be wilful. Therefore, any breach of an express or implied duty on the part of an employee, unless it be of a trifling nature, would amount to misconduct. If an act has nothing to do with the relationship of employer and employee or the latter's duty or work as an employee, it would not be a misconduct because it will have no effect on the terms and conditions of service of the employee. The rule of law is that where a person has entered into the position of an employee if he does anything incompatible with the due or faithful discharge of his duty to his master, the latter has a right to dismiss him. The relationship of master and servant implies necessarily that the servant shall be in a position to perform his duty duly and faithfully, and if by his own act he prevents himself from doing so, the master may dismiss him. What circumstances will put an employee into the position of not being able to perform his duty in a due manner, or it is impossible to enumerate. Innumerable circumstances have actually occurred which fall within that proposition and innumerable other circumstances which never have yet occurred or will occur, which also will fall within the proposition. This shows that any breach of an express or implied duty on the part of a servant, unless it be of a trifling nature, affords justification for a dismissal. The primary duties being obedience, fidelity, care, honesty, and punctuality, conduct opposed to the due fulfilment of these duties will entitle the master to dismiss. So, in order to decide as to what act is contrary to the faithful discharge of duties on the part of an employee, it has to be seen the basic nature of relationship of employer and employee and as discussed earlier, the test of employer and employee relationship is that the employee will abide by the instructions of the employer regarding the manner in which the work is to be done. The reason is that when a person enters into a contract of employment as an employee, he impliedly agrees to abide by the instructions of the employer in respect of the manner of performing his duties and obligations.

In every contract of service, there is an implied condition that the employee will work faithfully. If he does not work faithfully, the employer is entitled to ask for rescission of the contract. It is said to be an implied term of fidelity. It is also an implied term of contract that the servant will be subordinate and will work in accordance with the discipline set up by his employer. It is also an implied term that an employee will personally perform the contract and will not assign the performance of the contract to any other person. Another implied term of the contract under the common law is the obligation on the part of the employee to account for in respect of monies and properties received by him either from his employer or from anybody else on his behalf. The obligation to account for is a direct corollary of the obligation to faithfully perform duties. The obligation is assumed because in the absence of any such assumption the contract of employment will be unworkable or in any case it is an assumption based on equitable grounds in view of the peculiar nature of the contract itself. The liability of personal performance on the part of an employee gives rise to another implied term of the contract of competence. This means that the employee has warranted that he is reasonably fit for the job which he undertakes. In other words, if after entering into service he becomes incompetent for any reason then the employer is entitled to put an end to the contract. The concept of misconduct in employer and employee relationship is based upon the nature and relationship itself and implied and express conditions of service. Amongst others, the following acts on the part of an employee have been held to be misconduct:—

(1) any act or conduct which is prejudicial or is likely to be prejudicial to the interests of the employer or to the reputation of the employer;

(2) any act or conduct inconsistent or incompatible with the due or peaceful discharge of the workman's duty to his employer;

(3) any act or conduct of a worker which makes it unsafe for the employer to retain him in service;

(4) any act or conduct of an employee which is so grossly immoral so as to make him untrustworthy in the eyes of reasonable men;

(5) any act or conduct of an employee which makes it impossible for the employer to rely on his faithfulness;

(6) any act or conduct of an employee which is such as to open before him temptations for not discharging his duties properly;

(7) any act or conduct of an employee which disturbs the peaceful functioning at the place of work;

(8) use of filthy or abusive language against co-employees, officers or employer;

(9) insulting behaviour and in-subordination as to make it impossible to retain the relation of master and servant;

(10) habitual neglect of duties for which a worker is paid;

(11) neglect of the employee, though isolated which causes or tends to cause serious and harmful consequences;

(12) theft, fraud or dishonesty in connection with the employer's business;

(13) illegal strike;

(14) breach of duty, absence without leave, non-performance of job-duties, disobedience of orders;

(15) Breach of discipline, disrespect to or assaulting superiors or subversion of discipline, disrupting relations with co-workers;

(16) Delinquencies like telling lies, committing theft, fraud, dishonesty, disloyalty and corruption, damage to property or goodwill;

(17) Disabling or disrespectful conduct, disreputable outside conduct.

CHARGE-SHEET

The ordinary meaning of "charge-sheet" is a memorandum of charges, *i.e.*, acts of omissions alleged to have been committed by an employee. It consists of facts and allegations which the person issuing wants to establish against the employee committing a breach of rules or misconduct in terms of the standing orders or any act inconsistent with the fulfilment of the obligations implied in the contract of employment. In short, a charge-sheet is an allegation of misconduct, misbehaviour, indiscipline, lack of interest in work, negligence, etc., on the part of the employee. It is not used in the sense in which it has been used in section 410 of the Code of Criminal Procedure, 1973. It, therefore, follows that a charge-sheet is a memorandum of accusations which are levelled against an employee who commits a breach of any rules, regulations, standing orders or an implied term of contract. In other words, a charge-sheet is nothing but a paper or document containing the alleged acts of misconduct against an employee. The core of the matter is that no disciplinary action can be initiated against an employee or a workman unless he is first served with a charge-sheet containing all charges and their essential particulars.

The basic requirement of drafting a charge-sheet is that it should give to the employee a fair idea of the case which he is to face. So, while drafting a charge-sheet, care must be taken to see that it contains all the facts and for this, the standing orders as well as the service rules which define various misconducts must be read carefully. If a particular act, *e.g.*, absence without leave, late attendance or negligence, is a misconduct when it is an habitual one then the word, "habitual" is an essential constituent of the charge and must be mentioned in the charge-sheet. Similarly, if a particular act, such as affixing posters, riotous or disorderly behaviour or collecting subscription, etc., is a misconduct when it takes place on the premises during working hours then these are also essential elements of misconduct and must be mentioned in the charge-sheet. If gross negligence is a misconduct then the words, "gross" is also an essential part of the charge and must be mentioned in the charge-sheet. This shows that while drafting a charge-sheet, care must be taken to ensure that the charge-sheet mentions all the essential ingredients of a particular misconduct. Apart from the above, the charge-sheet should also mention the particulars of time, place and manner of the incident in order to make the charge specific, because at times they also form part of the charge itself. When riotous behaviour during working hours is a misconduct, then at other times it would not be a misconduct and so, in that eventuality, time would be a part of the charge. The reason is that if a particular act is misconduct when committed on the premises of the establishment, then the place is a part of the charge itself. So, while drafting a charge-sheet, an attempt should be to ensure that the charge mentioned in the charge-sheet is specific as well as complete in all essential constituents. The reason is that the charge is not an accusation made or information given in the abstract but a concrete accusation made against a person in respect of an act either committed or omitted to be done in violation of the law. When the charge is for striking work in contravention of the provision of law then the provision which is said to have been contravened must be mentioned in the charge-sheet otherwise the charge-sheet would be vague. If a person is in the habit of disobeying the instructions of his superiors then each act of disobedience must be mentioned separately in the charge-sheet so that the employee concerned knows the actual incidents with which he is charged. But when there is nothing to indicate that there are any rules of the establishment under which the employee is indicated to obey the orders then the charge of orders, which were not enforceable under any rules, can never be the basis of any order of dismissal or removal. While framing a charge, any document or record which is looked into or relied upon must be disclosed in the charge-sheet so that the employee may have the opportunity of dealing with it. The reason is that an employer cannot justify his action on any ground other than those contained in the charge-sheet. This shows that great care has to be taken while framing the charge-sheet against an erring employee.

Apart from the above, in the standing orders or service rules, there are certain offences or misconducts which have got specific name *viz.*, 'theft', 'criminal breach of trust', 'misappropriation', 'forgery', disobedience, 'strike', 'go-slow' and 'negligence', etc. While drafting a charge-sheet it is desirable that an act of misconduct be called in the specific name which is given to it under the standing orders or service rules. When the misconduct is "to go on strike" then it should not be called "stopping work in concert" because this does not give a clear idea which can be given by use of the simple word, "strike". In the same way, when the misconduct is of disobedience of orders, it should not be described as disregard or non-performance of orders. The reason is obvious. There are various distinctions between the meaning of one word and another and it is always safer to use language of standing orders in order to ensure that the same meaning is entertained. When the charge is that the employee took away new parts taking away of new parts is no charge unless theft is attributed. Similarly, when the behaviour of a particular employee was described as unmannerly or rude this does not amount to a charge of riotous behaviour. When it is mentioned in the charge-sheet that the employee was negligent and at the same time various warnings and suspensions which related to inefficiency were also referred to in the charge it would not amount to charge of negligence.

The whole object of drawing up a charge-sheet is to give an opportunity to the person charged. The principles of natural justice also require that the person charged should know precisely the nature of the offence so that he may be able to explain about it and prove his innocence in the matter. Vague allegations should also be avoided while drafting a charge-sheet and care must be taken to see that there should be no verbiage. The use of abbreviations such as "etc. etc." or "any other document" should be avoided and reference should be made to specific thing or person. Likewise, exceptions should also not be mentioned in the charge-sheet. When, however, the charge is of resorting to an illegal strike it must be remembered that the illegality of strike is a constituent part of the charge itself and so, it must be specifically mentioned in the charge-sheet. The contents of the charge-sheet should not indicate that the employee is guilty of a misconduct. Normally, the charge-sheet should be drafted in a language which the employee can easily understand, and while drafting a charge-sheet care must also be taken to see that it satisfies the following conditions:—

(a) the charge-sheet must specify the charges in the clearest possible language with full particulars;

(b) the charge-sheet must disclose the misconduct with which the employee is charged;

(c) the language used in the charge-sheet must be clear, precise, unambiguous and free from vagueness;

(d) it will not be enough if the employer informs his employee by means of a charge-sheet that he was wilfully slowing down the performance and on the contrary it is incumbent on the employer to furnish all necessary particulars of slowing down of performance before he is called upon to meet the charge;

(e) the charge-sheet should not contain unnecessary matters though mentioning of such unnecessary matters may not be fatal to the charge-sheet;

(f) the use of abbreviations *viz.* "etc. etc" or "any other document" should be avoided and instead, reference should be made to specific things or person;

(g) whenever, it is necessary to give the time of an incident in the charge-sheet the word, "about" must be mentioned;

(h) it must also be seen that there is no misdescription of any charge;

(i) in case of disobedience, the order disobeyed must be mentioned;

(j) in case of theft, full particulars of the goods stolen must be given;

(k) in case of mis-appropriation, all particulars regarding the amount misappropriated must be given;

(l) when the charge is of falsification of accounts, if the details of the particular items in respect of which the act of falsification of accounts was committed are not mentioned, the omission is fatal to the charge;

(m) it must also be seen that the charge-sheet is not devoid of essential particulars.

SERVICE OF CHARGE-SHEET

The service of charge-sheet on the employee concerned is a prerequisite to the validity of a domestic enquiry. The reason is that in case it is established that no charge-sheet was served upon the employee concerned the entire subsequent proceedings of the domestic enquiry would be absolutely invalid and ineffective. It is, therefore, of utmost importance to find out before initiating the domestic enquiry that there is sufficient material on record to show the service of the charge-sheet on the employee concerned.

The most common mode for service of the charge-sheet is by personal service. The charge-sheet may be handed over to the employee and his signatures in token of having received the same obtained on the office copy. In other words, when it is delivered in person, the signatures or thumb impression of the employee should be obtained on its duplicate copy. In case, he refuses to accept the charge-sheet, an endorsement to that effect should be made on it in the presence of two witnesses so that adequate proof of the same is available for evidence. Sometimes it also happens that when an employee is summoned personally in the presence of two or three witnesses by the competent authority to receive the charge-sheet and he receives it but refuses to sign or put his thumb impression on the office copy in token of having received the same, an endorsement to that effect must be made by the competent authority on the office copy of the charge-sheet and such an endorsement should be witnessed by atleast two witnesses. But when an employee insists on a cony of the charge-sheet being made out in Hindi or in any other _gional language this should be done though it is not obligatory to translate it in the mother-tongue of the employee unless such a language is declared as the official language of the State ' which he is employed.

POWER TO SUSPEND PENDING ENQUIRY

It is now well settled that the power to suspend, in the sense of right to forbid a servant to work, is not an implied term in an ordinary contract between the master and servant. Such power can only be the creature either of a statute governing the contract or of an express term in the contract itself. Ordinarily, therefore, the absence of such power either as an express term in the contract or in the rules framed under some statute would mean that the employer would have no power to suspend a workman and even if he does so in the sense that he forbids the employee to work, he will have to pay wages during the so called period of suspension.

Generally where there are 'Standing Orders' there is a provision in such standing orders for payment of subsistence allowance to the suspended workman. For instance, Model Standing Orders 14(4) in Schedule I to the Industrial Employment (Standing Orders) Rules, 1946, framed under Industrial Employment (Standing Orders) Act, 1946, makes such provision.

PROCEDURE TO CONDUCT A DOMESTIC ENQUIRY

The procedure to be followed in a domestic enquiry proceedings, is also not prescribed anywhere. Enquiry, of course, should be in conformity with rules of natural justice. What is natural justice is also not very clear, it has to be understood in the context of various case-laws. Before the start of domestic enquiry the date and place of the domestic enquiry should be communicated to the employee clearly. What should be the preferable procedure is beautifully delineated by Gajendragadkar, J. It is necessary to emphasise that in the domestic enquiries the employer should take steps first to lead evidence against the workman charged, give an opportunity to the workman to cross-examine the said evidence and then should the workman be asked whether he wants to give any explanation about the evidence led against him. Such procedure should be usually followed. When the charges are based on material on record and is accepted by the delinquent workman strict adherence to this procedure is not necessary. Witnesses should normally be examined in the presence of the employee in respect of the charges if statements taken previously and given by witnesses are relied on, they should be made available to the workman concerned. The workman should be given a fair opportunity to cross-examine witnesses. He should be given a fair opportunity to examine witnesses including himself in support of his defence and the enquiry officer should record his findings, based upon the evidence so adduced. The principles of natural justice in their journey through centuries have shed much of their glories and are now crystallised into four principles of justice—

(a) opportunity to both the contesting parties to be heard;

(b) hearing before an impartial enquiry officer so that no man can be judge of his own cause;

(c) decision made in good faith; and

(d) an orderly course of procedure.

REPORT OF THE ENQUIRY OFFICER

When the domestic enquiry is complete, the stage of submitting the report follows. This report is a very important document. Often this report comes to the scrutiny of the court and so it should be carefully written. Though inquiry proceedings before a domestic officer are not judicial or quasi-judicial reasons are not required to be stated out elaborately. It is always prudent that some brief reasons should be given in support of the findings. Report and findings should only be based on evidence adduced before enquiry officer and the material brought before it in support of the charges contained in charge-sheet. No extraneous considerations should come into play when enquiry officer comes to the conclusion or while writing the report. Strictly speaking, the enquiry officer is not entitled to bring in facts in his report which did not form part of the evidence. What type of punishment is to be given is entirely within management's discretion. An enquiry report, therefore, is a must after the domestic enquiry. If at the end of domestic enquiry the enquiry officer does not make a report, that itself introduces a serious infirmity in the enquiry and the Industrial Tribunal can in the case ignore the domestic enquiry and deal with the merits of the dispute for itself. It has been held by the Supreme Court in *Electronics Corporation of India* v. *B. Karunakar*, 1994 LLR 391, that submission of enquiry report to the delinquent employee will be imperative.

PUNISHMENT

For every misconduct punishment is a must. Any establishment or nation as a whole cannot progress without strict discipline in every walk of life. Industrial workers as a class form a small part of society and for smooth functioning of any industry and its progress discipline must be maintained at any cost. Now a days various theories of punishment are being propagated. It may be retributive, deterrent or reformative in character. Looking at the labour scene today, in the present context of economic affairs one cannot afford the luxury of reformative punishment and invite the trouble very often. Good human relationship should have some spine and firmness. It is always best to keep people under discipline. There should be no relaxing from the fundamental rule which must be enforced without fear and favour. It has been proved beyond doubt that employees will feel absolutely secure under the Iron-claw of discipline. The whole organisation is helped if you tell some trouble monger 'to go to hell' or even fire him, instead of trying to solve his inferiority complex, or compensate him for his wife's unfaithfulness. There can be no quarrel with those who treat their employees as human beings with hopes and desires, fears and tribulations, their wants and needs, their strengths and weaknesses. But we are remodelling our employees and spelling them beyond repair, all in the name of good human relations. We have, therefore, our quarrel with those responsible for enforcement of discipline who try and appease disrespectful and indisciplined employees because they threaten to go up to the highest boss. This case of fear, which paralyses many good intentioned officers is bound to sap office discipline. This is bad human relations. Office discipline must be maintained, come what may and if this is done then whatever we wish to do fulfilling good objects of human relations such as philanthropy, kindness, humanitarianism all will automatically follow. People forget that human relation is not a cult to be blindly followed; it is rather a methodical way of thinking and working together, so as to achieve the best results. It does not mean putting a premium on indiscipline. It is a language of discipline which enables us to reach the hearts of our employees. It has got to be learnt, studied and applied everyday in all walks of life.

Under the common law, punishment to be awarded was supposed to be entirely within the discretion of management. Under the Industrial Law also quantum of punishment to be awarded is the management's function to decide. Labour Court or Industrial Tribunal has no power to interfere with management's order, when the misconduct has been proved, except in a case where punishment is so disproportionate that a perversity can be inferred or punishment is to victimise an employee because of his union activity or other things.

Position has now been changed after the enactment of section 11A of the Industrial Disputes Act, 1947 under which power is given to adjudicating authority to interfere with the quantum of punishment.

POINTS TO BE CONSIDERED BEFORE INFLICTING PUNISHMENT

The termination of service of an employee for whatever reason, usually marks a critical moment in his life. Retirement can generate a deep sense of uselessness. Resignations can be filed with regret or bitterness, disciplinary termination means a social stigma as well as economic uncertainty. Retrenchment carries with it anxiety. Termination of service, particularly for the unskilled worker is usually catastrophe. The consequences both social and economic of the loss of employment can be so gross to him and his family that termination can be called social and economic capital punishment. In other countries, people can more easily from one job to another or find some relief in social security systems, but in India these facilities are not available. The implications for the Manager are obviously the greatest sensitivity to the consequences of an employee's termination, the paramount need of the social justice, the avoidance of the slightest trace of arbitrariness or impulsiveness, and the necessity of written documentation of each step leading to any termination. When the question of termination arises, the following considerations are generally reflected:—

(1) Human labour is not a commodity nor the employee a labour tool to be thrown away when his utility decreases. A new manager with the inefficient or an aging employee may need to recall the employee's manager must somehow patiently bear the consequences of poor selection by his predecessors where, through no fault of the employee the wrong person was selected and poorly supervised others.

(2) To a certain extent it can be said that the employee after years of service, acquires as it were property rights to a job. In a way similar to farmer acquiring land after cultivating it for many years, the post becomes his in a way that it is nobody else's.

Because of the gravity of the consequences of termination, the possibilities of retaining, transfer, or placement in another post should be explored.

RESIGNATION OF AN EMPLOYEE AND LEGAL IMPLICATIONS

'Resignation', in the dictionary sense, means the spontaneous relinquishment of one's own right. This is conveyed by the maxim *Resionatioiest juris propil spontanea refutatio* (*see* Earl Jowitt's Dictionary of English Law). In relation to an office, it connotes the act of giving up or relinquishing the office. To 'relinquish an office' means to "cease to hold" the office or to "lose hold of" the office (cf. Shorter Oxford Dictionary); and to "lose hold of office", implies to "detach", "unfasten", "undo or un-tie the binding knot or link" which holds one to the office and the obligations and privileges that go with it. In the general juristic sense also, the meaning of "resigning office" is not different. There also, as a rule, both, the intention to give up or relinquish the office and the concomitant act of its relinquishment, are necessary to constitute a complete and operative resignation (*see* American Jurisprudence, Second Edn. Vol. 15A, page 80) although the act of relinquishment may take different forms or assume a unilateral or bilateral character, depending on the nature of the office and the conditions governing it. Thus, resigning office necessarily involves relinquishment of the office, which implies cessation or termination of, or cutting as under from the office. Indeed, the completion of the resignation and the vacation of the office, are the casual and effectual aspects of one and the same event. From the above discretion, it emerges that a complete and effective act of resigning office is, one which severs the link of the resignor with his office and terminates its tenure.

Just as an employer can terminate the services of an employee, similarly, an employee can resign from service and in either case, nothing further is required to be done from both sides, because each side is *sui juris* and neither side is bound either to take or give service against its will. But it does not mean that an employee can snap the tie of service between himself and the employer by submitting his resignation the moment he wants to do so on the ground that he was entitled to do so at will just as an employer cannot force an employee to resign by coercion, undue influence, mis-representation, fraud, etc., or to dispense with his services contrary to the contract of service at his sweet will. In other words, resignation is a mode of putting an end of the contract of service by the employee like termination of service is the mode of putting an end by the employer and either of them does not require or need consent or acceptance of the other. In fact, resignation is an offer by the employee to the employer to leave the service and does not amount to termination till it is accepted by the employer. It is, however, open to an employee to withdraw or revoke the offer till it is accepted, but such revocation or withdrawal is to be communicated prior to the acceptance of the resignation. The law requires notice on either side for the termination of service. When the employer wishes to terminate the services of an employee, the purpose of notice is to give him time and opportunity to find other employment, without depriving him of his earning during the time; and when the employee wishes to give up employment, the purpose is to give the employer time and opportunity to find a substitute. Thus, the employee on the one hand and the employer on the other has the right to have notice and as that right is for his benefit, he can waive it. The question has sometimes been raised as to what is the effect of an offer of resignation upon a service contract. The law is that an employee has the right to resign from the offer or expression of intention to resign before it is accepted by the master. Once the resignation is accepted, the relationship ends. But mere expression of a desire not to serve any longer, by itself, does not stop the servant from changing his mind to serve again. However, once it is accepted the servant cannot insist to have the contract continued. But an offer of resignation at a future date is always revocable.

LAW RELATING TO RETIREMENT OF AN EMPLOYEE

The word, "retire" has been defined in the Concise Oxford Dictionary as "cease from or give up office or profession or employment." The meaning of the word, therefore, postulates a voluntary act on the part of the employee. In its use in the reflexive, the word "to retire" would mean "to remove from service". That would be a case of removal and not retirement, section 2(oo) of the Industrial Disputes Act, 1947 uses the words "voluntary retirement". It follows that, unless the termination of the service is the result of a voluntary move on the part of the workman, he cannot be said to have "voluntarily retired". A mere submission of the employee to the termination of service by the employer cannot be said to be a voluntary act of the former. This is particularly so in a case where the employer has the power under the terms of the employment to terminate the service, although such power has to be exercised after notice or on giving pay in lieu of notice. A voluntary retirement is the act of the employee, just as dismissal or removal from service is the act of the employer. Neither apathy nor submission on the part of a workman would alter the essential character of the termination of service of an employee. Retirement brings in the termination of employment or the contract of employment to an end. The definition of the term, 'retirement' as given in section 2(oo) of the Industrial Disputes Act, 1947 excludes from its purview the cases of voluntary retirement or retirement of the workman on reaching the age of superannuation, if the contract of employment between the employer and the workman concerned contains a stipulation in that behalf and termination of the service on the ground of continued ill-health as also termination of employment inflicted by way of punishment as a result of disciplinary action. Termination of service by way of retirement also amounts to retrenchment in certain circumstances.

Retirement or superannuation is an event which comes more or less in an automatic process. An age is fixed on the reaching of which the holder of office has no option but to go out of office. There is no volition involved in that act. The employer and the employee have notice of the matter long before the event is to occur and the event is such that it cannot be arrested by either one of the them if the rule is to be followed. Therefore, the word "retirement" cannot be regarded as conclusive of the question whether termination of employment includes retirement and superannuation. Prior to 17-1-1983, there was no reference to retirement in the Standing Orders to be certified under the Industrial Employment (Standing Orders) Act, 1946 but now sub-clause (3) of clause 10B of the Industrial Employment (Standing Orders) Central Rules, 1946 provides for age of retirement. Notwithstanding that the age of retirement will not be automatic but will have to be incorporated in the certified standing orders if such a stipulation does not exist.

CIRCUMSTANCES WHEN THERE IS NO AGE OF RETIREMENT EITHER IN THE APPOINTMENT LETTER OR CERTIFIED STANDING ORDERS

It is now well established that in absence of any provision either in the certified standing orders, contract of employment, conditions of service, letters of appointment, or the service rules as to the age of retirement, the workmen are entitled to work so long as they are physically and mentally fit to discharge their duties efficiently and diligently. It is also equally well-established that in the absence of any rule or standing order fixing the age of retirement, a workman cannot claim his appointment as one for life if otherwise he has become incompetent to discharge his duties efficiently and diligently. In cases, where such an age is fixed in some contract, it is the age so fixed in the contract which is the age of retirement and on the attainment of which an employee can be made to retire. If there is no contract but such an age has been fixed in the conditions of service or the terms of the appointment letter, it is that age which is the age, on the attainment of which the employee will be said to have reached the age of retirement. At the same time, it does not mean that in the absence of such a provision either in the appointment letter, service rule, standing order, an employee can be retired at any time. On the contrary, till the time an employee is physically and mentally fit to discharge his duties efficiently, he cannot be retired in the absence of such a provision in the contract of service.

PRINCIPLES FOR FIXING THE AGE OF RETIREMENT

The general considerations which should weigh with the industrial adjudication while determining or fixing the age of retirement in industrial employments are :

(a) what is the nature of the work assigned to the employees in the course of their employment;

(b) what is the nature of the wage-structure paid to them;

(c) what are the retirement benefits and other amenities available to them;

(d) what is the character of the climate where the employees work and what is the age of retirement fixed in comparable industries in the same region; and

(e) what is generally the practice prevailing in the industry in the region in the matter of retiring its employees. These and other relevant facts have to be weighed by the Tribunal in every case when it is called upon to fix the age of retirement in an industrial dispute.

However, in the case of an all India concern, it would be advisable to have uniform conditions of service throughout India and if uniform conditions prevail in any such concern, they should not be lightly changed. At the same time, it cannot also be forgotten that industrial adjudication is based, in this country at least, on what is known as the industry-cum-region basis and cases may arise where the conditions of service of an all India concern, are uniform. Besides, however, desirable may be in the case of an all-India concern, the industrial adjudication cannot abstain from seeing that fair conditions of service prevailing in the industry with which it is concerned. If, therefore, any scheme, which may be uniformly in force throughout India in the case of an all-India concern, appears to be unfair and not in accordance with prevailing conditions, in such matters, it would be the duty of the tribunal to make changes in the scheme to make it fair and bring it into line with the prevailing conditions, in such matters, particularly in the region in which the tribunal is functioning. But where an employer adopts a fair and reasonable pension scheme that would play an important part in fixing the age of retirement at a comparatively earlier stage.

RETIRAL BENEFITS TO EMPLOYEES IN PRIVATE EMPLOYMENT

Retirement or death is not a possibility but a certainty. Both have similarity with a stark dissimilarity. While the date of retirement is known to a person, the day he joins duty the death is mysteriously uncertain. Retirement is a contingency that is sure to happen sooner or later, and against which the individual of small means cannot effectively provide honourable sustenance by his own ability or foresight alone or even in private combination with his fellows. Our Constitution, therefore, has affirmed to all such individuals of small means the right to standard of living, adequate care for the health and well being of their own and of their families, including food, clothing, housing, and medical care and necessary social services and the right to security in the event of unemployment, sickness, disability, widowhood, old age, or circumstances beyond their control, by enacting various legislations like Employees' Provident Funds and Miscellaneous Provisions Act, 1952, Family Pension Scheme, Employees' State Insurance Act, 1948, Payment of Gratuity Act, 1972, etc. A brief information is being given below about the retiral benefits.

(i) **Gratuity.**—Gratuity is also a kind of retirement benefit like the provident fund or pension. Gratuity paid to workmen is intended to help them after retirement, whether the retirement is the result of the rules of superannuation or physical disability. The general principle underlying such schemes is that by their length of service workmen are entitled to claim a certain amount as a retiral benefit.

For purposes of gratuity 'retirement' has been defined in section 2(q) of the Payment of Gratuity Act, 1972 to mean termination of service of an employee otherwise than on superannuation. According to that definition, all cases of termination of service will fall within the ambit of the expression, 'retirement'. The Payment of Gratuity Act makes no distinction in cases of retirement or voluntary resignation in prescribing the qualifying number of years. In other words, a person who resigns his services or retires after putting in continuous service for five years, becomes entitled to payment of gratuity under the Act subject to the provisions of sub-section (6) of section 4. As soon as the services of an employee are terminated on his being so superannuated, gratuity becomes payable to him. Gratuity is also payable to a person whose services are terminated on account of his death or disablement due to accident or disease. Thus on retirement, superannuation or termination due to disablement or on resignation, an employee is entitled to get gratuity at the rate of fifteen days' wages calculated on the basis of the rate of wages last drawn by him for every completed year of service. For the purposes of the calculation, his wages will consist of the basic-wage plus dearness allowance and any bonus, commission, house rent allowance, overtime wages and any other allowances if being paid or payable to the employee will not be taken into account for the purposes of computing gratuity.

It is pertinent to clarify the position with regard to calculation of gratuity for an employee having served for 20 years and drawing salary of Rs. 2,600 per month will be as under:

"Rs. 2,600 per month last drawn salary Rs. 100 per day x 15 days x 20 Yr. of service — Rs. 30,000 gratuity payable."

The Payment of Gratuity Act has been amended by an Amending Act 34 of 1994 w.e.f. 24-5-1994 whereby the maximum gratuity has been fixed at Rs. 1,00,000.

(ii) **Provident Fund, Deposit Link Insurance.**—(a) Provident Fund is one of the basic social security measures which fulfils the

functions of restoration of the essential income of a worker to some
extent after retirement. The Indian Parliament created a fund
under the Employees' Provident Funds and Miscellaneous
Provisions Act, 1952 for the benefit of the toiling masses to provide
them to fall back upon in times of hardship *viz* death, retirement,
infirmity and sickness when a person is not able to earn his bread
by sweat of his brow. The corpus of this fund is created by the
contribution by an eligible employee, fixed under the Act together
with equal amount by the employer. This amount is invested and
the interest earned thereupon is also credited to the amount of the
member on pro-rata basis. When the member leaves the service/
retires or dies while in service, some more benefits accure to them.
In case of retirement the total amount which had been credited to
his account by way of his contribution together with the equal
amount contributed by the employer with upto date interest at the
rate declared by the Provident Fund authorities from time to time
is paid to him. The position of Private Provident Fund is more or
less the same.

In case of death there is minimum guarantee, *i.e.*, Rs. 3,500 is
assured to the member irrespective of the amount standing to his
credit in his account of Provident Fund, *i.e.*, the amount that falls
short will be paid from the Provident Fund itself. In case it is more
than that the full amount is paid to the survivors of the deceased.

Employees' Pension Scheme

A member can receive pension after putting in 10 years of
eligible service. This period of minimum service is not applicable
in the case of Widow's Pension/Disablement Pension/Children's
Pension/ Orphan's Pension.

The Widow's Pension, Children's Pension and Orphan's
Pension is payable after only 30 days of actual contribution.

A member can opt for discounted/reduced pension before the
age of 58 but not earlier than 50 years.

If a member opts for reduced pension his/her nominee or the
widow/widower can get benefit of capital return equal to 100
times of monthly pension is lump-sum along with pension.

Provision for nomination in the absence of the member's family
is made.

The option is also available to become a member of the
Employees' Pension Scheme, 1995 w.e.f. 1-4-1993 under certain
conditions.

On completing 33 years of pensionable service, the pension entitlement shall be 50% of the members' pay at the time of retirement.

60% entitlement of pay on completion of 40 years' pensionable service.

Family pension cover for widow/widower for life or until her remarriage, and to two children upto 25 years of age, upon death of the member, be it in service, out of service or after receiving the pension on retirement.

To further improve upon the benefits there is provision for valuation every three years by the Actuary.

(iii) **Medical care to the insured person and his spouse who has ceased to be in insurable employment on account of superannuation.**—The Employees' State Insurance Act, 1948 is a piece of social security legislation enacted to provide for certain benefits including medical care to the employees in factories, certain shops and establishments. The Law has been amended in 1989 by adding Rules 60 and 61 to the Employees' State Insurance (Central) Rules, 1950 *inter alia* providing that insured persons who cease to be in insurable employment on attaining the age of superannuation are eligible to receive medical benefits under the Act for themselves and their spouses. These Rules have come into force with effect from 1st February, 1991 by a Memorandum No.N.11/13/91-Ins-II dated 3-7-1991 and Rule 61 reads as under:

61. *Medical benefits to retired insured persons: An* insured person who leaves the insurable employment on attaining the age of superannuation after being insured for not less than five years, shall be eligible to receive medical benefits for himself and his spouse at the scale prescribed under the Act and the regulations made thereunder, subject to—

(i) the production of proof of his superannuation and having been in the insurable employment for a minimum of five years to the satisfaction of such office as may be authorised by the Corporation; and

(ii) the payment of contribution at the rate of ten rupees per month in lump sum for one year at a time in advance to the concerned office of the Corporation in the manner prescribed by it.

The Regional Directors have been advised to take immediate steps to provide medical benefits to these insured persons following the procedure laid down in Employees' State Insurance Act, 1948 Employees State Insurance (Central) Rules, 1950 and Employers' State Insurance (General) Regulations, 1950 alongwith the instructions contained in the aforesaid Memorandum.

Powers have been delegated by the Director General upon the Regional Director/Jt. Regional Director/Dy. Regional Director and the Local Office Managers *vide* orders dated 1-7-1991 to decide the title of the insured persons and their spouses for eligibility to receive medical benefits under the Rules. However, the following procedure may be followed for providing medical benefit:—

The insured person who desires to avail medical benefit shall submit an application to the local office Manager in the prescribed form alongwith a certificate/declaration from the employer in a prescribed form.

The Local Office Manager shall examine the application alongwith the enclosed documents with reference to the records maintained in the local office and shall satisfy himself that the insured person is eligible to receive medical benefit. After satisfying himself about the title of the insured person, the Local Office Manager shall record his order on the form prescribed on the reverse of the application. Also a certificate from the employer in prescribed form and a declaration by the insured person if corroborated by the records of the local office also shall be considered as a sufficient proof of his title for eligibility to the said benefit provided there is no evidence to the contrary.

If the Local Office Manager certifies title of the insured person to the medical benefit, the insured person may be asked to deposit the contribution at the rate of Rs. 10/- per month in advance for one year with the Local Office.

After the insured person has deposited the amount of prescribed contribution and receipt issued to him, he shall be issued a fresh Identity Card for himself and his spouse which shall be written/stamped on the top VALID UPTO .....". A new MRE shall also be prepared which shall also be written/stamped VALID UPTO .....". The period of validation shall be the same for which the insured person has paid the contribution. The MRE, as prepared shall be sent to the IMO Incharge of the concerned dispensary under ESIC 48-A.

(iv) **Retrenchment Compensation.**—Section 2(oo) of the Industrial Disputes Act, 1947 defining retrenchment incorporates the words, "voluntary retirement". It follows that unless the termination of the service is the result of a voluntary move on the part of the employee, he cannot be said to have "voluntarily retired". A voluntary retirement is the act of the employee just as the dismissal or removal from service is the act of the employer. Therefore in the absence of any terms of the contract of service providing for retirement of the employee on reaching a particular age or in the absence of any standing orders having statutory sanction regarding the age of superannuation, the termination of service of a workman on his reaching a particular age would not fall within exception (b) to section 2(oo) of the Act. Since retirement in the absence of any stipulation as to such age in the contract of service is termination of service within the meaning of section 2(oo) of the Industrial Disputes Act, 1947 and since such termination, on notice in accordance with the contract of service, will amount to 'retrenchment'. The employee will have to fulfil the requirements of section 25F of the Act. In other words, in the absence of any rule or contract of service as to age of retirement, the retirement of an employee for any reason including that he is beyond a particular age is termination of service and not the enforcement of any rule of superannuation and on such. termination the employee is also entitled to notice and retrenchment compensation in accordance with the provisions of section 25F of the Industrial Disputes Act, 1947.

(v) **Encashment of Earned Leave.**—Section 79 of the Factories Act, 1948 provides that if a worker is discharged or dismissed from service or quits his employment or is superannuated or dies while in service, during the course of the calendar year, he or his heirs or nominee, as the case may be, shall be entitled to wages in lieu of the quantum of leave to which he was entitled immediately before his discharge, dismissal, quitting of employment, superannuation or death calculated at the rates specified in sub-section (1), even if he had not worked for the entire period specified in sub-section (1) or sub-section (2) making him eligible to avail of such leave, and such payment shall be made to him where the worker is superannuated or dies while in service, before the expiry of two months from the date of such superannuation or death.

It is pertinent to refer to sub-sections (1) and (2) of section 79 of the Factories Act which provide as under:

"(1)   Every worker who has worked for a period of 240 days or more in a factory during a calendar year shall be allowed during the subsequent calendar year leave with wages for a number of days calculated at the rate of—

(i)   if an adult, one day for every twenty days of work performed by him during the previous calendar year;

(ii)   if a child, one day for every fifteen days of work performed by him during the previous calendar year.

Explanation 1.—For the purpose of this sub-section—

(a)   any days of lay-off, by agreement or contract or as permissible under the standing orders;

(b)   in the case of a female worker, maternity leave for any number of days not exceeding twelve weeks; and

(c)   the leave earned in the year prior to that in which the leave is enjoyed,

shall be deemed to be days on which the worker has worked in a factory for the purpose of computation of the period of 240 days or more, but he shall not earn leave for these days.

Explanation 2.—The leave admissible under this sub-section shall be exclusive of all holidays whether occurring during or at either end of the period of leave.

(2)   A worker whose service commences otherwise than on the first day of January shall be entitled to leave with wages at the rate laid down in clause (i) or, as the case may be, clause (ii) of sub-section (1) if he has worked for two-thirds of the total number of days in the remainder of the calendar year."

SUBJECT INDEX

A

Absence

pregnancy, 155

Accident

Factories Act, 1948, special
provisions, 95

fatal, 252

notice of, 166

Accident book

ESI, Act, 1948, 58

Accounting year

bonus, 198

***Ad hoc* allowance**

bonus, 203

Adjudication

dispute, ID Act, 1947, 110

Adult workers

working hours under Factories
Act, 1948, 90

Age

particulars of, 59

report to local office or medical
officer, 58

retirement 284

Allocable surplus

bonus, 198

Annual leave

wages, 93, 191

Apprentice

bonus, 7

contract of, 3, 5

ESI, 7

graduate, 6

hours of work, 7

hours per day, 7

not governed by labour laws, 5

not workman, 5

obligation of employer, 6

obligation of employee, to
accept employment, 5

provident fund, 7

regular post, claim for, 5

skilled craftsman, 6

stipend, 10

technician, 6

termination of, 9, 10

trade apprentice, 6

training, 6

training, period of, 3

violation under Apprentices
Act by employer, 9

Apprentices Act, 1961

amendment in, 2

appearances rules,
amendment, 3

objects of, 2

penalties, 11

Appropriate government

Contract Labour (Regulation
and Abolition) Act, 1976, 19

Employment Exchanges
(Compulsory Notification of
Vacancies) Act, 1959, 68

Arbitration

dispute, 112

Available surplus

bonus, 199

B

***Badli* workman**

ID Act, 1947, 119, 128

293